Tony Fletcher recentl[...] [Inspec]tor in charge of the [...] Crime Department a[...] Manchester Police. H[...] Criminology at Manch[...] and acts as a consultan[...] [tele]vision crime programmes.

TONY FLETCHER

Memories of Murder

The Great Cases of a Finger-print Expert

GRAFTON BOOKS

A Division of the Collins Publishing Group

LONDON GLASGOW
TORONTO SYDNEY AUCKLAND

Grafton Books
A Division of the Collins Publishing Group
8 Grafton Street, London W1X 3LA

Published by Grafton Books 1987

First published in Great Britain by
Weidenfeld & Nicholson Ltd 1986

Copyright © Tony Fletcher 1986

ISBN 0-586-07210-1

Printed and bound in Great Britain by
Collins, Glasgow

Set in Times

I wish to dedicate this book
to the memory of my father, Thomas, and to my family

Contents

Acknowledgements

A first-time author needs help and this I have received in abundance from Alex MacCormick and Allie Morrison of Weidenfeld, and from Mary Turner, who typed the manuscript, corrected grammatical errors and gave me the benefit of her experience as a local historian.

T.F.

Illustrations

The photographs on illustration pages 2, 5, 7 and 8 are reproduced by kind permission of the Chief Constable, Greater Manchester Police; those on page 6 (below) courtesy of the Department of Medical Illustration, Manchester University.

1

For Those in Peril on the C

Stockport was a market town in Cheshire, but it has for a long time been part of Manchester's suburban sprawl. It is a thriving place and for the last couple of hundred years has been an industrial centre – cotton processing being important until quite recently. The River Mersey starts there and provided power for the once thriving industries. Sometimes houses on the banks of the river have tumbled in and archaeologists have been quick to look at what was beneath their foundations, because Stockport's history embodies an ancient settlement and a ford used by the Roman forces in the first century A.D.

My father Thomas was a builder there when I arrived on the scene in 1928. Eventually there were five brothers in all, and for reasons of her own my mother did not want any of her sons to go into the building trade, perhaps because it can be financially very uncertain. So, influenced by my mother and backed only by an elementary education, I went into the office of a chartered accountant in the centre of Manchester, ten miles from home. When my father was conscripted into the Army, my mother persuaded me to leave the accountancy business and join my elder brother, who was training locally as a draughtsman in an engineering office. For five years I was a square peg in a round hole, but my life altered considerably when I was sworn in as a Constable in the Manchester City Police, a change I never regretted.

The swearing-in ceremony was brief, but impressive, and the twelve recruits that day were taken by Black

Maria to Number 1 District Police Training Centre at
Bruche, near Warrington. It sounds grander than it was:
built as a US Air Force base during the war years, it did
not look much different on 13 September 1948.

Recruits to the police service had thirteen weeks of
basic training, covering the rudiments of law, police work,
first aid, civil defence (still relevant), unarmed combat
and some, including myself, passed a swimming test in
life-saving. On returning to Manchester I was posted to
the C Division as Constable C96, and thus I remained for
the next eight years.

In those days the City of Manchester was some twelve
miles from north to south, but perhaps no more than five
miles wide at best. Like all big conurbations Manchester
has its points of contrast: on its southern side there are
big houses built by the cotton barons and rich Jewish
families, which were joined towards the end of the
nineteenth century by small enclaves of reasonably good
terraced housing; on its northern side there were rows
and rows of poor housing, which ran close to the heart of
the city. But it was on the eastern side that the centre of
my working life lay: C Division. In mediaeval times there
had been little there except a great house or two with
extensive lands, and a hamlet here and there. But of
course much of what happens to an area depends on
what nature has provided, and in this case there were
rivers and streams to drive factory wheels, a number of
coal mines, a good quantity of excellent lime and room
for the arriving masses to be accommodated in never-
ending terraces of working-class housing.

By the time I was posted there, the air we had to
breathe was a rich amalgam of the coal dust of a hundred
years, leaks from the coal-gas works, the stench of more
than one glue works producing adhesives from animal

carcases and the fumes from chemical factories, Beyer Peacock's railway engine works, and many electrical engineering and motor engineering enterprises. It didn't leave much room for oxygen, and natural sunlight had something of a struggle. Small wonder that asthma, bronchitis and other chest infections fuelled by the worst offenders of all, the domestic hearths and personal smoking habits – made for long queues at the doctors' surgeries and ensured full employment at the cemeteries.

It all sounds grim. In many ways it was, yet I can truthfully say that in working-class streets there was more going on, more life being lived, than there is in most places today. Society has changed so much. Television keeps indoors people who once would have been standing on the front step engaging in neighbourly gossip. Cars were less common in 1948 and certainly most crime was strictly local, because it had to be. Neighbours were aware of who was 'inside' or due out, and it was quite natural that the local bobby should get to know his local backsliders. In a few years of circulating through the beat system, moving from station to station, one acquired quite an amount of knowledge and expertise. If Fred Murphy of Gorton was on Stockport Road, Levenshulme (an adjoining district) and seemed to be making for Stockport, a beat Constable would wonder which of the big houses was vulnerable, because one thing would be certain – Fred would be looking after his own interests.

The area of the C Division hasn't changed much and covers Levenshulme, Longsight, Ardwick, Chorlton on Medlock, West Gorton, Gorton, Ancoats, Beswick, Bradford, Openshaw, Higher Openshaw, Miles Platting and Clayton – one of the most heavily industrialized areas on this planet for most of this century. In my time the Division was run by a Superintendent, assisted by a Chief

Inspector; there were three reliefs – 6 A.M. to 2 P.M., 2 P.M. to 10 P.M. and 10 P.M. to 6 A.M. Each relief had a Charge Office Inspector and a Patrolling Inspector. There were six sections in the Division, each controlled by a Section Sergeant and each section consisted of five beats.

What the general public called 'police stations' were sometimes referred to as 'section houses' – a distinction without a difference. Brunswick Street Section House accommodated the first and second sections, and was manned twenty-four hours a day by a Section House Officer on each of the three reliefs. Levenshulme Section House did the same for the third section, and Gorton Section House for the fourth. The fifth and sixth sections occupied the divisional headquarters at Mill Street, manned throughout the twenty-four hours by a station Inspector and a clerk on each of the three reliefs. There was a fixed point system, each beat had four, and the beat bobby was expected to be at each one in turn at half-hourly intervals in the daytime and at forty-five-minute intervals at night.

When first issued with his uniform, the young policeman was also handed his appointments – not a list of arrangements for spending his time, but part of his equipment: note book, staff or truncheon, snaps or handcuffs, whistle and chain, and a leather dog-lead, which reminded him that the handling of stray dogs was part of his duties.

Each Sergeant and Inspector had his own stick. It was an essential part of his accoutrements, and he either had his own made specially or one was handed on to him by grace and favour. These sticks, often of perfectly serviceable ash, but sometimes and more expensively of lignum vitae, are still made on Great Ancoats Street, Manchester, at the shop which has produced them as long as anyone can remember. The stick was most valuable at night: if the Sergeant was perhaps a little late or the Constable had been detained at an incident, it would be tapped on the pavement and, under favourable conditions, could be heard over an amazing distance, perhaps as much as a mile, because granite sett pavements provide a first-class sounding board. A Constable could respond by tapping his staff on the pavement, if he needed to. People now may think this rather primitive, but bear in mind that there were no personal radios and few telephones either public or private. Natives in Africa banging on drums were not the only ones to utilize the percussive value of sound through the atmosphere, especially the damp one with which Manchester is said to be perpetually blessed.

At strategic points on the C Division were thirty-six police boxes left over from a system which had operated a decade or two earlier; each had a telephone and a flashing light. If an officer was wanted, the divisional telephonist would cause the box light to flash and response was expected to be rapid and effective.

When a Constable made an arrest he had no means of summoning assistance directly from a police station, though of course he had his whistle, but if he blew that he might only summon a hostile crowd which he could well do without. So he had to manhandle the prisoner, very likely struggling like mad, to the nearest police box and that could be up to a mile away; he had to subdue and hold on to the prisoner whilst opening the box with a key attached to his whistle chain which, in turn, was hooked on to a button of his tunic; next he had to put the prisoner in the police box and then, if he had enough breath left, use the telephone to summon the prison van.

One acquired a certain knack in this procedure, but there were hazardous moments.

Each division had its own CID and plain-clothes officers. The plain-clothes staff deal mostly with prostitution, obscene publications and the licensing laws. In a way it serves as a training ground for the CID, which deals with crime, serious and trivial alike. Many young officers have dreams of joining the CID, but for most it doesn't come quickly, if at all. It has always been a very different life from being a uniformed officer and it is essential to walk the beat for some years if transfer is to be successful. It is only by walking the beat that one learns about that side of human behaviour which is concerned with the preservation of peace, the maintenance of law and order, and above all the art of public relations. Some police, men and women, never have aspirations to join the crime offices; rightly, they see that it means irregular hours, covering a very seedy side of life, and many spouses get understandably anxious if left with young families for periods far longer than they feel is fair.

At any hour of the day or night the C Division was manned by upwards of fifty police officers, all male, the majority of whom would be working the beat. As they walked through the grimy, but mainly cheerful, streets most of them cut an impressive figure, giving members of the public an impression of sternness, justness, sobriety and Christian endeavour, and certainly not of men who were to be meddled with or taken lightly.

Assisting the professional lawmen was a sprinkling of Special Constables and a few dedicated lady telephonists. Supernumerary to the C Division's establishment was a middle-aged lady who at night patrolled the main roads of Gorton, checking that all the lock-up property was secure and later reporting to the beat Constable any suspicious circumstances. She was K11. Whilst supernumerary to establishment she rarely took a night off, and was more diligent than many officers.

To maintain his image it was essential that the policeman had pride in himself, in his appearance and, above all, in the service he represented. As old heads do not grow on young shoulders, and pride usually comes before a fall, many is the time that for a brief moment the image was tarnished and pride dented, usually in the most trivial of incidents. You could be patrolling the district's main shopping street on a summer's day, walking erect and with measured stride, only to lose your helmet by colliding with a shop sunblind which had been lowered less than the statutory eight feet above the footpath. Members of the public always found this amusing and it added to the young officer's discomfort if he happened, as was often the case, to be using his helmet for carrying eggs or tomatoes intended for his refreshments. (Some trades or occupations have lunch hours or dinner hours; policemen 'take refreshment'. The question, 'Where were you at 10.12 A.M.?' being legitimately answered by, 'At Mill Street, sir, refreshing', which sounds rather odd!)

It is not only young policemen who suffer embarrassment, as I discovered in circumstances so unusual that I shall never forget them. I had paraded for duty at Brunswick Street Section House on the afternoon relief. The Sergeant, Tommy Alker, said he would accompany me and another young Stockport lad, Roy, to our respective beats. Roy and I had joined less than six months previously. I was on the beat on the eastern side of Hyde Road, Ardwick, and Roy was on the western side. Literally bridging these was the railway, which was known at that point as the Fenian Arch. (On 18 September 1867, a Sergeant Brett was murdered there as the prison van which he was accompanying was attacked to rescue the Fenian prisoners – for which crime Allen, O'Brien and Larkin were later hanged. They became known as the Manchester Martyrs. That was a long way in the past.)

Tommy was the salt of the earth. About forty-five years old, he had a red face and a barrel chest. As he walked along Hyde Road with a young Constable on either side, he held forth on his favourite topic, education, and in particular the education of his sons; he was very proud of them.

As we got to the Fenian Arch we were approached by a middle-aged woman, who said, 'You'd better go and have a look at the school, Sergeant. The flaming kids are pulling it to pieces.' The children were on school holiday. 'Follow me', said the Sergeant and away he went, leading the pair of us along a maze of cobbled streets. His face was blood-red, his chest pushed out, his stick tapping the pavement with every stride – bluntly, he was in full cry. He looked majestic and soon the word was out that he was on the warpath. Front doors opened and young women scuttered out of the two-up-and-two-downs at the thought of their children being exposed to retribution.

When we reached the school, it was a sight to behold. The school playground was grey, bounded on three sides by six-foot-high green railings and on the fourth side was the school itself, red-brick Victorian stability with a blue slate roof. On the opposite side of the school yard was the playground shelter. But it was the kids who caught our eye. There were boys everywhere: some were balanced on the railings, some were ripping the slates off the shelter roof, windows were tinkling into slivers, some had climbed the fall pipes and were on the school roof – boys were everywhere and not one up to any good. Already

For Those in Peril on the C   19

grouped near the school railings were their mothers, each one hollering to her offspring, trying to rescue him (or them) before the storm broke.

Too late. Tom arrived at the scene and, having no regard at all for the circumstances in which the children had been conceived, he raised his stick aloft and shouted, 'The bastards, the flaming little bastards!' Feathers ruffled like those of a turkey-cock, he rushed to the school railings, where the anxious mothers redoubled their efforts in encouraging the children to escape. 'Quick, number eleven,' he shouted to Roy, 'get round to the other side of the railings. Don't let any of them escape.' No sooner was Roy dispatched than Tommy shouted at me: 'Ninety-six, watch this side of the railings. Keep it well posted. I'm going over.'

With that he tucked his trousers into his socks, leaned his stick against the railings and climbed over. There was instant panic in the playground as the mothers continued to scream and, with Roy posted on the far side of the railings, the only means of escape was over the school roof. Some twenty boys had perceived this and were busy shinning up the fall pipes. Tommy had collected his stick from where he had left it and commenced the chase. I knew immediately that no arrests were imminent; corporal punishment was to be applied. Nowadays we see little of it, but on the C Division in 1949 it was quite acceptable. As Tommy raced round the playground he looked fearsome, a wild man in a blue uniform, a throwback to an ancient Briton. Every time a boy's buttocks came within reach he landed them one with his stick.

The pursuit went on for a full three minutes and the scene was both hysterical and hilarious. The children were shouting warnings to each other, the mothers were yelling, Tommy was roaring, and Roy and I were bent

double laughing. Suddenly, puffing and panting, his face
as red as a beetroot, Tommy started chasing one thirteen-
year-old monster the full length of the playground in my
direction. As they neared the railings, he caught the boy
with his left hand and raised him from the ground,
preparing to give him a smack across the buttocks with
his stick. The woman standing next to me shouted to
Tommy, 'Leave him alone, you big fat pig, leave him
alone, he's mine.' Tommy glared at her. 'Don't touch
him, sir, please don't hit him, sir.' Tommy had changed
from a big fat pig to a sir within seconds. 'Don't touch
him, sir,' she continued, 'he's been misled.' 'Don't touch
him?' roared Tommy, 'I'll bloody well kill him, missis!'
and with that he raised the lad until his head was six feet
from the ground and he was staring down into the
Sergeant's poppy-hued face. The boy was wearing a grey
jersey and grey below-knee length short trousers, the
fashion in those days, plus long grey socks and black
boots.

Tommy glared at him. This Ardwick kid had never
been so frightened in his life. His face screwed up. 'Mam,'
he said, and with that he peed straight on Tommy Alker's
broad chest. It ran down the front of his uniform. 'You
dirty little sod,' shouted Tommy, and dropped the lad
forthwith.

A crowd of women standing near to me looked aghast
until one of them shouted, 'He's pissed on the Sergeant,
he's pissed on the Sergeant!' and with that they all roared
with laughter. Suddenly there was not much else to do
but retrieve a little pride. The Sergeant climbed back
over the railings, pulled his trousers out of his socks,
adjusted his helmet, smoothed his damp tunic and raised
himself to his full height. 'Right oh, number eleven, right
oh ninety-six, that's taught them a lesson, that's how we

do it,' and with that he led us away along the rough streets to the main road and our respective beats.

Nowadays each force will have its Community Contact department, even though that department may be known by another name, and great store is set by this contact between the police and the public. In earlier days such departments were unnecessary as the vast majority of police officers were in direct contact with the community as part of their everyday duties.

With no traffic wardens or school-crossing patrols, the business of regulating the flow of traffic and seeing to the safety of the children was a police function. The benefits gained by having police officers manning the school-crossing points was enormous. The children grew up with far more respect for the police than is evident today. They knew the policeman they saw every day to and from school; he changed from time to time, of course, so that they may have known several policemen quite well by sight, but each was 'the policeman'. More importantly, all the children thought that the policeman knew each and every one of them.

Not only did the police supervise their journeys to and from school, but officers were also in attendance when the children's matinées finished at the main-road cinemas. There was never any need to ask what the main feature had been. If it had been a science fiction, all the budding Dan Dares would pour out off the cinema, raise their arms outstretched to shoulder level and rocket off along the footpath with open mouths emitting sounds similar either to police sirens or aero engines under fierce acceleration, dipping or raising their wings as they dashed past the elderly shoppers, and braking violently at road junctions both with legs and vocal cords. When you got to know children at such a young age, it was rare for them to think of assaulting you in later years, even if you did have occasion to tan their backsides once in a while.

A third recruit posted to the C Division at the same time as Roy and myself was Jock, a quiet and cheerful Scot, who had spent his previous ten years as a deep-sea trawlerman. Within his first few weeks on the C Division, he became the first policeman I knew to question a person about 'unauthorized wire-tapping', some twenty-five years or so before President Nixon made the subject topical.

After spending his early life either at sea or in a remote country district in the North of Scotland, he entered the police training centre, where he was taught the need to keep a sharp look-out for suspicious characters and to net less tasty fish than he had previously been used to. On his first tour of night duty he was alerted when, in the early hours of the morning, illuminated only by the street lights, he saw the shadowy figure of a man who, dressed in a long raincoat and flat cap, was shuffling along the darkened streets carrying a pole. Keeping well in the shadows, Jock tagged along with the suspicious character under close observation.

Suddenly, all the young Scot's suspicions were confirmed when the man stopped and then started testing the bedroom window of a house by tapping it with the end of his pole. The Constable raced forward to question him and then found he had caught up with one of a policeman's companions of the night, the knocker-up.

Companion of the night he well might have been as the original knocker-up was the Watch, who, in turn, with the introduction of Manchester City Police in 1839, passed the duty on at the request of the mill-owners to the first police officers. This continued for a while until the Chief

Constable of the day instructed that the practice be stopped. In the 1890s a retired Salford Inspector related how, in his early days, policemen used to wrangle fiercely about who should have the lucrative working-class beats, because at threepence a week it could equal a week's pay. Incidentally, these officers didn't carry a pole with wires at the top – it would hardly have been suitable – their alternative was a pea-shooter and a pocketful of marrowfats.

Inevitably, privatization took over and a bond grew between the bobby and the knocker-up, a fact which Lancashire author Walter Greenwood recognized in *Love on the Dole*. An early chapter opens with the night Constable meeting Blind Reilly who, armed with a twelve-foot bamboo pole with wires fixed to one end, went round his beat, usually from 3 A.M. onwards, knocking up bakers, railwaymen and mill-workers by the simple expedient of tapping on their bedroom windows with this bunch of wires.

Quite often police officers are confronted with situations and events for which the law fails to provide a remedy or even a bit of support, and others where applying the letter of the law seems a bit much. In those days policemen did not come under such close scrutiny as they do nowadays and usually solved their problems by using initiative and imagination, invoking two little-known but much-used Acts. The Ways and Means Act covered most eventualities in which the law was not crystal clear, and the Mingling of the Sexes Act gave extraordinarily wide powers of entry into places where there might be goings-on, as one might say.

My first application of the Ways and Means Act came in my first year of service. Being a newcomer to the C

Division, I had been offered an exciting choice of summer leave: April or October. I'd picked October. In August I had arranged that on one of my weekly rest days I would have a day out in Blackpool with my current girlfriend. We were to go on a Thursday early in August. I was on the 2 to 10 P.M. relief, the weather was fine and the forecast for the rest of the week was excellent.

On the afternoon before the proposed day out I was walking along Ardwick Green when I saw a man doing a balancing act along the tram tracks, much to the annoyance of motorists and the amusement of most pedestrians. He was very drunk. Suddenly, the effort became too much for him and he lay down and slipped into dreamland.

My position was crystal clear: it was my duty to arrest and charge him with being drunk and incapable. The problem was that, instead of sampling the breezes and delights of Blackpool, I would have to spend the following morning in the magistrates' court. Still, all was not lost. I could go through his pockets and, if I could find an address, I could get him over my shoulder and hump him home. A quick check, no address. It was now either the police station or the park, both an equal distance away. With all eyes on me I hoisted him on to my shoulder and carried him into Ardwick Green Park, where I laid him to rest on one of the benches. At tea time he was still there, at eight in the evening he'd gone. The Blackpool day out was saved!

The Ways and Means Act was frequently used by officers not wishing to attend court with trivial offences. When a dog reaches the age of six months, its owner is required to take out a dog licence. As each licence cost 7s 6d (37½p), which was probably more than the dog cost, they were in short supply. So when a dog had been killed or injured in a road accident, the officer would often reduce the age of the dog to five months.

When the owner of a dog was being interviewed by a Constable who asked to see the dog licence, there would be a diligent but fruitless search through the sideboard drawers, a hopeful root in the Toby jug, a worried glance and a sad shake of the head, which usually caused the Constable to make the necessary adjustment to the animal's lifespan, sometimes reducing the dog's age by upwards of twelve years. A Manchester Chief Constable once observed that five months was a dangerous age for most dogs in the city and it could be anticipated that many would meet with fatal accidents.

From a vantage point on the C Division it would have been difficult to count the many thousands of chimneys. A much easier task would have been to count those which were regularly swept. Most bobbies had experience of being approached in the street by an elderly and distraught person shouting, 'You'd better come quick (officer, sir, bobby), me chimberley's agate.' What was required when someone's 'chimberley was agate' was that the fire brigade be summoned to extinguish the chimney fire. Incidentally, 'to set agate' is a Lancashire dialect expression meaning 'set to work', so the chimney being agate meant that it was working – that is, on fire.

A great number of the division's residents were unsure who footed the bill when the fire brigade turned out and were reluctant to contact the fire station themselves, but would enlist the help of the nearest policeman. Payment by individuals for the fire brigade's services had ceased many decades earlier, but the myth persisted from the days when it was sixpence for a fireman and a shilling for the horse which pulled the water tender.

If the offending chimney had not been recently swept and the fire was due to the neglect of the householder, it was required that he or she be summoned for 'allowing his chimney to catch fire'. That word 'allowing' used to make me smile, because the firing of chimneys was often deliberate to avoid paying a chimney sweep. Not wishing to go to court for a chimney-fire case, the officer would invoke the Ways and Means Act and report that the cause of the fire was a 'pocket of soot igniting in a defective flue', which satisfied both honour and the householder.

At the scene of one such incident I was pleasantly upstaged by a leading fireman. One Sunday lunchtime a gentleman had returned home from the pub after consuming copious draughts of Chester's Fighting Ale. On arrival he found that his 'chimberley was agate' and the house was in a state of turmoil. He immediately threw a few buckets of water into the firegrate, which extinguished the domestic blaze, but did nothing at all to the chimney fire.

Not thinking too clearly, he knelt down, put his head into the fireplace and then gazed up the chimney to assess his problems. As he did so a pocket of hot, burning soot fell on to his head, causing him considerable discomfort. I arrived at the house at the same time as the fire brigade and saw that the householder, who was sobering up rapidly, was feeling very sorry for himself. After the fire brigade had done their worst, I was standing on a sodden carpet seeking particulars from the leading fireman. He looked at me rather pointedly. 'Defective flue, I suppose?' was what he said. I glanced at the householder, saw his head covered with small burns, and said, 'Defective head, as well.' The fireman looked at him and then back at me, 'Aye, in more bloody ways than one.'

* * *

In the immediate post-war years there were several reported sightings of a naked man running around the C Division in the early hours of the morning. He never molested anyone nor were any complaints received that he had exposed himself to any women. On one or two occasions he had been chased by policemen, but had managed to evade capture. Most of the sightings had been in the Gorton and Openshaw areas.

About 1 A.M. on a spring morning I was patrolling along Hyde Road, Gorton, and had just passed its junction with Church Lane, when I saw a man's head emerge from a side passage some sixty yards in front of me. He gazed along Hyde Road in the opposite direction. As he did not turn his head and look in my direction it seemed obvious that he was not a villain 'keeping nick' whilst his partners in crime were busily engaged. As I got nearer, I stayed close to the buildings, keeping as quiet as I possibly could.

Suddenly the head reappeared, again looking away from me. It then withdrew. At that time I thought it was a man awaiting the arrival of either his wife or his girlfriend who did not wish to be seen. When twenty or so yards away from the entrance to the alley, I saw the head pop out yet again, completely unaware of my silent approach. My arrival at the alleyway coincided with the head's reappearance and I do not honestly know who was the more surprised. From a distance of four feet I was staring at a naked man. As I was in night uniform, which had black buttons, helmet badge and flashings, he must have thought he was looking at the 'Man in Black'. For what seemed an eternity, but in reality could not have been more than a second or two, we stared at each other. Suddenly he fled, with me close behind. It was rather like a scene from the Keystone Cops. The advantage of speed lay with me: I had been a schoolboy sprint champion a few years before. However, as he had no clothes on, I found it difficult to catch hold of him. I therefore brought him down from behind in a football tackle and dived on top of him. It was a foul, true enough, but what else could I do? It is a bad time in a policeman's life when he realizes he is tangling with someone who is stronger than himself. This now happened to me. As I grasped his upper arm I found, with a nasty shock, that I had hold of good hard muscle. Lying on top of the naked man in a back entry in the early hours of the morning was bad enough, but to find that he was both fit and muscular was too much. It was like music to my ears when he said, 'OK, I'm glad you've caught me. I'll be no trouble to you.' We both started to breathe again. I put my cape round him and walked him to Gorton Section House. He was a nice man, some ten years older than I was. He told me he was a blacksmith's striker who had served most of the war years with the 14th Army in Burma. His naked nocturnal wanderings had started shortly after his demobilization and he could not say why or how they had come about. I went to his home and enlightened his wife to some extent about what had gone on, collected his clothing from where he had left it, which was in the outside toilet of his home, and along with his wife took him to Manchester Royal Infirmary, where he was treated as an out-patient. There were no more sightings of the naked man.

Five years later, one Sunday morning, I met him again out walking with his young daughter. I was prepared to nod and walk past, but was more than a little pleased when he stopped to chat.

* * *

My years on the C Division were eventful and enjoyable ones, and with eight years' service I found myself happily married and a father, a condition which had earlier caused me to study for and pass the examinations necessary for advancement within the service.

I was now looking about me with a view to achieving these aims and was soon to leave the uniform branch and serve a further twenty-seven years in a far different capacity.

Whilst at the police training centre in 1948, my attention had been attracted to the trial and subsequent execution of Peter Griffiths for the murder of young June Anne Devaney at Blackburn. My interest was aroused in the detection of crime by finger-prints and it lasts to this day.

With my promotion examinations behind me and a reasonable knowledge of the finger-print classification system obtained by private study, I was accepted for a vacancy in the Finger-print Bureau. After a short time there, I was expected to talk to both members of the public and police recruits about the system of finger-print identification and I chose, as the basis of those early lectures, the Blackburn murder, the only time that the entire adult male population of a town was asked to volunteer its finger-prints.

2

The Homespun Man

The Second World War was a time of hardship, death, disaster and yet of enormous public spirit and great self-discipline amongst most people. As always after a war, a new world had to be built. The men in the forces, coming home after demobilization, voted in the general election for the first time for many years, and they put a Labour Government in power. The Government chose to retain rationing, believing it to be the fairest system until a free market with ample supplies could be established. Some resentment about this was certainly felt by many, because in what had been occupied Europe free markets began almost immediately, their belief apparently being that supplies would rapidly reach demand, if demand were not restricted. They may have been right.

It was against this background that in May 1948 there occurred in Blackburn a most brutal murder. It resulted in what is arguably one of the finest enquiries involving finger-prints in the history of criminal investigation.

Policing goes back over 600 years in this country, but it developed in a somewhat piecemeal fashion. Indeed, in the mid-nineteenth century many local police forces had as few as fifty men. One thing about them is certain; the force would know its own villains. Thieves have always travelled, but mobility has been relative to the times. If a man with stolen property hitched a lift on a slow-moving wagon he could be caught by a rider on a faster horse. A thief on a fast horse, knowing his own moors and by-ways, could get away.

It is also startling to remember that the first juries were composed specifically of men who knew the offender, because they alone were in a position to judge whether he was guilty and whether anything could properly be said in his defence. Nowadays, of course, every endeavour is made to collect a jury which does not know any of the contenders in a case and can therefore be impartial. Even magistrates are supposed to declare any private interest that might cloud their judgement. Things change but slowly, and it is only in looking back that change can be properly assessed.

In 1969 a Royal Commission on Local Government reported that 'England needs a pattern of local authorities with clear responsibilities big enough in area, population and resources to provide first-class services.' Thus came the death knell for several (in most cases efficient) small police forces. They were soon replaced by fewer but larger, if not more efficient, police forces. As technology has developed, so police forces, fire brigades and local government have increased their equipment; there has not been any alternative. But such expertise has to be shared and its use cover a wide area. Where expenditure is heavy, the huge police forces we have today do in fact share facilities. This is a responsible and sensible approach.

Prior to this reorganization, if a murder occurred in a small borough and the Chief Constable decided that he did not have the necessary resources to deal with the situation he would seek assistance from New Scotland Yard or from a larger neighbouring force. How the newspapers loved it when the 'Yard' were called in! The placard writers worked overtime, and outside all the newsagents' shops would be the enticing words 'Murder – Yard Called In'. How many thriller writers have made a decent living out of the intrepid 'Yard' man, whizzing up (or down) from London to take charge. What calling in the 'Yard' usually meant was the arrival of two experienced officers, one of whom would be senior and expected to control the investigation, and the other his reliable right-hand man. They would need to be pretty diplomatic, too, because the local Chief Constable, having called them in, had probably offended his own head of CID. If a neighbouring force gave help, it was usually by way of extra manpower or some equipment.

Whilst not denigrating this kind of help in any way, it must be emphasized that it is the local policeman with knowledge of the area, the nature of the community and its criminals, the reaper of casual information, known and it is hoped respected by the local populace, on whom the success of the enquiry depends. In the case of the Blackburn murder, such a man was Inspector William Barton.

Blackburn has always been important to Lancashire, being a mill town with a skilled labour force, turning out high-quality goods for export all over the world. Manchester is surrounded by a network of such towns and, when their goods were technically finished, they would come into the big Manchester warehouses to be run through the measuring machines, checked for faults, labelled and packed according to each customer's requirements, and shipped overseas. Blackburn, Bolton, Oldham, Burnley and the rest had been busy during the war years and, whilst some man-made fabrics had been invented and more were yet to come, cotton was still important. But, like so many other places, these towns had suffered bombing, and house repairs had had to go by the board because the men and materials necessary were not available. By 1948, however, a start had been made on bringing about the improvements we all hoped for, but it was not always easy.

Blackburn lies in a hollow, though it is higher above sea level than one might think, not far from windy moorlands. There were still cobbled streets here and there, and some gas lighting. Clogs were still being worn because they were practical for many trades. Blackburn was noted for good weavers and in 1948 there were about 110,000 inhabitants in the town. Most of the 35,000 houses were of the working-class type, set in compact terraces. A large proportion were two-up-and-two-down, with a backyard and an outside lavatory, though in some cases a small row would have their lavatories set next to each other in a common courtyard. On high ground, south-east of the town, stands Queen's Park Hospital overlooking Blackburn itself. It was in this hospital, on 15 May 1948, that the events which caused so much public interest, concern and co-operation took place.

Like most of the public hospitals built in Victorian times, Queen's Park consists of several buildings in grounds covering some seventy acres. A high stone wall surrounded most of it except for a small portion in the north-west corner, where there was a disused quarry. Part of the wall had collapsed at this point, but to serve as a protection a six-foot-high chestnut paling fence, with interwoven wire, had been erected. The main entrance had a porters' lodge where legitimate callers entered, stating their name, address and business.

In accordance with the custom of the times, the local public assistance committee controlled the hospital's affairs, catering for mental patients, aged and infirm persons, maternity cases, general illness cases – and children. Naturally, separate wards were maintained for dealing with these specialities. Emphasizing the role of the public assistance committee was the continuing presence of a casual ward, where vagrants or tramps were accommodated for the night – mostly around ten on any one night. In all the hospital housed about 1,200 people.

The events of the day in question revolved around ward CH3, which was a children's ward at the furthest point of the hospital from the lodge entrance. There were twelve cots in it, though only six were occupied, and June Anne Devaney, almost four, was in fact the oldest patient.

She had been admitted to the ward ten days earlier, suffering from pneumonia. The only child in the room who could talk, she was a big girl for her age, and when seen in bed she could have been taken for six or seven years old. June had recovered well in the hospital, and her parents were expecting to take her home during this particular Saturday.

About twenty minutes after midnight the night nurse in charge, Gwendoline Humphreys, went round all the cots, saw their occupants were safely asleep, and then went to the kitchen near the ward to start preparations for their breakfasts. She had been in the kitchen about twenty minutes when she heard a child's voice. She went quickly back to the ward, but found nothing amiss, so she returned to the kitchen – little children quite often call out in their sleep. At twenty minutes past one she noticed a draught. She went to the porch doors and found them open, but did not worry about it because the outer door had a faulty catch and a strong gust of wind could have opened it. Then she went into CH3 ward to see to one of the babies. She saw that June was not in her cot. The drop side of the cot was still in its raised position and, as it was about four feet above the ground, it was not likely she would or could have climbed out. She appeared to have been lifted out, very neatly.

On the floor, by the side of June's cot, was a Winchester bottle. This kind of bottle comes in several sizes and this particular one was quite large. When the nurse had last seen it, an hour earlier, it had been in its usual place on a trolley at the end of the ward some six yards away. A quick glance round showed some footprints on the polished floor, one near June's cot – and they seemed to Gwen Humphreys to have been made by someone in bare feet. This was a frightening situation for her.

A quick alarm and a rapid search by hospital staff of adjoining wards and the hospital grounds did not reveal anything useful. At five minutes to two the police were told. A squad of officers carried out a systematic search of the grounds and one hour and twenty-two minutes later, at 3.17 A.M., June's body was found lying near the boundary wall some 283 feet away from the ward. The Chief Constable, the police surgeon and Detective Supertindent Woodmansey of Lancashire Constabulary arrived at 4 A.M. They saw little June lying, face down, in the grass. Her nightie was lifted a little and was dirty as though she had been rolled about on the ground. It was obvious she had been brutally raped, her left buttock had been severely bitten and she had been battered to death by being swung against the stone wall by her ankles.

The hospital area was sealed off. The immediate help of New Scotland Yard was sought and the Chief Constable of Lancashire placed the whole of his large force and its equipment at the disposal of the Chief Constable of Blackburn. The Assistant Chief Constable of Lancashire and officers manning radio cars arrived quickly. Even hardened officers can be deeply moved by the killing of a young child, and this abduction of a three-year-old girl from her bed, and her violent and nasty death, were worse than most.

A bloodhound was brought to the hospital. It was given the scent from the child's bed and the footmarks on the ward floor. It sniffed around a bit and then led its handler to the child's body; no further. Police officers followed the trail directly to where the boundary wall joined the paling fence, where there was a small gap. It was possible to climb through this gap and to reach a small ledge skirting the edge of the quarry. It needed careful manoeuvring not to fall sixty feet into the quarry before reaching Queen's Road, but somebody had done it, and got away.

A forensic scientist joined the team; he came from the Home Office Laboratory at Preston, which now operates from Euxton, near Chorley. Colin Campbell, Officer in Charge of Lancashire Constabulary's Finger-print Department, also arrived. The usual photographs were taken of the child's body and its immediate surroundings, and she was then taken to the police mortuary. At that time Colin Campbell was one of the country's foremost finger-print experts, a man of vast and useful experience.

An ordinary chap cannot imagine himself taking a little girl from a hospital cot, carrying her outside the building and killing her. Nevertheless, any investigating officer has to imagine himself doing just that; to cast round for the slightest disturbance, scratch, scuffmark, fibre, that will throw any light on the actions of the intruder.

Together with Mr Looms, the Chief Constable of Blackburn, Colin Campbell stood outside the children's ward. Both men peered through a window near the cot which had been occupied by June Anne Devaney. As they did so, Mr Looms briefed the Chief Inspector as to all known human circumstances in the case, particularly drawing his attention to the Winchester bottle standing on the floor near June's cot.

The ward, about forty feet long and eighteen feet wide, had in it twelve empty cots. Once the murder was discovered the remaining children had been moved to another ward. A quick tour of the outside of the building showed there was a verandah on the west side of the ward; on the east, a concrete path. In each of the west and east walls of the ward were three glass doors that were never locked. At the ward's northern end was a small office containing three windows, and two of these were left open for ventilation. At the southerly end was a corridor which gave access to bathroom and kitchen, and another short corridor, at right-angles, led to the ward where toddlers were accommodated.

Obviously, there had been many open doors and windows available to the intruder, so it wasn't surprising that Colin Campbell didn't find any signs of forcible entry on which attention could be concentrated.

After this quick tour Campbell and Looms stood in the corridor at the southerly end of the ward. They stared into the ward, looking particularly at what seemed to be a trail of bare footprints which had been made on the wax-polished floor. On more detailed examination it was seen that the foot had not been bare, as the nurse had thought, but had been stockinged, the pressure of the foot making shallow impressions in the thin layer of wax polish.

This trail appeared to begin at the door leading from the office at the north end of the ward. It travelled to the first cot on the west side, then to an instrument trolley standing against the north wall, recrossed to the west side of the ward and to the second cot from the door. At this cot the footprints were implanted side by side on the floor, as if made by a person standing alongside the cot, looking at its occupant. Similar footprints were found

alongside the third and fourth cots, this latter being the
one from which June had been taken. The toes of these
footprints were at right-angles to the cot side and actually
under its edge, showing their maker was standing very
close to the cot. From there the footprints went down the
ward and stopped about two feet from the south door.
There, they seemed to turn round and traverse the entire
length of the ward in a straight line right up to the north
door. There were no footprints on the east side of the
ward. It was pretty clear what this evil human being had
done.

Colin Campbell selected the most distinct right and left
footprints and asked for them to be photographed.

Now it was time to concentrate on the Winchester
bottle found near June's cot. It was labelled 'Sterile
Water'. It also bore twenty finger and palm impressions.

Some of these impressions appeared to have been made
recently, whilst others seemed fairly old. And if you ask
me now, after so many years of experience of my own,
how a finger-print officer can tell the age of a print, I
have to confess it is almost impossible to put into words.
A print can have a 'new' look; the sweat which has made
it somehow looks fresh. It has not been changed by
atmospheric dust molecules. One can be wrong in this
judgement of a 'fresh' print, but it's rare. Most important
in the case of this Winchester bottle was that the recent
impressions were much larger than the other, older ones.
Colin Campbell took the Winchester bottle back to his
own force headquarters and in the Finger-print Department the impressions were quickly photographed. After
the smaller, older impressions had been eliminated as
those of the nursing staff (their prints having of course
been obtained for comparison) a large-scale search began
in the department's files.

Whilst the Detective Chief Inspector had been examining the Winchester bottle in the ward, the Home Office forensic scientist, Mr Jones, had also been busy. He scraped the wax from the floor where the footprints were implanted. Certain fibres, invisible to the naked eye, were later found embedded in these scrapings. He also measured the footprints. They were ten and a quarter inches long: not a small foot. The next examination he made was of one of the three windows which formed the bay in the small office at the north end of the ward. It had been left open, and it overlooked a concrete area at the rear of the ward. There were marks on the window which were consistent with a person having climbed through it. Adhering to the wooden window frame the scientist found fibres. He collected them, and with the other specimens took them back to the laboratory.

A special squad of officers had been established in the hospital, under the control of Detective Chief Inspector Bob McCartney. They screened the movements of all inmates, staff and patients alike. All persons who had legitimate access to the ward were finger-printed and the finger-print forms were given to Colin Campbell for elimination purposes. And providing an extra bit of news for the papers, Detective Chief Inspector John Capstick of New Scotland Yard, a name well recognized now, came with Detective Inspector Daws. Mr Capstick took control of the enquiries.

There had to be a post-mortem examination. Although it can be very distressing to relatives, it is an essential part of the enquiry. The pathologist found that June's death was due to shock caused by a fractured skull and extensive injuries. The bite on her buttock had been made before death, as had a bruise in each groin. Internal injuries were consistent with rape. Specimens were taken not only from the body but also from various places at the scene of the enquiry. Those which proved vital were:

Fibres from the window of the room adjoining the ward.
Blood and hairs from the boundary wall of the hospital.
Fibres found on the child's body.
A single pubic hair found on the child's body.
The child's nightdress.
Various swabs.
Fibres taken from the footmarks in the ward.

Add to these the finger-prints on the Winchester bottle and the footprints found in the ward, and you have an idea of the material on which the police had to work.

The hospital staff and local people were much concerned. They began to think, and think hard. Quickly came the news that, at about a quarter past eleven on the night of Friday 14 May, some nurses in the nurses' home about a hundred yards from ward CH3 saw what tradition describes as a peeping Tom peering into a window on the ground floor. When a nurse told him to go away, he put a finger to his mouth and said, 'Hush, don't tell anyone.' Naturally, this looked helpful, but on 19 May he was traced and interviewed, showing that though he might have been up to no good he was not the man who had left the finger-prints on the Winchester bottle.

On 18 May a taxi driver came forward to say that just before midnight on the 14th he had picked up a man in the town centre on a road which leads to the hospital, and had set him down in Queen's Road near the quarry. When he got out of the taxi, the man had run across the quarry and was last seen going in the direction of the hospital. The taxi driver could not describe the man in any detail, but thought he had a local accent.

After giving a great deal of thought to the evidence

in the ward itself, Detective Chief Inspector Campbell deduced that the murderer had entered the ward by the north door and had peeped into the first cot; he had then crossed to the instrument trolley, where he had picked up the Winchester bottle, before crossing to the second and third cots, where he had gazed at the sleeping children. He had then walked to the fourth cot, put the Winchester bottle on the floor, lifted June from her cot and had carried her to the south door. He had there presumably heard a noise and had turned and retraced his steps, walked the length of the ward and carried the child out through the north door.

A conference was called on 18 May at the Central Police Office. All officers concerned in the investigations were present.

Chief Inspector Campbell gave his assessment of the situation. He said that after the most exhaustive comparisons with both finger and palm prints of all persons who had access to the hospital, all the finger and palm impressions found at the scene had been eliminated with the exception of ten prints found on the Winchester bottle. These ten were the fresh marks which had been made by a person with a large hand.

He believed these impressions consisted of a left thumb print, a sequence of left fore, middle and ring fingerprints and a left palm print. There were two impressions which appeared to have been made by right middle and ring fingers. The remaining three were partial fingerprints which could not be allocated to any particular finger. Whilst he would not make a guess as to the murderer's age or as to whether he was right- or left-handed, Campbell did say that having regard to the span of the sequence of finger-prints left on the bottle, the clarity of the ridge detail and the absence of coarseness or temporary injuries, he believed they were made by a biggish man who was not old and did little or no manual work.

For some hours all the available evidence was discussed by those present at the conference and eventually the following four conclusions were arrived at. Firstly, the finger-prints on the bottle were undoubtedly those of the murderer, as all males in the hospital and all persons with legitimate access to CH3 ward had been eliminated. Secondly, the wanted man was someone living locally, who knew the hospital and its surroundings, particularly in view of the taxi driver's evidence. Few people could take off into the darkness and successfully negotiate the edge of this quarry; and it seemed a return trip had been made the same way. Thirdly, the man had to be reasonably tall. A small person could not have lifted June cleanly out of the cot without dropping the cot sides, and there was no evidence that this had been done. Furthermore, a small man would not be likely to have feet ten and a quarter inches long. Fourthly, the person's clothing would be bloodstained.

The big question now was how the finger-prints could best be used to trace the murderer. All prints filed in the bureaux were being examined, but this would take several weeks and, in any case, the wanted man might not have been recorded in general criminal files; and whilst this search was proceeding the trail would be going cold.

The problem was huge. A bold and courageous decision was taken to deal with it. All male persons of sixteen years or over known to have been in Blackburn on 14 and 15 May 1948 would be finger-printed. The manpower, the time and the paperwork could be provided; a matter of logistics. What was disturbing was the knowledge that at least one person in Blackburn had a good reason for not having his finger-prints taken and might be expected to do whatever he could to avoid putting himself on record. Of course many men could have left Blackburn for perfectly legitimate reasons: to work elsewhere, join the army, or even to die and be buried in the cemetery or be cremated. All these things can be checked, but it takes time.

Inspector William Barton of Blackburn Borough Police was allocated the most demanding task of all, that of ensuring that no man in the town of Blackburn slipped through the net of the finger-printing officers. It was an enormous responsibility, though he was comforted by the fact that the finger-prints on the Winchester bottle were clear and could be matched without difficulty if their maker were traced. If and when the time came there would not be a grain of doubt. Inspector Barton picked his small staff and gave them a simple instruction: 'No adult male must be missed.'

On occasions such as this the newspapers can be particularly helpful and through them the Mayor of Blackburn appealed for men over the age of sixteen to volunteer their finger-prints. Alongside this the Chief Constable assured everybody that such prints would not be used for any other reason and that when they had served their purpose they would be publicly destroyed. Public feeling was running very high indeed. The nation had just come through a long and bloody war which had been impossible to avoid; the hospital incident was an unnecessary and evil thing, and people were quick to help. When the special squad of finger-print officers made their first visits to houses in the vicinity of the hospital on Sunday 23 May, eight days after the killing, they found everybody on their side. This is a heartening feeling for any officer of the law.

Plans were made to obviate overlapping of visits. Thoroughness was essential. The electoral registers were used to ensure that every house in Blackburn, some 35,000 dwellings, was visited. Not every house is on the roll, but as one goes round a street armed with such a list any omissions are obvious. The registers at that time recorded all those over the age of twenty-one and thus entitled to vote. When visiting a house an officer could ask about other, younger members of the family. You might think to yourself that a member of a household could easily suspect a brother or son and omit him deliberately. True enough, but a check with neighbours either side will reveal discrepancies.

Armed with the Blackburn registers, divided into fourteen voting divisions, subdivided into sections and then alphabetical street and road order, the finger-print squad went into action. Carrying finger-print cards and inked pads they worked to a predetermined pattern until every house in every street was covered. Whilst doing this, enquiries were made to obtain information about persons not normally resident in the town but who were there on the night in question. Public co-operation was truly magnificent. Each night all the gathered information was handed in to Inspector Barton along with completed finger-print cards.

This mass of detail meant enquiries had to be made in all parts of the United Kingdom via local police, and to forces in Australia, Singapore, India, Egypt, South Africa, Canada, the USA and almost every country in Europe. People were located in all these places and finger-printed for elimination.

The finger-print cards were cancelled against the appropriate entry in the electoral roll and then sent to Chief Inspector Campbell for comparison. It didn't take long to check an individual card, but it took a long time to examine all the thousands. After checking, each card was stamped 'Cancelled' and filed in strict alphabetical order at police headquarters in Blackburn.

At the same time Detective Chief Inspector Capstick of New Scotland Yard was seeing that other lines of enquiry were being pursued regarding the peculiar nature of the crime and its implications. You will realize how extensive these enquiries can be when you study the following types of people who were seen and finger-printed. Much of this line of enquiry is not pleasant, but it has to be done. The human psyche is a complex and often secretive thing.

1 About 3,600 persons discharged from mental institutions in the northern half of the country, the nature of the crime suggesting a person of low mentality. Many of these persons had been convicted of offences involving indecency.

2 About 3,000 male persons of uncertain nationality; prisoners of war and Polish Army men living in camps within twenty miles of Blackburn. This line of enquiry arose from the biting of the child, not normal in Great Britain, but fairly often committed on the continent in crimes of indecency. Lancashire Constabulary officers conducted this part of the investigation.

3 Epileptics and sufferers from schizophrenia who might have committed such a crime during a temporary black-out.

4 Persons suffering from venereal disease, so far as the confidential treatment of such persons would permit. Some sufferers from this kind of disease believe, wrongly of course, that sexual intercourse with a virgin or young child will effect a cure.

5 Persons known to commit or suspected of committing sexual offences contrary to nature, that is homosexuals and the like (though the phrase 'contrary to nature' would now be hotly disputed, I don't doubt). Many people in this category were the subject of anonymous letters to the police.

6 All persons having recently committed suicide and remaining in mortuaries, and those who had recently attempted suicide.

7 Casuals and other people forming the moving population of the district, who might have stayed at the casual ward on some previous occasion and thus be familiar with the hospital.

8 All persons missing from home at the relevant period.

Working on these eight groups was quite an undertaking, and indeed it is likely that some people came into more than one category. Assaults on young children are, regrettably, not uncommon and it is carefully amassed local knowledge about the kind of people who commit such crimes which can be helpful not merely to trace a wrongdoer but also to eliminate the rest.

After about eight weeks of intensive finger-printing work most of the houses in Blackburn had been visited, but no clear lead had as yet been established.

There was another source of information in 1948 which would not, so far as I know, be available to us now, and Inspector Barton did not hesitate to take advantage of it. To do whatever was possible to ensure that every person in the borough would be finger-printed, the records already obtained were compared with the records kept by the local registration officer for the issuing of food ration books. In 1948 these would be reasonably up to date, because between 30 June and 18 July 1948, new ration books had been issued to everybody in response to the completion by each person of a reference leaf from the previous year's books. If this was not done, a new ration book was not issued. The reference leaves gave the name, address, date of birth and national registration of the holder, all filed in strict alphabetical order of surname at the registration office.

On 18 July finger-printing was suspended. The next three weeks were spent by Inspector Barton and his squad in the registration office. They compared each finger-print card with its counterpart in the registration files. When this had been done, the remaining ration book reference leaves showed the balance of the population which still required to be finger-printed. A good deal of clerical work followed, producing new lists, separated into the sub-divisions of the borough wards.

House-to-house finger-printing restarted on Monday 9 August, but now the officers had lists giving particulars of specific persons whose prints were needed to complete the check.

On the night of Wednesday 11 August one of the squad obtained the finger-prints of Peter Griffiths, aged twenty-two, at his home, 31 Birley Street, Blackburn. His card, with others obtained that day, was sent in the normal way to Chief Inspector Campbell at the Lancashire Constabulary Finger-print Bureau, arriving at about 3 P.M. on Thursday 12 August 1948.

One of the experts, making the comparisons, spotted on Griffiths's card the finger-prints exactly as they appeared on the bottle. It was quite a moment. He could hardly believe his own eyes. He double checked and then exclaimed, 'I've got him! It's here!'

In addition to his name and address, there was national

registration number NBA 6917–188, indicating he was an
ex-serviceman. News of the identification quickly went to
the Chief Constable of Blackburn. His name would not
have been found in the electoral register, as he had not
qualified for inclusion when the last list was prepared on
30 June 1947.

Friday 13 August 1948 was not Peter Griffiths's lucky
day, but it was a good one for the police. He was arrested
near his home and brought to police headquarters. He
admitted his guilt in the following statement:

I want to say that on the night the little girl was killed at the
Queen's Park Hospital, it was on a Friday night, the Friday
before Whitsun. I left home that night on my own about six
o'clock. I went out to spend a quiet night on my own. I went to
the Dun Horse pub or hotel and bought myself about five pints
of bitter beer. Then I went to Yates' Wine Lodge and had a
glass of Guinness and two double rums. I then had another
glass of Guinness and then went back to the Dun Horse again. I
then had about six more pints of bitter. I was on my own and
came out of there at closing time. I walked down to Jubilee
Street off Darwen Street and I saw a man smoking a cigarette
sitting in a small closed car with the hood on, with wire wheels,
they were painted silver. I did not know him. I had never seen
him before. I asked the man for a light as I had no matches to
light my cigarette. I stayed gabbing to him for about fifteen
minutes. He said to me, 'Are you going home?' I said, 'No, I'm
going to walk round a bit and sober up first.' He asked me
where I lived and I told him. He said, 'Well get in, open the
window and I'll give you a spin.' He took me to the front of the
Queen's Park Hospital and I got out opposite to the iron
railings. I don't know what happened to him, I never saw him
again. I must have got over the railings, for the next thing I
remember was being outside the ward, there were some children. I left my shoes outside the door, which had a brass knob.
I tried the door and it opened to my touch and I went just in
and heard a nurse humming and banging as if she was washing
something so I came out again and waited a few minutes. Then

I went back in again and went straight to the ward like, I think I went in one or two small rooms like, like a kitchen, and then I went back into the ward again. I then picked up a biggish bottle off a shelf. I went half way down the ward with it and then put it down on the floor. I then thought I heard the nurse coming, I turned round sharply, overbalanced and fell against a bed. I remember the child woke up and started to cry, and I hushed her. She then opened her eyes, saw me and the child in the next bed started whimpering. I picked the girl up out of the cot and took her outside by the same door. I carried her in my right arm and she put her arms round my neck and I walked with her down the hospital field. I put her down on the grass. She started crying again and I tried to stop her from crying, but she wouldn't do, like, she wouldn't stop crying. I just lost my temper then and you know what happened then. I banged her head against the wall. I then went back to the verandah outside the ward, sat down and put my shoes on. I then went back to where the child was. I like just glanced at her but did not go right up to her, but went straight on down the field to the delph. I crossed over the path alongside the delph leading into Queen's Park. I walked through the park and came out on Audley Street. I went down Cherry Street into Furthergate, then I went down Eanam to Birley Street and got home somewhere around two o'clock on Saturday morning. It would be somewhere about that time. I went into my house, took me collar and tie off and slept in me suit on the couch downstairs. Mother and father were in bed and did not know what time I came in. I woke up about nine o'clock, got up, washed and shaved, then pressed me suit because I was going out again after I had had my breakfast. I went out then down the town, had a walk round, then went to the Royal Cinema in the afternoon, came out of the pictures at five o'clock, went home and had my tea. I looked at the papers and read about the murder. It didn't shake me, so that I just carried on normally after that. My mother and father asked me where I had been that night and what time I came home and I told them I had been out boozing and had got home at twelve o'clock. This is all I can say and I'm sorry for both parents' sake and I hope I get what I deserve.

Shortly before midnight on Friday 13 August 1948, he was charged with the murder of June Anne Devaney. His finger-prints were again taken, and also palm prints and impressions of his stockinged feet. A comparison resulted in ten of the twenty finger-prints found on the bottle being identified as his.

There was more to come. All possible samples were taken and examined by forensic scientists. Certain clothing was removed from his home. His suit, which he had worn on the night of the murder, was recovered from a pawnbroker's pledge office, where he had pawned it on 30 May. Tests showed that fibres from the window were identical with those of the suit. Fibres taken from the child's body were found to be made of wool ranging in colour between blue and violet, and agreeing exactly with threads from which the suit cloth had been woven. Other wool fibres agreeing with those of the suit were found on her nightdress. And fibres taken from the footprints in the wax on the floor of the ward were found to match a sock taken from Griffiths's home.

Human bloodstains, sufficient for grouping purposes, were found on the lining inside the trousers at the bottom of the fly. This blood was of group A, the same as that of the child. There were more bloodstains on the linings of both trouser side pockets, on the lining at the bottom of each jacket sleeve, on each lapel, on the right front above the top button and inside the right edge, on the top button and near to the right shoulder, and inside the right bottom front.

It was interesting that the speculative conclusions arrived at during the conference had proved substantially correct, because Griffiths was not only local, and five feet, ten and half inches, but also had a good knowledge of the hospital grounds as between the ages of ten and twelve he had been a patient in the very block of buildings from which he had taken the little girl. And he was later identified by the taxi driver as the man set down near the quarry on the fatal night.

The due process of law followed: first the magistrates' court and then on Friday 15 October 1948, he entered a plea of 'not guilty' before Mr Justice Oliver at Lancaster Assizes. Many people not versed in law may wonder why anybody, having admitted guilt, pleads not guilty. In fact, this plea ensures the hearing of all evidence during the trial and a jury verdict, followed by sentence if found guilty. If a guilty plea is entered, even though a jury may be present, the judge conducts proceedings rather differently: an outline of the evidence is given, the judge makes sure that the prisoner has full knowledge of the circumstances in which he is placed, and then sentences him.

On the first day of Griffiths's trial the prosecution evidence was presented in total. It was pretty damning and the defence appeared to accept it almost without question, because there was little or no examination of the Crown witnesses. The case was then adjourned until the following Monday.

From the defence point of view the case was desperate, but Griffiths's counsel was honour bound to try and find a way out for him. An attempt was made, using medical witnesses, to prove that he was schizophrenic and therefore insane when he committed the crime. It was also given in evidence that Griffiths's father had been an inmate of a mental hospital for six months after the end of the First World War and that young Peter's condition could have been inherited. However, a medical officer from Liverpool Prison said he had had Griffiths under almost continual observation since his admission there on 14 August and his conclusion was that Griffiths was sane when he committed the crime.

On the second day of the trial, after only twenty-three minutes, the jury returned a verdict of guilty. It had been a short trial, but it was not surprising in view of the forensic evidence.

When pronouncing sentence, Mr Justice Oliver addressed Griffiths thus:

Peter Griffiths, this jury has found you guilty of a crime of the most brutal ferocity. I entirely agree with this verdict. The sentence of the court upon you is that you be taken from this place to a lawful prison and thence to a place of execution and that you there suffer death by hanging and that your body be afterwards buried within the precincts of the prison in which you shall have been confined before your execution. And may the Lord have mercy on your soul.

The sentence of the court was carried out at Liverpool Prison at nine o'clock on the morning of Friday 19 November 1948.

The people of Blackburn had co-operated magnificently in this enquiry and the promise of destruction of finger-prints was kept: on 3 November about 46,500 finger-print cards, several hundred finger-print forms and numerous other documents were pulped at a local paper mill. The destruction was an event of great local interest, attended by the Mayor of Blackburn, journalists, press photographers and a newsreel cameraman. There had been a press announcement that if persons applied for their finger-print cards to be returned to them this would be done. Some five hundred people did so. No doubt many of these are still preserved in sideboard drawers and the popular old wooden document boxes as a memento of an event in which thousands of innocent people were caught up.

Most murders are of a domestic nature and quickly

detected, and do not arouse much discussion amongst the general public. This case was different. Griffiths, of course, knew what he had done, and many people unversed in the ways of criminals thought he had been stupid to remain in Blackburn and risk detection by being finger-printed. It may be of interest to readers to outline what police reaction would have been to some of the things he could have done.

Firstly, he could have refused to have his prints taken. It will be appreciated that there are people who, being innocent and uninvolved in an event, will refuse to have their finger-prints taken on the grounds of it being their legal right. I do not think Peter Griffiths had this sort of intelligence. If he had refused, his movements on the night in question would have been very carefully looked at. If, in the likely event of his saying he was at some place other than the hospital during the relevant time, he would certainly have qualified as a major suspect when this proved false.

Secondly, he could have left the district. This again would have meant he would come under strong suspicion.

Thirdly, he could have committed suicide, but you will remember that bodies were examined and finger-printed.

Fourthly, he could have engineered an accident to his fingers. Local hospital staff were aware of this possibility and, if he had gone for help having injured the inner surfaces of his hands, subsequent enquiries would have raised suspicion. In any case his normal finger-prints could most likely have been obtained from surfaces in his home. Peter Griffiths took a chance when he volunteered his prints, and lost. He may indeed not have been bright enough to know exactly what he was risking.

A few more thoughts may occur to the reader when considering what Griffiths actually said in his statement and what came out in the course of the enquiry. He may or may not have been confused about the identity of the vehicle in which he was taken to the quarry. He says he had eleven pints of beer, two glasses of Guinness and two double rums between 6 P.M. and the closing time of local pubs; quite an intake, if it were true. If it were so, could he have negotiated the quarry edge so easily? When interviewed after his arrest he would have been closely questioned in great detail. In his statement he glides over the actual attack on the child, probably preferring to push it all to the back of his mind. This is not uncommon in sordid crime.

The vast majority of murder enquiries are solved by team-work. This Blackburn investigation is a perfect example. Each officer, from the highest rank down to the beat Constable and Detective Constable, was but a small cog in a powerful machine. Each officer played his or her part to the full and in so doing gained tremendous support from the entire population of a town.

3

Death Down a Lift Shaft

Over the years many parts of Manchester have changed enormously, sometimes reflecting change in social habits and sometimes changes in trade. For instance, when I was younger, Oxford Street, near the city centre, was a lively place, particularly in the evenings; now it is often deserted. Joining Oxford Street is Whitworth Street, which is also often deserted. Its buildings are magnificent examples of building and architectural skills when cotton was king. Have you ever been in a cotton making-up warehouse? Making-up is the simple but rather elegant process by which cloth, usually printed, is made up into lengths, measured, ticketed and exported. At least, it used to be like that; nobody seems to do it in quite the same way now. A good maker-up was worth his weight in gold. Customers had their own signs and symbols, and these were added to each piece. The maker-up would take the piece from the machine man, roll out the last few yards again along the wide, polished and clean table, re-roll it tightly, tuck in the cut end, and then perhaps wrap round it one or two printed bands of the customer's design; he might then also add an oblong ticket lightly glued to the front. When velvet comprised the order, the turned-in end was often embellished with a gold cut-out paper edging, a very handsome affair. Woe betide the junior who did this job. Blobs of glue where they were not wanted made that youngster highly unpopular with the foreman. The pieces for export were put into lovely white boxes with tissue liners and quite reverently packed in chests to be collected by the railway carter, who was always fond of his horse. He'd draw up underneath the hoist and the containers would be lowered on to his cart, ready to go to the docks.

Tab-ends and bits of waste would gather in big boxes under the work-tables. There was always a market for them. Fent and rag merchants bought them, but if a handy woman wanted a piece for trimming something she could usually have it. Warehouse workers usually were able to buy anything they wanted. Many a yard was sold pre-war for a sixpence and workers never bought third-rate material because they knew what was what.

You'll appreciate that the processing of cotton left a distinct flavour in the air, proclaiming the trade of these huge buildings. The big warehouses in Whitworth Street and surrounding thoroughfares were wonderful monuments to the Victorian age, and the trade gave tremendous numbers of people regular employment.

Princess Street is a major road with one-way traffic and it bisects Whitworth Street. Its function was much the same as that of Whitworth Street in its prime, the appearance of its buildings a little less imposing, and at number 82, in 1961, was Asia House, which still stands today. These large offices and warehouse buildings were mainly occupied by the representatives of the countries with whom Manchester traded world-wide. They had chosen to make their homes in Manchester and it is to such people that she owes much of her varied culture. Asia House had one hundred offices and thirty-six ware-rooms.

A familiar sight in the Manchester of 1961 was the office cleaner arriving at 5.30 in the morning. Work of this kind had to be done before the staff arrived and in those days they started at 7.30 or 8 A.M. Irene Macken was such a cleaner. It was Tuesday, the last day of

February, when she arrived at Asia House to find she could not get in; the side door she normally used was firmly locked and bolted. Sam Rowney, the night watch-man, had usually unlocked this door by the time she got there. Bewildered, she stayed by the door for a full half hour, knocking repeatedly to attract Sam's attention, but in vain. Finally, she went to the front entrance in Princess Street.

The steel-latticed gates were normally securely pad-locked across the front of the door, but this was not a normal day – they were six inches apart. She pushed them further apart and then went through the unlocked front door. She found her way to the rear of the ground floor. Sam Rowney's body was hanging upside down in the lift shaft. His clothing had caught on the top of one of the metal railings which surrounded the old-fashioned shaft. One glance was enough to tell her he was dead.

Irene Macken raced out of the building to Whitworth Street police station nearby and breathlessly told the night-duty Sergeant what she had found.

Police Sergeant Alan Cotton, a close friend of mine from earlier C Division days, went immediately to Asia House with other officers. They could see that Sam was dead and immediately started a search of the building. Quickly they discovered that the trellis gates to the lift shaft on the fifth floor were wide open; not only that, the lattice gates to the shaft were open on the ground floor, and the lift car itself was there.

A solitary electric light bulb was burning inside the lift car whilst the rest of the six-storey building was in utter darkness. Near the lift shaft on the ground floor was a canvas shoe and in a nearby room used by Sam Rowney was a bent screwdriver. It appeared to Sergeant Cotton that Sam had plunged down the lift shaft from the fifth floor. It could, of course, have been an accident; but there was something odd, something not quite right, about the situation.

Samuel Rowney was a sixty-three-year-old bachelor who lived in the Longsight area of Manchester. He had spent thirty years working for the City Surveyor's Department of Manchester Corporation, and had then taken this night watchman's job. For rather less than twelve months he had been responsible for the security of the building between 7.30 in the evening and 7.30 the following morning.

On the evening of Monday 27 February, a few hours before all this had occurred, a Mr Lindsay worked late in his office on the ground floor of Asia House. As he was leaving, at five to nine, he saw Sam standing near the front entrance. He was the last known person to see Sam alive.

Sergeant Cotton regarded Sam's death as highly suspicious and officers of the CID were quickly sent for. They made a more detailed examination and asked for Finger-print Bureau staff. I was sent. It was to be the first murder investigation I worked on, and the first murder trial at which I subsequently gave evidence.

At 9.55 A.M. on 28 February, along with other members of the finger-print team, I saw Sam Rowney's body in the same position in which Irene Macken had found it less than four hours earlier. As I stood in front of the lift shaft I could see the body hanging, head downwards, between the right side of the lift car and the heavy metal balustrade surrounding the shaft. The head was about four feet clear of the ground in the well of the lift shaft, and facing towards the front of the lift.

Sergeant Cotton voiced his suspicions and pointed out that there appeared to be one or two small blood spots on the floor of the lift car and that two parallel scratch marks, which had been made on the linoleum floor, led from the lift shaft, along the corridor, through the telephone operator's room and into the typists' office of the Oxford Packing Company, where they ended at a swivel chair with metal castors, which was standing in a corner of the office.

Similar tracks and a spot of blood were found on the stone floor immediately outside the open lift-shaft gates on the fifth floor.

The typist whose chair it was worked for the Oxford Packing Company. Her name was Mary Richardson and she proved of great assistance in the early stages of the enquiry and at the subsequent trial. She said that when she left work the previous day the chair was not only in a different position to that which it now occupied, but that a piece of white cotton cloth had been covering the seat, secured by a number of drawing pins. This piece of white material was now missing, although the drawing pins were still in the underside of the chair, with fragments of the white material stuck to them. Despite a lengthy search, the material could not be found. She also pointed out that the seat of her chair appeared to have been wiped and that there were small bloodstains on it.

The early examination continued, and the newspaper reporters clustered around the main entrance to Asia House. Gerald Alexandri Fontes, a director of A. Fontes & Company with offices on the first floor of Asia House, came forward to complain that money had been stolen from a petty-cash box kept in a locked safe inside his office, and that another safe in the next office appeared to have been opened, even though no forcible entry could be found to any of his offices. If there had been any lingering doubt that Sam's death had been other than accidental, it now evaporated. It was obvious we were investigating a case of murder.

Examination of the circumstances I have already described led to the conclusion that the watchman had been attacked on the ground floor, then placed in the typist's chair and dragged to the lift, in which he had been taken up to the fifth floor. The killer had then taken him out of the lift car, sent it up to the sixth floor, reopened the lift-shaft gates on the fifth floor and tipped the watchman down the shaft. As I have explained, the equipment was old fashioned and, instead of being completely enclosed by a solid wall, it had an ornate metal fence around it at each floor. The railings of this fence did not reach completely to the ceiling and the watchman's left sock had caught on one of the spikes on the ground floor, leaving him suspended, upside down, just above the bottom of the lift shaft.

My part of the enquiry was to work in the Fontes offices on the first floor. Someone had opened two safes and money had gone from a cash box. A detailed examination was called for.

My luck was in. Most of us like to see shining brass-work, particularly if it is not our job to clean it. The cleaner for this company was meticulous and the brass-work was her pride and joy. She polished it every evening after the staff had left. For a finger-print officer at the scene of a murder investigation it was like manna from heaven, providential help.

I began by examining the swing doors leading from the first-floor staircase to the office corridor. On each of these swing doors was a large, beautifully polished brass handle. I carefully removed the handles from the swing doors and on the left one I found two finger-prints which were still glistening with perspiration. I put this handle to one side. In the general office was a floor-standing safe alongside the far wall. It was wide open. On the floor of the safe itself was a cash box from which both money and property had been stolen. Careful examination and a little discreet powdering brought further finger and thumb impressions to light.

In the next office the careful cleaner had been just as busy. There was another safe, allegedly opened by the murderer. In the centre of the safe door was a highly polished brass knob. I carefully removed it from the door and on the back of it found two finger-prints, again freshly made and glistening with sweat.

On a safe in a third office I found a portion of palm print on the left-hand front edge near the door. Due almost entirely to the diligence of the cleaning lady I had the good fortune to collect a number of finger-prints which I confidently believed to have been left by the murderer. With a highly polished brass handle, an equally highly polished brass knob and a cash box I made my way back to the Finger-print Bureau at police head-quarters, where other members of the team were grouped around the typist's chair. From the back of it they had recovered a portion of a right palm impression made, they hoped, by the killer. Quickly the finger-prints and palm prints of all the employees at Fontes and the Oxford Packing Company were taken. A swift check was made. The prints we had collected from the chair, the brasswork and the cash box were still outstanding. We were confident we had found the murderer's prints.

At 3.30 P.M. the same day, a managing director of Cousins & Company, whose offices were on the second floor of Asia House, discovered that his brown leather brief-case had vanished. His name was Kenneth McEwen

Copeland; the case bore his initials K.M.C., and contained pencils and tracing cloth. He had last seen it four days earlier. No forcible entry could be found to these offices.

This was the break we needed though we did not know it at the time. We looked set for a long and detailed enquiry; diligent slogging seemed to be the way we would reach the killer and the next day we began the first stage of that routine.

An early task was to finger-print all the people who worked in this large office block. It could be that the person responsible was a man with inside knowledge of both building and security procedures. Another officer and I began next morning with all the people who worked on the ground floor. As we finger-printed each person I compared the prints taken with the photographs of the prints found on the safe door and the cashbox. It was the first part of a long and tedious job.

All the daily papers that day contained reports of this bizarre murder hunt and described the missing leather brief-case with the initials K.M.C. embossed on it in gold.

At lunch time that day, in Piccadilly railway station, Manchester, the left luggage attendant, George Glasgow, was poring over his daily paper as he finished the remains of his lunch. Naturally, he read about the murder. Suddenly he stopped when he read the description of the brief-case; he knew that an identical case had been handed to him at the left luggage office that very morning.

George Glasgow immediately told the police. Detective Sergeant John Sparks hurried across to Piccadilly station to investigate. He examined the case; yes, it was embossed with the initials K.M.C., and it contained pencils and tracing paper. George Glasgow told the

Sergeant that the case had been handed to him by a taxi driver acting upon the instructions of a third person. Immediately a team of detectives began enquiries to trace the taxi driver. Every rank in the city centre was visited and the drivers questioned. It was crucial to find him, because obviously he held the key to the entire set of circumstances surrounding the death.

Quite quickly the driver was found and interviewed. He was Francis Wilson. At 9 A.M. that day he had picked up a male passenger in Albert Square and taken him the short distance to the junction of Princess Street and Whitworth Street, within a hundred yards of Asia House. The passenger had got out of the cab and asked the driver to take a brief-case to the left luggage office at Piccadilly station and deposit it there. He doubted whether the staff would accept the case and said so to his passenger, who then said, 'Well, please take it and tell them that Mr Singleton will call and collect it in two hours.' With that the taxi driver took it to Piccadilly station.

Sergeant Sparks returned to Asia House, where Mr Copeland identified it as the one stolen from his office. The description and name supplied by the taxi driver fitted a seventeen-year-old man who worked in Asia House. Discreet enquiries revealed that Sydney Singleton worked as a warehouseman for P. and G. Fabrics Limited and had finished work at 5.05 P.M. on the evening of the murder. At 5.40 P.M. he spoke to the commissionaire employed at Asia House, who agreed to place a bet for him on a dog race. Singleton handed the commissionaire six shillings and a betting slip.

At about the same time, Thomas Sheerin, an employee of Oxford Packing Company, was standing near the front

entrance of Asia House in Princess Street when he saw
Singleton re-enter the building.

On the day the murder had been discovered, and at
the time Mr Copeland was reporting the theft of his brief-
case, Sydney Singleton was being interviewed in a nearby
office by Detective Constable Thorpe as part of routine
enquiries. He was shown a photograph of the murdered
man and asked if he knew him or could give any details
as to his associates. Singleton denied knowing Sam
Rowney and said, 'I've told you, I don't know anything
at all about the old geezer. Anyway, it was an accident,
wasn't it?' But the chance of passing off the incident as
an accident had long since gone.

Finger-prints would confirm or refute our suspicions.
Singleton's prints were taken and rushed to the Finger-
print Bureau, where an instant check was made. The
palm print on the swivel chair, the palm print on the safe,
the finger-prints on the brass safe knob and the brass
door handle, and the finger- and thumb prints on the
cash box were all identical to those of young Sydney.

At 4.55 P.M. on 1 March 1961 Sydney Singleton was
interviewed at Asia House by Detective Superintendent
Eric Cunningham, who had been placed in charge of the
investigation only that morning. During this interview a
negative statement was obtained from Singleton. In it he
denied ever having been in the offices of A. Fontes &
Company, something we could prove to be false. He
later admitted that after he had finished work on the
Monday evening he had returned to Asia House in order
to place a bet with the commissionaire, but insisted that
after doing this he went straight home. After further
questioning he changed his story completely and told
Superintendent Cunningham that he had gone to Belle
Vue Greyhound Track, where he had met a Birmingham

man. He could not name the man, but went on to say that they had agreed to break into Asia House to steal cash. They had entered the building and he, Singleton, was on the fifth floor when the other man brought the watchman up to that floor on a chair.

Suddenly young Singleton stopped talking, looked at Superintendent Cunningham, and said, 'It's no use, is it? You don't believe me. Come upstairs to where I work. I'll show you the bar I hit him with.' Superintendent Cunningham escorted Singleton to the second-floor premises of P. & G. Fabrics, but found them locked.

'It's after five o'clock,' said Singleton, 'they've all gone home. The iron bar is inside. However, you will want this.' He then produced a wallet. 'There's twenty-five pounds in there. Last night I went to the dogs with the money that I stole from Fontes, and won.'

Keys were obtained for the premises of P. & G. Fabrics and an iron bar was recovered from beneath rolls of cloth in the warehouse. Singleton identified the bar as the one he had used to attack the night watchman. He then went on to make a written statement in which he confessed to the premeditated attack on the night watchman in quite chilling detail.

In his statement, he said that during the previous nine months he had become addicted to gambling and that he had been placing bets on both dog racing and horse racing, and that he had gambled away his savings and his holiday money. Not only that, he had decided to leave his job at Asia House and to steal money from there before he left.

He admitted that at 5.45 on the evening of Monday 27 February he had re-entered Asia House. Because the lift was being used by other people, he had used the back staircase and had gone into the office of Cousins &

Company on the second floor, using a key he had stolen some weeks previously. Quietly he had settled down for the night. He saw the brief-case which had been left by Mr Copeland and a plan formed in his mind.

At 10.45 that night he telephoned Sam Rowney from the office where he was concealed. He told Rowney that he was Mr Copeland, speaking from home. He said he was worried because he had mislaid his brief-case, that he may have left it in his office, and asked Sam to go along to the office to see if he could find it for him. Singleton said that Sam agreed to find the brief-case if he could, and ring Mr Copeland to tell him the result of the search.

Singleton replaced the receiver and quietly went down the back staircase to the office of Oxford Packing Company on the ground floor, part of which was used by Sam. As Singleton was creeping down the back stairs Sam Rowney was using the lift to go to the second-floor office of Cousins & Company.

Singleton was concealed in the typist's room of Oxford Packing Company, near the swivel chair, when he saw the watchman return with the brief-case. The town-hall clock had just struck eleven when Sam sat down in the telephonist's office with his back to Singleton, who was concealed in the next office, and picked up the telephone and began to dial a number.

Before he had finished dialling Singleton crept up behind him and struck him on the back of the head with an iron bar he had obtained from his own warehouse. The watchman was knocked unconscious. Singleton put him in the swivel chair and dragged him to the lift, taking the iron bar with him. The two of them went up to the fifth floor in the lift. No sooner had he dragged him out of the lift car than Singleton saw that Sam appeared to be regaining consciousness. This presented a threat to this nasty young man; Sam Rowney had to be silenced. Singleton set about him once more, hitting him with the iron bar about the head and shoulders, and told the police that he must have struck too hard because he slumped forward and the chair rocked. Rowney then fell through the open lift gates, down the lift shaft, as, according to Singleton, the lift car had moved upwards of its own accord. The poor man had not fallen straight down but had banged about from side to side.

After Sam had fallen down the lift shaft, Singleton said the lift car had come down again to the fifth floor and he got into it and travelled to the first floor. He walked down the stairs to the ground floor, looked at Rowney and saw that he was dead.

Removing the cleaner's keys from the office of Oxford Packing Company, he went into several offices, but did not steal anything until he came to A. Fontes & Company. There he unlocked the swing door and went in. Searching around, he found a cardboard box containing keys to the safes. Using these, he opened the safes and stole money. Leaving the office, he carefully locked the swing door behind him and replaced the keys in Oxford Packing Company's offices.

On his way out of Asia House he picked up the brief-case that Sam Rowney had brought down. As he tried to leave the building by the front entrance he found that the heavy metal trellis gates there were secured by a padlock and chain. Using a screwdriver taken from the watchman's room he tried to force the padlock, but instead merely bent the screwdriver, which he returned to its rightful place. He then concealed the murder weapon beneath rolls of cloth which he knew would not be moved for some time, and finally he let himself out of the building using the keys of the dead watchman. As he walked home from Manchester to Salford he threw the keys together with the padlock and chain into the River Irwell.

He concluded his statement by saying that he thought it quite ridiculous that there should be only one watchman in a building the size of Asia House and that if there had been two watchmen on duty he would not have attempted to steal anything and no one would have been killed. A neat but hardly justifiable line of thought to transfer his guilt to somebody else.

William Lambie, a service superintendent of the long-established Otis Elevator Company, made various tests on the Asia House lift. His opinion was that, when the lift car had been stopped, it was extremely unlikely that it would continue to move in an upwards direction.

When Singleton committed the crime he was four months short of his eighteenth birthday. Later that year, at Manchester Assize Court, he was found guilty of the murder of Samuel Rowney. Although hanging was still the penalty for murder at the time, he could not be executed as he was under eighteen when he committed the crime and so he was accordingly sentenced to be detained until Her Majesty's pleasure be known.

4

Death of an Expatriate

Moss Side, Manchester, has been well known outside Lancashire since it featured prominently in television programmes in 1981 as a place of riot and disorder. But in the 1850s Moss Side was in the country, a low-lying place popularly known as Twenty Pits because the ground was rather wet, irregular and indented with pit-like depths. When Manchester's industrial expansion began, such land was drained and houses built. Many of them were substantial and of high quality, occupied by merchants in the city, who kept all the servants they needed and had carriages to take them into town to their places of business. Moss Side was a township, contiguous to the townships of Hulme, Chorlton on Medlock and Rusholme. Many of these big houses were in the area around Whitworth Park, not far from Owen's College, which later became Manchester University, and close to the then new Manchester Royal Infirmary.

Another kind of house, nowadays described as 'large terraced', appeared by the thousand in long uniform streets. Until the 1930s this kind of dwelling was occupied by well-paid artisans, teachers, bank clerks, chief cashiers of a firm, commercial travellers and 'comfortable' tradesmen.

During the years of the Depression, more and more of these people found it necessary to take in what were at first termed genteel guests, then lodgers, in order to make ends meet. In some cases, rooms were let with the provision of meals, or partly furnished for self-catering.

Many of these lodgers were university students and the-
atrical people. During the war years these rooms were
occupied by the ever-changing populace working on
munitions or other essential duties; some tenants were
immigrants who had left Europe before the war or who
had escaped since and needed a place to live. Often
alongside them were houses vacated by their owners and
requisitioned as billets for wartime soldiery.

After the war those who wished to move and could do
so made their escape to more salubrious parts, nearer
the Cheshire boundary, and the whole area began to
deteriorate. Eventually entire houses, often with twelve
or fourteen rooms including cellars and attics, were let
room by room to individual tenants. The landlord or
caretaker would have perhaps two rooms and then keep
an eye on as many as ten other tenants, taking weekly
rent from them and emptying the gas and electricity
meters which were set to charge high rates for supply.
The bathroom and lavatory would be shared by all.
Rooms sometimes had a small gas stove and a sink, a
curtained alcove for clothes, a bed, a table and a couple
of chairs, but little else. The rooms in the bigger houses
were often well proportioned and ornately ceilinged in
their shabbiness. Moss Side had become an easy place in
which to remain anonymous if one so desired.

Many kinds of people moved in following the war years
and the result was a mixture of tongues, colours and
creeds, interspersed with the occasional house still occupied by one family, keeping up appearances: the curtains
clean and starched, the glass polished, the front steps
donkey-stoned, and waging eternal war against damp,
falling plaster and the depredations of beetles and mice.
At nearly every street corner was a grocer's shop licensed

to sell beer, wines and spirits, which stayed open until late at night and supplied every reasonable need.

Thus Moss Side in 1950 had no trouble in absorbing Jadwiga Uhryna, née Skotarek, when she went to live with her mother at 66 Darcy Street. Her life story was not uncommon in the history of Poland, but was very different from that of the new and fluctuating population on The Moss.

The unfortunate woman was born on 15 May 1915 in Horodziej, Poland. In 1938 she married Mieczyslaw Bienkowski, an engineer. In 1939, when Poland was invaded by Germany, Jadwiga became sympathetic to the aims of the Polish underground army and was in Warsaw at the time of the 1944 uprising, being taken prisoner in September and put into a German concentration camp. She was released the following April and, after returning briefly to Poland, she then joined the Polish Forces in Italy where, in October 1946, she became mentally ill. In November 1946 she arrived in the United Kingdom with her husband.

We shall never know whether her experiences in Europe contributed to her mental illness, nor does it matter now. Not every person can survive unscathed the horrors of seeing their homeland ravaged or of a stay, no matter how short, in a concentration camp. She stayed with her mother, Weronika Skotarek, at a Polish resettlement camp in the Midlands and just over a year later was admitted to Iscoyd Park Mental Hospital near Whitchurch, Shropshire. Whilst there, she was attacked by another patient and received severe, disfiguring injuries to her nose.

Nine or ten months later she was transferred to Denbigh Mental Hospital, where a prefrontal leucotomy operation was carried out on her brain, its purpose being to relieve pressure, inhibiting that part of her brain which exhibited the strong and irrational feelings which disturbed her, enabling her and those around her to lead a more tranquil existence.

Evidently her condition improved and in December 1950 she came to live with her mother at 66 Darcy Street. The improvement was not wholly maintained and seven years later she was admitted as an in-patient at Prestwich Mental Hospital, Manchester, being discharged some twenty-seven days later. She subsequently sued the Ministry of Health for the injuries to her nose received in Iscoyd Park Mental Hospital and obtained a settlement of £950.

A sharp reminder of the effects of inflation is that with part of this money she purchased a house at 4 Lincroft Street, Moss Side. Certainly a substantial house, perhaps needing repair, could be bought in Moss Side around 1960 for five or six hundred pounds.

There is an old Latin tag that every man is the architect of his own fortune; if pressed, most of us would admit to being the architects of own misfortunes too. It is, of course, less true of those with mental disability. It is in the nature of humans to wish for company and, though Jadwiga was cared for by her mother, she evidently wished for male companionship and in 1954 she put an advertisement in the matrimonial column of a Polish newspaper. She thus met Stefan Uhryna, who was cited in 1956 by her first husband, Mieczyslaw Bienkowski, in an application for divorce.

Jadwiga married Stefan Uhryna on 19 March 1957 and together they lived in the house in Lincroft Street, occupying the front ground-floor room and the front bedroom on the first floor. The remainder of the house was sub-let. The rooms were furnished, after a fashion, and in the front window they put a small card advertising the availability of the rooms. Any income would contribute to their own living costs, and indeed by this time Jadwiga had become obsessed about money, a story not uncommon amongst displaced persons whose only security has been their money and jewellery. Money became the cause of dissension between Jadwiga and Stefan, and obviously her mental history made her a difficult person to live with, cloistered as they were in two rooms. The neighbourhood reluctantly accepted her as a pernickety and bad-tempered woman.

In 1960, following yet another argument about money, they agreed to separate. Stefan left, staying away for about three months. He came back for a short while, but in August 1961 left again, choosing to live in Burnley near to his work at Bank Hall colliery, where he still worked at the time of his wife's death.

Jadwiga had a reasonable figure for a woman of forty-six and was very fond of clothes. This perhaps was a reflection of her erratic and uncertain life in war-time Europe when the possession of stylish clothes was unlikely unless one had access to the black market or had friends in privileged places. Her wardrobe reflected this, and she was evidently ambitious to improve her lot because she studied at Openshaw Technical College on the course leading to the General Certificate of Education. Perhaps her need for security is reflected, too, in her taking a course in judo at Princess Road School not far from her home.

Polish women can be very beautiful, and a number of them have become famous in the lucrative world of beauty treatment. It cannot be said that Jadwiga was beautiful, but she certainly had been reasonably attractive before the appalling injury to her nose. She had developed an interest in beauty treatment, and so she took a course of instruction and set herself up in business as a beautician in her home. Another notice in the front window joined the one advertising rooms to let.

Her business did not do well. Few people are apparently willing to go to a woman whose own appearance, even though through injury, was less than prepossessing. Nor was the interior of the house attractive: it was unclean and poorly decorated. The entrance hall itself was depressing. The elaborate plaster work of the ceilings was a stark contrast to the worn linoleum, the painted Lincrusta some four feet up from the skirting boards, and the stairs covered in the centre of each tread with a patterned plastic runner, a cheap post-war innovation.

On 29 September 1961, the first-floor middle bedroom was occupied by Thomas Kirkham. The two attic rooms were rented by Anne Josephine Fay and her five children. These seven people were away from the house for most of that day.

Next door, in rooms at 2 Lincroft Street, lived another Polish expatriate, Maria Bronislawa Chaczko. At 3 P.M. on this same day Mrs Chaczko was about to go into her lodgings when Jadwiga Uhryna spoke to her and invited her into the front ground-floor room of number four. Jadwiga said she was going out to a pawn shop to pledge two ladies' wrist watches and a wedding ring; this certainly indicates that affairs were not prosperous. She asked Maria Chaczko to look after the house whilst she was away, in case anybody arrived for a beauty treatment or the telephone engineer called to move her telephone from the kitchen to the front room. Maria had lived next door for some time, but the two had only recently got into conversation, which is somewhat surprising as they were both Polish.

Jadwiga went on her errand and Mrs Chaczko sat on the divan bed in the front ground-floor room of number four. Whilst sitting there, she heard what she thought were steps on the floorboards somewhere above. She thought it was probably one of the lodgers. When Jadwiga came back, Maria asked about the woman lodger, Mrs Fay, saying she was very quiet. Jadwiga replied that Mrs Fay and her five children had all gone out and that Mr Kirkham was at work.

It was conventional and friendly to offer a guest a cup of coffee, and Jadwiga made two cups in the kitchen, carrying them back to the front room, closing the door behind her. The radio was playing, and she and her neighbour Maria continued their conversation.

Whilst they were talking, Maria heard the noise of a movement outside the room but said nothing, thinking it was a lodger, and Jadwiga did not appear to have heard it. Noting that the time by the electric clock was 4.00 P.M., Maria got up and prepared to leave. (The clock, when later tested, was found to be correct.) As Jadwiga showed Maria out of the front door, she kept looking behind her along the lobby as though she had either seen or heard something from that direction. Maria Chaczko then went home.

At about 5 P.M., Maria was in her room, the one corresponding to Jadwiga's front living-room, divided only by the party wall, when she heard, she says, someone moving about on the other side of the dividing wall. At about 5.55 P.M. she left her house to go to the local Polish club and, on her way out, knocked at Jadwiga's front door. There was no reply, but the radio was still on.

The pattern now changes. At 6.40 Thomas Kirkham returned from work. His key would not open the door. Naturally, he knocked on the door, rang the bell; no reply. He could not understand it. At 7.30 he went round to Moss Lane East police station and asked for assistance to get into the house.

Police Constable Sydney Smith went with Thomas Kirkham to the house in Lincroft Street. They tried the key again in the front door lock, had a bit of a push and shove, and then went round the back. An entry at the end of the block led to the back alley serving the even-numbered houses in Darcy Street as well as those of Lincroft Street, which ended in a cul-de-sac almost at the backyard gate of number four.

There were no lights showing in the house and the backyard gate was open. Constable Smith went into the yard, Kirkham following him. The back door of the house was ajar. This kind of house always had sash windows and the upper half of each sash window at the back was open, which seemed very odd.

They both went into the kitchen. All appeared to be in order. They continued along the passage towards the front door. The front ground-floor room, Jadwiga's living room, was in a very disorderly state.

Next they had a look at the Yale-type lock on the front door and found the locking catch was in operation on the inside. They released it, tried Thomas Kirkham's key, and found it worked perfectly. There were no signs of a forcible entry into the house. Later, Jadwiga's husband said she sometimes put a bolt on the front door, but never used the safety catch on the Yale lock.

The policeman and Kirkham went upstairs. They looked into the bathroom and then went to the back bedroom. In an ordinary one-family household it would be unusual to see, on the outside of a bedroom door, a padlock and hasp; in multi-occupancy houses such a lock is not merely usual but vital. A padlock was closed over the hasp on this door, but was not locked. The officer took the padlock from the door, pushed it open and saw Jadwiga Uhryna's body. She was lying diagonally on the floor, on her back with her feet towards the door.

She was a pathetic sight. Her fair hair was untidy, her eyes partly open, her mouth open too as if in protest. An apron familiar to Mr Kirkham was loosely round her neck. Her slacks and panties had been drawn down to her ankles. Her other clothes had been drawn up to her waist. Her knees were splayed outwards and her body was completely vulnerable. There were scratch marks on her neck. Jadwiga's own bedroom, at the front of the first floor, was in a state of disorder.

When Constable Smith reported the circumstances, the whole investigative process began, headed by Detective Chief Superintendent Eric Cunningham. Before the body was moved, it was examined by Dr Manning, a Home Office pathologist. When it was raised, a considerable amount of dirt from the floor adhered to the buttocks. Later, in the central mortuary, Dr Manning carried out a post-mortem examination, following which he said death was due to strangulation. There were about eight ounces of ingested food in the stomach, but the bladder was empty. The lavatory of the house was in the bathroom, next to the room in which Jadwiga's body was found.

Outside the bathroom door was a cigarette on the floor, fractured in a 'greenstick' manner. Jadwiga had been a heavy smoker, invariably seen with a cigarette in her mouth and, indeed, forensic tests later showed that this cigarette had been in her mouth. Its position on the floor indicated that an encounter may have taken place in the passage outside the bathroom and the rear bedroom door.

Substantiating this belief were a number of scuff marks

on the surface of the linoleum covering the landing. A senior finger-print officer, mindful of the possibility of a struggle, powdered the linoleum along the line of the scuff marks, hoping to find a finger-print or footprint, but without success. However, whilst kneeling on the floor he found, on the Lincrusta wall covering, slightly to the right of and about three feet above the broken cigarette, a right thumb print.

He recognized this as being of the twinned loop pattern, not altogether common, but the sort that can narrow down a search. The thumb print was photographed, the Lincrusta panel was carefully taken from the wall and carried to the Finger-print Bureau. There was not, of course, anything to indicate that this thumb print had any connection with Jadwiga's sudden death at the hands of another person, but it went forward for investigation along with photographs of two hundred and more other prints collected from the house. It might be innocent, but its proximity to the broken cigarette raised our hopes a little.

When a murder enquiry gets under way investigations in many directions are carried out simultaneously, each backing up the other. First the house had to be examined. The only disturbance to furniture and property was in the two rooms occupied by Mrs Uhryna, that is the front ground-floor room and the front bedroom on the first floor. In the scullery there were two gas stoves, each with its own prepayment sub-meter. There were no locks on these two coin boxes, and neither contained any money.

In the cellar the gas and electricity mains meters were of the quarterly kind, but there was also an electricity prepayment sub-meter, again without a lock or cash contents. Strangely, there were no signs of recent interference with any of these meters.

So, it looked as though an intruder had searched for money or valuables, but there was nothing to tell the team whether in fact anything had been stolen.

In your own home there may be hundreds of examples of finger-prints of yourself, your family, visitors, callers with legitimate access such as gas and electricity meter readers, workmen and so on, and because of this perfectly normal situation you will appreciate that enquiries to trace everybody with access to 4 Lincroft Street were under way without delay. All were traced, their finger-prints voluntarily given and checked against the vast number which had been photographed inside the house. Many were eliminated. Of course, any detective knows prints are not necessarily left by every visitor, legitimate or otherwise. Not only that, prints can be retrieved from suspect premises but never matched to a known visitor.

At 4 Lincroft Street there was a finger-print on a bottle of vinegar which could not be identified as belonging to any visitor there, so the search was taken right back to the factory where the bottle had been produced. The print was traced, much to his surprise, to the man who had packed the bottle. It is as important to eliminate the innocent as it is to find the guilty. You might think these were incredible lengths to go to, but they are necessary for everyone's peace of mind.

Day after day, the checking went on until the comparison of finger-prints in the house with those of people with legitimate access had eliminated all but one: the mark found on the Lincrusta wallpaper, close to the broken cigarette. An added difficulty was that this mark was far from perfect because of the grained surface of the painted Lincrusta: it did not lend itself to the reception of a good mark.

As I write, it is twenty years after the event. It may be

that in times to come computerization of the immensely complicated indexing of finger-prints will speed up the process. In 1961 there was no alternative but for six finger-print men to spend the next six months comparing this imperfect mark with every finger-print held in the Bureau. It would be the same today.

The angling of light on a mark, an identation or other impression can make a tremendous difference to the detail revealed. This is why graveyards are visited at night by family historians checking against parish burial registers, because worn headstone inscriptions are more easily read by artificial light. The piece of Lincrusta wall-covering was put on a special table in the photographic department which could be tilted to enable light to shine across it in many different directions. Each time the position was changed, the print was photographed in the hope that every detail would be revealed. Eventually fluorescent powder was used to enhance the thumb print, subjected to ultraviolet light and the print rephoto-graphed. The clearest print possible was enlarged to about eighteen by twelve inches. This huge photograph was constantly in front of the six searchers as they made their laborious but necessary way through the files. When we drew a blank, the searchers were left with the daily task of comparing the finger-prints of new prisoners with the unidentified thumb print.

In spite of massive enquiries nobody could throw any light on who was responsible for killing Jadwiga Uhryna. This right thumb print remained the only clue we really had. The whole matter was irritating and disappointing, and the print itself could not tell us who it belonged to. A mere glimpse of an intruder could have produced a description: the hearing of a voice could perhaps have helped. There was nothing like that, so we waited.

Fourteen months later, in the early hours of 10 November 1962, somebody broke into and stole property from 24 Oxford Grove, Chorlton on Medlock, the district adjoining Moss Side on the eastern boundary. The burglary was first investigated by a young probationary Constable who was being advised by a newly promoted uniformed Sergeant who had considerable CID experience, a distinct advantage at times. The intruder had entered the premises by breaking a pane of glass in the kitchen window, putting an arm through and withdrawing the bolt at the rear door. A gentleman's eighteen-carat gold Bulova wrist-watch and some American dollars were stolen from the house. It was noted that the watch was running slow. Such watches were not common then, certainly not in Chorlton on Medlock, and a special circulation was sent out to jewellers and pawnbrokers in the Manchester area.

On examining the broken glass from the kitchen window the Sergeant found a thumb impression on a small piece still adhering to the window frame. No doubt the young Constable learned something from watching how this piece of glass was carefully removed from the frame and brought to the Finger-print Bureau, where it was powdered and photographed. The photograph was then dropped on my desk.

It was not a moment I will easily forget. Staring up at me was the right thumb print we had found in the home of Jadwiga Uhryna. We had searched for it for months. After searching for six months it was easier for me to recognize that finger-print than perhaps it was for me to recognize a neighbour. Finger-print officers get like that.

This correlation still did not tell us who the killer was, but it told us that he was alive and kicking in our area again, and still committing crime. We reset the stall accordingly. There was every chance that, having got away with the watch and the dollars, he would try to get rid of them and then break into more houses.

It is not always possible to say by which sex finger-prints have been made, although experience engenders educated guesswork. By this time we did not have any thought of looking for a woman; we had the two right thumb prints from 4 Lincroft Street and 24 Oxford Grove, and we were all on the look-out. An interesting series of links came about.

A few days after the break-in at 24 Oxford Grove, the home of Mabel Anderson at 109 Warwick Street, Hulme, was feloniously entered between 12.30 A.M. and 6.45 A.M. on 13 November 1962. Someone broke a pane of glass in a rear ground-floor window, put a hand through and released the catch on the back door. During the night Mrs Anderson had been wakened by the sound of breaking glass. She switched on the light, but did not investigate further.

When she got out of bed at a quarter to seven in the morning and went downstairs she found the signs of forced entry, but could not tell if anything had been stolen. Later, the finger-print officer found impressions on glass from the broken window. On one piece, a right thumb and right forefinger; on another, the left thumb, left forefinger and left middle finger. The right thumb impression on the broken glass was identical with the right thumb at 24 Oxford Grove and the one on the Lincrusta wall covering at 4 Lincroft Street.

What prints had we so far from these crimes? Right thumb, right forefinger, left thumb, left forefinger, left middle finger: five out of ten. We could not, of course, say with certainty at this point that the right-hand impressions necessarily had any connection with the left-hand impressions. The burglar may not have been operating alone, but we had something to work on and we could get the ball rolling.

The newly obtained finger-prints enabled us to do a lot of back-checking and we found that the next link had occurred just four months after the murder.

At 7.15 on the morning of Friday 19 January 1962, Mrs Minnie Trevor, who was sixty-eight years old, woke and went downstairs in her terraced house at 65 Darncombe Street, Moss Side. She opened the back door of her house and went into the yard, where she opened the back gate so that the dustmen could come in and empty her refuse bin. She went back in the house, shut and bolted the back door. She said that all the windows were secure and at that time nothing had been disturbed from when she had gone to bed the night before.

She got back into bed. When you are sixty-eight years of age, and retired, getting back into bed is a luxury to be relished. Her bedroom was at the front on the first floor. In the back bedroom on the same floor was her mother, Mrs Betsy Kirkham, who at the time was the respectable age of ninety-three. Not long after Minnie had returned to bed, her mother Betsy, with the persistence of routine which many old folk have, went into her daughter's room to remind her it was the day for the dustbin men and then returned to her own bed.

Half an hour later Mrs Trevor heard a noise, but thought it was the neighbours. The next second she felt a heavy blow on the head and something running down her face. She picked up pieces of a broken milk bottle, the neck of which had some flannel round it. She looked around slowly only to see the bedroom door closing. Obviously injured, but plucky, she told her mother what had happened and then went downstairs where she found the living-room door half open and the room disturbed. It was only just becoming light outside, so to see better inside the house she tried to put on the electric light, but could not do so, and later found it had been turned off at the main switch in the cellar. She also found that a bottle of sterilized milk had been taken and this was what she had been hit with. Nothing had been stolen from her house, for which she was probably thankful.

When the finger-print officer called to examine the scene, he searched and found one poor print on the drainpipe near the ground-floor window at the rear. It was photographed and found to be a left-thumb print which we could now connect with another left-thumb mark which had been obtained from 109 Warwick Street, Hulme.

Back-checking went on. Most of Hulme and a good portion of Moss Side consisted of rows of seemingly identical two-up-and-two-down houses with a lavatory in the back yard. Perhaps this is why in Lancashire so much care was given by working-class women to their front curtains, the exact arrangement of the lace nets, the pattern and colour of donkey-stoning the steps. It could be their only way of asserting their individuality, of impressing their personalities upon the somewhat drab, soot-encrusted and monotonous environment of their daily lives.

The checking quite quickly led us to identify prints from many burglaries in Hulme and Moss Side, most of which had occurred in those small terraced houses. Such houses usually had a window in the scullery, nowadays called the kitchen, at the side of the back door. We were now almost certain that the man we were so anxiously seeking was working alone. In the early hours of the morning he would climb over either the rear wall or gate, break a pane of glass in the scullery window, release the catch, open the window and climb through, or else break the pane sufficiently for him to insert his arm, lean through the window and release the bolts or the catch on the back door. He then entered and ransacked the house, looking for money, jewellery or both.

His victims were as much creatures of routine as he was. At that time few people were paid by cheque for their work; most were paid in cash on Thursday or Friday evening and thousands of men went to bed with their wages, less perhaps the cost of a few pints, in their trouser pocket. In the normal way of things a man would take off his shirt and trousers and put them over a chair near his bed. The man we were searching for knew this, because, after breaking into the house and ransacking the ground-floor rooms, he invariably entered the bedroom, took the trousers downstairs, stole from them and left through the back door.

As the staff working in the Bureau were busily engaged with the checking, so those finger-print officers visiting the scenes of recently committed burglaries were kept busy seeking fresh evidence, and along with the rest of the staff I visited dozens of such houses searching for prints. It was a most exciting time and I can vividly remember one damp Saturday morning in November talking to an old chap who told me what had happened in his house and who, incidentally, provided the first description of the intruder.

This old man had the sort of build which was common at one time and is, through improved health care, much less common nowadays; he had bandy legs, a result of childhood rickets and long hours of work, often the fate of the industrial Lancastrian.

At his home the scene had a familiar look about it: the

scullery window was broken and the back door wide open. The intruder had as usual broken a pane of glass in the window, inserted his arm, released the bolts on the back door, entered and ransacked. Our old Lancastrian was by this time a pensioner, extremely spry and I would think rather aggressive if his feathers were ruffled, as they were when he was disturbed in the night and woke to find an intruder searching through his trouser pockets. Well aware that his money was in them, he grabbed one leg of the trousers, and as the burglar had hold of the other leg a tug of war began which the pensioner actually won. He said to me, 'If I'd caught him, I'd have bloody killed him!' but at this stage, knowing how dangerous the intruder was, I couldn't help thinking that, brave as the old man was, he might so easily have been the next victim. The description he provided of the intruder was very valuable.

He actually tried to chase the burglar, and I will never forget his words when describing the burglar's agility: 'He went downstairs just like a phantom. He didn't seem to run, he just seemed to disappear . . .' For the first time, we knew that the man we sought was black, about five feet eleven, slim and wiry. Incidentally, there's nothing about finger-prints which tells us whether a person is white, red, yellow or black.

The *modus operandi*, MO for short, of many burglars is common knowledge to detectives and is important when determining who has committed certain offences as well as linking crimes committed by an otherwise unknown criminal.

Further checking showed that between 7 September 1961, that is shortly before the murder, and 19 December 1962, a period of some sixteen months, 161 house-breakings of similar MO had occurred in Moss Side and Hulme, and we still did not know who the burglar was.

During November 1962 a complete set of finger-prints found at the scenes of many of these offences was sent to all finger-print bureaux in the country and to bureaux abroad. We could add that we knew the man was black, fairly young and lithe. Nothing helpful came of this initiative; few overseas bureaux replied at all and we got negative replies from all the British bureaux. So much for that.

Detectives and all supporting groups need and welcome a little bit of luck. The breakthrough came at nine o'clock on the morning of 15 December 1962, when a black man, Rudolph George Robinson of 46 Richmond Street, Moss Side, took a gold Bulova watch for repair to David Bloomenfield, a director of Freedman (Manchester) Limited, jewellers. He said it was running slow. You will remember that such a watch had been taken from the home of Patrick Egan of 24 Oxford Grove, Chorlton on Medlock, on 10 November 1962, and that its description had been circulated to all jewellers and pawnbrokers.

Mr Bloomenfield thought there was very likely a connection between the watch he was asked to repair and the stolen one, so he informed the police. The matter was investigated. Mr Egan identified the watch as the one stolen from his home. Rudolph George Robinson said he had bought it from a black man, whom he described, on the afternoon of Saturday 10 November 1962, in Moss Lane East, Manchester – within hours of the time of the burglary – and also that this same man had offered to sell him American dollars. You will remember that Mr Egan had suffered the loss of similar currency.

This new information was collated with the already known finger-print details. At 12.45 A.M. on Friday 21 December, Detective Inspector Mellor, Detective Constables Heath and Arnfield, accompanied by an understandably nervous Rudolph, visited Monton House Club,

Moss Side, a familiar place to most local officers. At one time it had been an exceedingly nice house, suitable for a gentleman with family and servants; it was detached and had formerly had attractive gardens.

The outside of the house was stuccoed and it was sad to see its deterioration in 1962. The officers went with Robinson into the basement. Amongst a number of black persons Robinson pointed out a particular man. The officers said they wished to speak to him and invited him to sit outside in the police car.

He was forthcoming enough to give his real name, James Jacobs, and said he was an ex-policeman from Saint Kitts in the West Indies, which proved true enough. He was shown the watch and told its possession had been traced to him. Yes, he had seen the watch before, because he bought it a week before he had sold it to Robinson. It might have been a blow when Jacobs was told he was supposed to have sold it to Robinson the day it was stolen from Mr Egan, and that he would now be detained for further questioning and, it was hoped, some answers.

A quick comparison of his fingers and his physical description indicated he was similar to the person responsible for house-breaking in the district. He was partly searched and found to be wearing two pairs of socks. Tucked between the legs of the socks were a screwdriver, torch and other house-breaking implements. He was cautioned and detained at Bootle Street police station in Manchester city centre, where the search was completed. He admitted he had broken into 24 Oxford Grove and had stolen the watch and dollars from Mr Egan. Presented with other facts, he later admitted breaking into many other houses. His finger-prints were taken and an expert sent for.

Naturally, there was more to come. Jadwiga Uhryna's

death was still under investigation, and there was that right thumb print from the Lincrusta wallpaper, which the expert now positively identified as that of Jacobs.

Detective Chief Superintendent Eric Cunningham joined the group of officers and, well aware of the evidence available to him, he questioned Jacobs closely as to Jadwiga's death. Jacobs finally admitted being responsible for her death, but denied killing her deliberately. He said he had pushed her away only, and agreed to make a statement.

Before writing his statement he was asked to describe how he had pushed her. In demonstration he grasped Detective Inspector Mellor by the neck with his hands, applying considerable pressure, and he shook the inspector's head violently. Not what most of us would call a push. Jacobs made his statement after due caution and, when it had been read over to him and he had read it himself, he signed it.

Next he was questioned about his widespread housebreaking activities and about these he made a further statement under caution. He admitted breaking into over one hundred houses including that of Mrs Trevor at 65 Darncombe Street, and hitting her on the head.

When charged with the murder of Jadwiga Uhryna, he replied, 'I did not murder her at all.' He was also charged with wounding Mrs Trevor with intent to cause injury, five cases of burglary, possession of house-breaking implements by night, and in addition he asked for over one hundred other offences to be taken into consideration if he should be found guilty.

On 27 March 1963, at Manchester Crown Court, Jacobs was convicted of the manslaughter of Jadwiga Uhryna. He was sentenced to two years' imprisonment. On the charge of wounding with intent he received a sentence of three years' imprisonment, the two sentences to run consecutively. On the five burglary charges he was sentenced to two years' imprisonment on each, to run concurrently with each other and with the sentences for manslaughter and wounding. Thus, his total prison sentence was five years.

James Jacobs behaved himself in prison and because of this he was released in 1966. This was the first time he had been in prison, but it had not made him see the error of his ways.

Our phantom burglar returned to the same area, operating in the early hours of Friday and Saturday mornings. At five minutes to five on 9 December 1966, when of course it was still dark, a police officer was on duty in the back entry of Parkfield Street, Rusholme, when he heard breaking glass. Quickly having a look round, he found that the rear ground-floor window at 86 Parkfield Street was broken and that Jacobs was standing just inside the house, close to the window. The officer tried to get through the back door but, whilst doing so, glanced through the window and so saw Jacobs trying to open the front door.

The policeman immediately ran around to the front and saw Jacobs dive head first through the ground-floor window. Jacobs ran off. By this time another policeman had arrived, so together they chased Jacobs into a nearby entry and held him. He was searched and had with him a pair of gloves and a knife. When interviewed at the police station, he admitted the offence and later made a voluntary statement.

Appearing yet again at Manchester Crown Court, on 12 January 1967, a little less than four years after his earlier, and first, appearance, he had to answer charges of burglary and possessing house-breaking implements by night. On this occasion it was Jacobs's wish that sixty-nine other offences should be considered when sentence was passed. For the burglary he got six years' imprisonment and for possession of the house-breaking implements by night two years, both to run concurrently, that is six years altogether.

Over the past hundred years Moss Side has in truth become something of a melting pot and in the history of the area it is regrettable, but not particularly unusual, for people born on opposite sides of the world, decades apart, to cross paths and for one of them to die undeservedly at the hands of the other.

5

A Show-off Killer

Easter is, for most people in this country, the first holiday of the year. The weather can be fair or foul. Whatever it is, Easter is the time of spring, with bulbs coming into flower, and summer just round the corner.

But Easter 1962 was not a holiday for many detectives and finger-print staff recalled to duty to investigate a most brutal murder case, and I was amongst them. Indeed, the whole set-up was quite bizarre. Just before lunch time on Easter Sunday the mutilated body of William Nelson was found in his first-floor bed-sitting room at 1 Oakleigh Avenue, Burnage.

Burnage is a nice suburb of Manchester, a mixture of building and social styles. Burnage Lane itself winds a little and is quite leafy, and some of the houses lining the road are large, standing in their own grounds. There are many early Edwardian semis and terraced houses down the side roads. Further away from the city is a large area of council houses built in the early 1930s, and many of the other roads are wide, spacious and tree-lined. There is the Duchess of York Babies' Hospital and a quite lovely charitable housing estate, known as the 'garden village'.

Not, one would think, an obvious scene for a murder, and not a place of bed-sitting rooms either; but these big houses had long since lost their original tenants and were far too large to be occupied by single families. Letting rooms was often the only answer to paying the rates and providing funds for minimal upkeep of the fabric. The story is fairly typical of many cities now.

The house where the murder occurred has long been demolished, I am glad to say. When we got there we could see it was a substantial semi-detached, Victorian house, standing in a spacious garden which was neglected and overgrown with grass and weeds. It was at the junction of Burnage Lane and Oakleigh Avenue. This once beautiful home had been converted into a lodging house. The ground floor and first floor each contained three large bed-sitting rooms and the attic held a three-roomed flat. On the first floor were a toilet and bathroom shared by all the residents.

William Nelson, forty-eight years old, occupied one of the first-floor bed-sitters. Born in Scotland, he was a confirmed bachelor and regarded as a quiet and thoughtful man. Since 1957 he had been employed as a telegraphist by British Rail at Victoria Station, Manchester. He had finished work at one o'clock on the afternoon of Thursday 19 April 1962, and was due back there until four o'clock on Monday afternoon, the 23rd. He was presumably looking forward to spending the Easter holiday in his own quiet and unobtrusive fashion.

On the Saturday morning, Carol Bent, a young girl living in the attic flat, noticed that the door of Mr Nelson's room was ajar. She had passed this door three times on Good Friday and had noticed that the door was slightly open and the light switched on. It was not unusual enough then to arouse anxiety, but when the light was still on at 11.45 the following morning, and the door still ajar, she was puzzled. It seemed to the girl obvious that something was amiss; could Mr Nelson have been taken ill? She went for help.

Raymond Bale was an ambulance driver who lived in

one of the ground-floor rooms so it seemed sensible to knock on his door and ask him to check whether anything was wrong. He tapped repeatedly on the door, still partly open; there was no response, so he peeped in. He could see William Nelson lying in bed. Thinking he might be ill, the ambulance man went towards the bed and pulled the bedclothes away. There was a blood-stained cloth covering his face. He moved the cloth and saw that it had been viciously battered. He immediately called the police and a full-scale murder hunt began.

A thorough examination was at once made of the victim's room. The key to the room was in the lock on the outside of the door. The electric light was switched on and the curtains were drawn across the window. To the left of and behind the door was a single divan bed, its headboard near the door. The body was lying on its back on the bed and was partly clothed. The headboard appeared to have been badly damaged by the same instrument which had caused the fatal wounds, but there was no sign of a struggle.

On the polished side of the headboard, to the left of the damage inflicted by the murder weapon, were the clear impressions of two thumb prints, or, at least, two prints of the same left thumb. Their position indicated that this was where someone had stood to aim the blows at the head of the sleeping man. It appeared that the killer had held on to the headboard to give himself greater leverage and add force to the blows. The two prints suggested a slight change in position as he aimed blows at a slightly different part of the head and face. The wounds indicated that the murder weapon had had a serrated edge, which was a little unusual. The pathologist was able to say that nine blows had been struck, but he could not give any opinion as to what the murder weapon could have been. No one had seen wounds like them before. The bedsheet on which William Nelson was lying was badly blood-stained; but more unusually there was a mark, in blood, of a definite pattern. This was of six adjoining squares, each side of which was half an inch long. Extremely puzzling indeed.

There was one more significant discovery. On top of the bedclothes was a pillow. On the blood-stained pillow slip was a palm print in blood. The lines of the palm gave the unmistakable outline of the letter E.

Partly because of the time of the year and partly because of this letter E in the bloody palm print the case became known as the Easter Murder and there was little doubt in the minds of the investigating officers that we had found the prints of the killer. What was not clear was why he had killed; such a case hardly fitted the reasonably quiet environment of Burnage.

It was soon found that the forty-eight-year-old victim was an ex-soldier. Near to his body was a framed case containing the medals he had been awarded as a member of the Royal Scots Fusiliers, bearing mute testimony to his service. It seemed likely that he had invited someone back to spend the night at his flat. In those days it would be typical of an old soldier to offer help to somebody down on his luck. He would be happy to share what he had and provide accommodation for the night.

But it looked as though on this occasion the ex-soldier's kindness had cost him his life. Directly beneath the damaged headboard of the bed was a gabardine raincoat, which was identified as William Nelson's property. It was badly blood-stained and from the position of the blood spots it was assumed that the coat had been worn by the murderer at the time of the attack.

In the Finger-print Bureau yet another search began

through the print index in a desperate bid to identify the killer. Our efforts did not produce anything useful. Meanwhile, members of the Murder Squad tracked down everyone who had ever had cause to visit the flat. More than three hundred people were interviewed and finger-printed for elimination purposes. None of these prints matched the left thumb print found on the headboard. We seemed to have come to a dead end, not a comforting place for a CID officer to be.

Two months later something happened which changed the whole course of the investigation. On 23 June 1962, a pencilled letter was received at police headquarters, Manchester. It was addressed to Detective Crowe, was written in a code and referred to the Easter Murder of William Nelson.

It is not unusual for such letters to appear on the desks of investigating officers when there's an unsolved murder – cranks abound. First impressions were that this letter was from one of them.

Nevertheless, they each felt that it could not be disregarded. Work began to decipher the code and unravel whatever mystery it contained. Any doubts still lingering in the minds of certain detectives that the coded message had come from a crank were dispelled and the job got top priority when, on 4 July 1962, eleven days after the coded message had been received, another envelope arrived. It was addressed in pencil to police headquarters, Manchester. There was no stamp on it. When detectives opened it, they found it contained a plan marked 'The flat of the late William Nelson'.

It was clear that whoever had drawn the plan had been in William Nelson's room at about the time of the murder. The door, window, sink, bed and mantelpiece were shown in their correct places. The lazy switch by the side of the door, the campaign medals in their case on the shelf to the right of the door and, even more significantly, a new white shirt on a chair by the side of the bed were all indicated. Such details left no room for doubt that the coded message and the plan were sent by a man who had been in the room and was almost certainly the killer.

Cracking the code became absolutely vital. It was a mixture of letters and numbers, and appeared to be something the killer had developed himself. Almost every officer engaged on the case had a try at it. At every spare moment, all those officers not actually assigned to breaking the code were working away at their own copies, intent on solving the problem not only to help the case along but for the personal satisfaction it would bring. However, no one succeeded.

The whole tantalizing affair was solved when at 11.12 P.M. on Monday 13 August, a 999 call was received at the information room in police headquarters. The caller, who identified himself as Frank, sounded very drunk. He demanded to know what the police were doing about the William Nelson murder. He taunted the Sergeant receiving the call, by saying, 'I did it. Come and get me for the William Nelson murder.' Then he rang off – seconds too late. The call had been traced to a telephone booth at Piccadilly railway station. When detectives arrived at the station, the telephone booth was empty, so they searched the platforms for anybody who looked suspicious.

Minutes later another call was made to the same Sergeant at police headquarters. He identified the voice. 'I'm still here,' it said, 'I'm not a bloody fool. You can't keep me talking.' Whilst he was calling, detectives went back to the booth and closed in on him. They opened the door quickly. The drunken man handed them the

telephone, saying, 'Do you want to speak to your mates?'
One officer took the telephone and identified himself to
the Sergeant at the other end of the line; and for a short
time they thought they had arrested a drunken crank.

The man was taken to the police office at Piccadilly
station, where he identified himself to the arresting
officers as Frank Goodman, twenty-two years of age,
who lived with his widowed mother in a small house at
Radcliffe, some eight or nine miles north of Manchester
city centre.

Goodman was searched. In his hip pocket was found a
piece of paper on which were written letters and figures
which appeared to be the key to a code. He was questioned about it. Rather scornfully he replied, 'If you don't
know what this is, then you know nothing about the job.'

A finger-print expert was quickly sent for. He obtained
Goodman's prints and immediately checked the left
thumb print with left thumb impression found on the
damaged bed headboard in William Nelson's bed-sitting
room. They matched perfectly. Frank Goodman was the
man we were seeking. He was now rapidly sobering up,
but still wanted to talk. He told the interviewing detectives that he had met Nelson in a public house on Easter
Friday (although it was felt it was almost certainly on the
Thursday evening they had met). He then began to cry,
and blurted out that he had killed Nelson and could
prove it.

He calmed down and then said he had gone with
Nelson to his room, which was up one flight of stairs and
to the right of the passageway. He went on to say that it
was not a blunt axe, as had been reported in certain
newspapers, which he had used to kill him – it was an
iron bar. He had struck Nelson about eight times on the
head and face with this iron bar, and on one occasion he

had missed his aim and struck the headboard. He further admitted responsibility for sending the coded letter and the plan of the murder scene. He was concerned as to whether he had got all the particulars of the plan correct as he had only been in the room on the one occasion. Human nature is a curious thing: there he was confessing to a horrible murder, yet anxious that he had got such details right!

As Frank Goodman was extremely co-operative, he was invited to decode the mysterious letter which had baffled detectives so completely. He was happy to oblige, but before he was halfway through the task he handed the pen to a senior officer, saying, 'That's it. You can finish the rest off yourself.' Using the key found in Goodman's hip pocket detectives completed the decoding of the message:

DET. CROWE
THE EASTER MURDER
OF WILLIAM NELSON
AT HIS FLAT IN BURNAGE

IF YOU SORT THIS LOT OUT YOUR HALFWAY THERE. IT CAN BE DONE.

YOUR INVESTIGATIONS INTO THE MURDER OF WILLIAM NELSON HAFE NOT GONE TO WELL ASK ASK DENNIW CRONNIN WHO IS IN CRUMPSAL HOSPITAL A FEW QUESTIONS HE MAY BE ABLE TO HELP.

IF BY THE 1ST JULY YOU HAVD NOT CAUGHN THE PERSON RESPONCER-BLE FOR THIS MURDER I ATUURE YOU HE WIKK STRIKE AGAIN

I R P
YOU WONT FIND
ANY FINGERPRINTS
ON THIS PAPER

OVER 6 FOOT
FAIR
TATTOO LEFT ARM
AGE 28

You will see that literacy was not his strong suit, and this alone would have made deciphering the message much more difficult.

Goodman was asked about Cronin. He stood up and said, 'Dennis Cronin, Ward 3C, Crumpsall Hospital', and went on to explain that two weeks before the murder of William Nelson he had attacked Dennis Cronin on a train near Bury. Using the same iron bar which he had wielded on Nelson, he had knocked Cronin unconscious, robbed him of £10 and had then thrown him off the train.

Urgent enquiries now began into that incident. It was true that early on Friday 6 April 1962, Dennis Cronin, thirty-five years old with an address in Bury, was found lying between the railway lines at Hollinghurst Bridge, Radcliffe, North of Manchester. He was badly injured and was taken to Crumpsall Hospital, where he was found to be suffering from severe head and facial injuries. The gross fractures of the skull and the deep lacerations to his head had led the surgeon at the hospital to suspect that the severity of the injuries could not have come about merely through Cronin's having fallen from the train. The surgeon felt that some of the injuries could have been caused by a heavy, blunt instrument, and Lancashire police decided to investigate. Cronin was suffering from post-traumatic amnesia and could not help the police, so the file had remained open.

Goodman, for reasons of his own, misled the police when he told them that he had committed both crimes using an iron bar which he had thrown away in the Burnage area after leaving the scene of the Nelson killing. Accompanied by several police officers he led them on a wild goose chase in Burnage, searching for the particular garden into which he had, he said, thrown the murder weapon.

The gardens, which incidentally had all been searched after the discovery of the Nelson death, were again thoroughly gone over, but nothing useful was found.

The police searched Goodman's home at Radcliffe. In his bedroom they found a long, threaded bed bolt, twelve and three-quarter inches long. This kind of bolt was common in the old-fashioned type of bed which had a wooden frame supporting coiled steel mesh springs, upon which the mattress was placed. After use, the mesh tended to sag somewhat and this bolt was used to tighten the mesh on the frame.

The implement was taken to the forensic science laboratory. It gave a positive reaction to a chemical test to see if it bore traces of blood. The mystery of the blood-stained pattern of six adjoining squares on the bedsheet was solved. When a sheet was wrapped around the hexagonal head of a bed bolt it produced a similar pattern. It was also established that this large threaded bed bolt with its curious serrated edge could have caused the unusual injuries to Nelson.

Obviously, we had found the murder weapon. We also had a left thumb print from the bed headboard, which put Goodman in the flat where the murder had occurred.

There remained the last piece of evidence which proved, beyond reasonable doubt, that Frank Goodman had been there at the time the murder had been committed: the blood-stained palm print found on the pillow slip.

When we examined this portion of blood-stained palm print we found that most of the papillary ridge characteristics, which are normally used in the process of finger/palm print identification, had been obliterated by the heavy blood-staining, leaving insufficient ridge characteristics to provide evidence of identification by traditional methods. What was still visible, however, was the pattern of the lines of the palm, the skin creases used for centuries by palmists to deduce a person's character and destiny. Clearly visible in the centre of the palm print were the skin creases forming the letter E in a most distinct manner.

Goodman's palm prints were now examined. There, in the centre of his left palm, was the same distinctive letter formed by the hand lines. Enlarged photographs were made both of Goodman's left palm print and of the portion of blood-stained palm print found on William Nelson's pillow slip. A chart was carefully prepared showing thirty similarities in the skin creases. To the best of my knowledge this was the first occasion on which evidence of this type had been prepared and introduced in a court of law, and the unusual features it displayed have remained of interest to officers engaged in finger-print work.

After statements had been obtained Goodman was committed for trial, charged with the murder of William Nelson and with the attempted murder of Dennis Cronin. Goodman was described as having been a schoolboy footballer, an avid reader, keen on angling and kind to his mother.

On 3 December 1962, eight months after the com-mission of these awful crimes, Goodman appeared at Manchester Crown Court. Rather dramatically, proceed-ings were delayed for almost an hour whilst lawyers talked to him in his cell. Finally he appeared in the dock. The court was crowded, and hushed. It could be seen that he was a tall and good-looking man.

Many members of the public make a point of attending murder trials because they hope to revel in ghoulish details. Any such folk who attended the Goodman trial must have been acutely disappointed. It took Mr Justice Brabin just ninety seconds to sentence Goodman to life imprisonment. First, Goodman quietly but firmly told the judge, 'I plead not guilty to capital murder, but guilty to murder.'

Then the judge was addressed by Mr Joseph Davies, QC, who accepted the plea as it stood. Mr Alexander Karmel, QC, representing Goodman, addressed the judge, saying that he had explained the consequences of the plea to his client who was adamant that this was the plea he wished to make.

The judge gave his verdict, life imprisonment, in what was the shortest murder hearing court officials there could remember.

These were most unusual proceedings and you may welcome an explanation of the procedure if it is outside your own experience.

First let me deal with Goodman's plea and the prosecuting barrister's acceptance of it. In 1962, some few years after the death penalty had been abolished for most types of murder, and before the Murder (Abolition of Death Penalty) Act of 1965 declared that no person convicted of murder in this country shall suffer death, it was still possible to be executed if convicted of one of the acts which constituted capital murder. Murder in furtherance of theft was one such crime.

When Goodman made a statement admitting to the murder of William Nelson, he also admitted stealing a wage packet containing £12 and was therefore charged with capital murder. In the court he was prepared to plead guilty to murder only, as unlike capital murder it no longer carried the death penalty. The prosecution counsel were prepared to accept this plea because the only evidence to substantiate a charge of capital murder had been supplied by Goodman himself in a statement made to the police, a confession he would probably have been able to retract with little difficulty.

When Goodman's counsel told the judge that he had explained the consequences of the plea and that his client was adamant that this was the plea he wished to make, he was referring to the fact that no trial would occur, no witnesses would be examined and cross-examined, no exhibits would be produced and no jury would decide the outcome. Justice would not be seen to be done.

Nevertheless Frank Goodman escaped with his life. Dennis Cronin never recovered from his severe injuries. He died three years later, unaware of what had happened to him on that fateful train journey.

6

A Winner, a Loser – an Unpaid Bet

When people speak of 'the oldest profession', they are usually referring to prostitution. I believe that a profession of equal antiquity must be that of the thief, and wherever a thief has been active there has always been someone interested in his detection.

Historically, crime has been solved by using three sources: those who witnessed the crime being committed; the interrogation of those suspected of its commission; and information supplied by informers. These traditional means of crime detection have served law enforcement agencies well over the ages and are still much in evidence today. Recently, though, all three methods have come under careful examination and the professional informer, who now charges far more than the biblical thirty pieces of silver, comes under very close scrutiny indeed.

However, since the turn of this century science has played an increasingly important part in the continuing war against the criminal, and to this end dactyloscopy, the science of finger-prints, has been well to the fore. Today, along with many other aspects of forensic science, the study of finger-prints makes a vital contribution to many areas of police work.

Whilst England deserves great credit for leading the world in the use of finger-prints in criminology, firstly with the identification of criminals for record purposes and later as an aid to the detective engaged in his enquiries, it sadly lagged behind most other European countries in its appreciation of the need to establish a chain of forensic science laboratories throughout the country.

That England led the way in the development of a system of finger-print identification for forensic purposes was mainly due to the excellent work of two early dactyloscopical pioneers, William Herschel and Henry Faulds. In the latter part of the nineteenth century Herschel was a district officer serving in Bengal, India, where part of his duties entailed the payment of pensions to retired government workers.

As most of these employees were illiterate, he would obtain from each of them a thumb print in lieu of signature to show receipt of their earnings. He was quick to appreciate the uniqueness of each print and soon realized that this provided the means of easily identifying an individual, something which could be of the utmost importance in matters relating to the law.

About the same time as these thoughts were occupying the mind of Herschel, the Scottish-born physician Henry Faulds, who was working in Japan, had observed the same phenomenon, and in 1880 was prompted to write a letter to the magazine *Nature* stating, 'When bloody finger marks or impressions on clay, glass etc. exist, they may lead to the scientific identification of criminals, or help in medico-legal investigations when only the hands of some mutilated victim are found.'

A short time later, back in England, Sir Francis Galton, an eminent anthropologist, physician and scientist, was appointed by the Home Office to examine various means of identifying the individual with a view to finding one which would, for all practical purposes, prove infallible. His appointment had been made against a background of mounting public concern about the matter. A case of particular interest was that of Adolf Beck. In a case of mistaken identity, Beck was serving a lengthy prison sentence for fraud, after being identified by several witnesses (as well as by the trial judge) as John Smith, the man responsible for those frauds. The innocent Beck served five years in prison before he was released with £5,000 compensation after the real John Smith had been arrested and identified. Beck could find little consolation in the fact that he and Smith were almost identical in appearance.

Galton was soon pursuing his task with great vigour, and not satisfied with the Bertillon anthropometrical system which identified people by taking various bone measurements, he invited Herschel to come to England to assist him in the enquiry. Galton was hoping that together they could introduce a system of identification based upon a criminal's finger-prints. Unfortunately they hit a stumbling block which neither was able to surmount. Whilst Galton agreed that for identification purposes finger-prints were infallible, neither he nor Herschel could produce a classification system which would allow the finger-prints to be filed and retrieved. It was left to another Englishman living in the Far East to solve the problem. Edward Henry, the Inspector-General of Police in Bengal, came forward with a classification so good and so easy to apply that it is still in use to this day.

In 1901, when Henry's classification system was first put into use at New Scotland Yard, he was offered the position of Assistant Commissioner of the Metropolitan Police. He gratefully accepted; it had all come a little late for the unfortunate Adolf Beck, because he was released from jail only a few weeks after Henry had taken up his appointment.

* * *

Forensic science could be described as the application of scientific methods in order to provide evidence for the law courts. Services are now available for police forces in England and Wales in a most efficient network of laboratories at Chorley, Wetherby, Nottingham, Birmingham, Chepstow, London and Aldermaston. There are five main areas in which the laboratories specialize: biology, chemistry, firearms, documents and photography. Each laboratory will have three main objectives, which are firstly to identify, secondly to measure and thirdly to compare.

Scientists at the laboratories may be asked to identify drugs, poisons or explosives, to measure the amount of alcohol in blood or urine, the amount of poisons or drugs contained in certain organs of the body in cases of suspicious death; they may be asked to compare samples of handwriting, hair (human and animal), fibres, blood, footprints, glass particles, flakes of paint, soil, mud, seeds, and so on.

Often when the detective officer utilizes the services of the forensic laboratory, he is hoping to find scientific evidence which will link an offender with a person, a place or an object. He may wish to link the burglar with the scene of his crime, the rapist with his victim, the arsonist with inflammable materials, a robber with a firearm or a murderer with the murder weapon. When a member of the uniform branch consults the scientist, he may be hoping to connect a particular vehicle with a serious road accident or to provide evidence to substantiate a charge of drunken driving.

Contrary to what many people imagine, there is little glamour attached to the laboratory, but a great deal of hard work, with a fair amount of the chemist's time being spent on the examination of paint and glass, while the biologist is kept busy examining blood, body fluids and fibres.

Until 1932, when the first forensic science laboratory was established in Nottingham, the police were required to seek out forensic experts who would act on their behalf. They called upon the services of pathologists, analytical chemists and biologists from many of the country's leading hospitals, and engineers and textiles experts from various industrial institutes. Whilst this system produced several famous figures who became household names – Sir Bernard Spilsbury, Professor Francis Camps, Sir Sidney Smith for instance, and others such as the gunsmith Churchill – it was found far from satisfactory. In 1931 a committee was formed under the auspices of the Home Office to enquire into the need to establish a number of laboratories to assist the police in the scientific investigation of crime.

Unlike the finger-print bureaux which are controlled by the police service, when the forensic science laboratories had been established their control was vested in the Home Office. The role of the laboratories as an independent examining body was defined as early as 1935 by Mr L. C. Nickolls, the then director of the Metropolitan Police Forensic Science Laboratory, who wrote:

Whilst it may seem that laboratory staffs, appearing in court as witnesses called by the prosecution, must be in favour of the prosecution, this is not so. When the laboratory finds evidence indicating the innocence of the subject, as often happens, this evidence is rarely given in court since the police do not, in such cases, continue to take court action.

Even when the laboratory records negative findings, these are offered to the defence in case they may be of some value to them. As Mr Justice Humphreys remarked, 'The expert is not a witness for the prosecution nor the defence, but is the witness of the court.'

Whilst most laboratory staff strive to maintain this image of complete impartiality, it must be said that the people representing the defence do not have access to the laboratories' facilities.

A case which fully illustrates how science can not only assist in the detection and conviction of the guilty but also in removing suspicion from the innocent occurred in 1962, when Mrs Isabella Cross was murdered in her small corner sweets and tobacco shop in Miles Platting, Manchester. Not only did a finger-print found at the scene of the crime result in the arrest of the murderer, it was also instrumental in eliminating from the enquiry a man who had been arrested after falsely confessing to the crime. Additionally, a small piece of glass found in the murderer's home some weeks after the killing was fitted jig-saw fashion into a mineral-water bottle, one of the murder weapons, which had been reconstructed at the North-Western Forensic Science Laboratory from broken pieces recovered from the scene of the attack. This small fragment of glass established that the accused was present when the murder was committed, something which the finger-print did not.

The circumstances of the affair illustrate yet again how all too easily innocent people are drawn into events which seize the public imagination and hit the headlines in the newspapers. At 4.25 on the afternoon of Friday 4 May 1962, Mrs Cross signed for a delivery of cigarettes to her shop at the corner of Hulme Hall Lane and Iron Street. Nine-year-old Stephanie Howarth, who was visiting her married sister nearby, went to the shop five minutes later for some sweets. Nobody came to attend to her as she stood in the shop, so she peeped over the gate which led into the house. She saw 'Auntie Bella's' body lying on the floor behind the counter. Perhaps, when you come to think of it, it was Stephanie's lucky day: if she had been a couple of minutes earlier, the killer might have felt the need to silence her as well.

The little girl ran back to her sister, who, with another woman, went quickly to the shop and saw fragments of glass bottles scattered about, but they could not see the terrible injuries which Isabella Cross had suffered, because her blue overall was pulled over her head. The two women went quickly to the nearby sub-post office, where George Howard rang for the ambulance and the police. The man in charge of the investigation was Detective Chief Superintendent Eric Cunningham, an excellent detective with the ability to co-ordinate the various departments involved and a great believer in forensic science.

He quickly sent for the scenes-of-crime team, who had a lot of immediate work to do. Vast experience is needed by all members of this team, because, if the samples – and the range is wide, including finger-prints, blood, fibres, hair, and in this case the thousands of bits of glass, and of course a complete photographic record – are not taken at the time, then later can be too late.

It seemed fairly clear that 'Auntie Bella', the children's familiar friend, had been battered to death for the contents of the till. Consultation with her husband, David, who had been at his job at the Royal Ordnance Factory, Patricroft, gave Detective Chief Superintendent Cunningham a good idea of how much there was likely to be in the till.

Five large, full mineral-water bottles had been used to batter Isabella Cross; her clothes, the glass fragments and the floor around were completely saturated. Similar bottles were on a low shelf behind the counter. The till was open. A few coins lay about the floor.

The killer had not been satisfied with the till contents. The door leading from the shop to the living room was open and he had evidently tampered with a desk there. An inner drawer had been pulled out and traces of blood were on it. The next door, from the living room to the kitchen, was open; the door to the back yard and the back-yard gate were open. Easy enough to see how he had made his escape. Normally, the back-yard gate and rear door were locked and bolted from the inside. Other traces of blood were found on the rear door of the premises.

When the swabs taken of the bloodstains were examined they were found to be of Mrs Cross's blood group. Many finger-prints were found and photographed, only to be eliminated later, which was easy enough when one considered the number of people who would have had legitimate access to the premises. But fate played into the detectives' hands, because David Cross had recently been doing some household painting and only two days previously he had painted the door leading from the kitchen to the living-room. On the opening edge of this door were three finger-prints in sequence. They were not Mrs Cross's and they were not those of her husband David – so whose were they?

With great care the door was taken from its hinges and removed to the Finger-print Bureau at police headquarters. Teams of experts were already searching the files and when the prints on the door had been photographed the details were passed on to them. Prints from the glass fragments were also being examined and searched for in the files. The fragments themselves were photographed and then taken to the Forensic Science Laboratory at Preston, though it was felt the best hope of identifying the murderer lay with the finger-prints on the newly painted door. Detective Chief Superintendent Cunningham considered, rightly as it turned out, that the killer was local. He ordered house-to-house questioning in the area, with finger-prints being obtained from all likely people.

At Preston, Detective Chief Inspector Louis Allen started what was eventually seen to have been an extraordinary task, notable in the history of forensic science. Using a tube of glue and his own infinite patience, he painstakingly rebuilt the broken mineral-water bottles. Hour by hour, piece by piece he glued together the jagged edges, making what the forensic people call a 'physical fit'. The Chief Inspector knew that the making of glass involves tremendous heat and this results in striation or stress marks. They are highly distinctive and vary from piece to piece. Using his microscope, he matched the glass not only in physical fit but in striation too.

Another enquiring detective thought that his moment of glory had come when, a few days after the crime had been committed, he discovered a man loitering in the back yard of the sweet shop on Hulme Hall Lane. Embedded in the soles of the man's shoes were particles of broken glass and, when questioned, he admitted to the detective that he had murdered Mrs Cross. He was able to supply details not only about the interior lay-out of the combined shop and dwelling but also of the killing which had occurred there. It is not unknown for a criminal to revisit the scene of his crime and so the man was arrested and taken into custody.

His finger-prints were taken and a police motorcyclist

rushed them to the Bureau, where they were found not to be those recovered from the living-room door. It was most disappointing, particularly for the vigilant detective who had taken the man into custody. It is not uncommon for false confessions to be made. Nothing this man had to say could not have been obtained from reading the newspapers and looking through the windows of the shop. On the other hand, there was no real proof at this stage that the prints on the door had been left there by the killer. So, although there was doubt, every aspect of the case had to be carefully considered at what proved to be a long and somewhat anguished conference between all those involved in various aspects of the investigation. Courts are interested in proven facts, as are all detectives and supporting agencies. Nevertheless, human instinct does come into play, a feeling, a gut reaction about a situation. Cunningham felt this man was lying; nevertheless, it took considerable courage for him to disregard the man's confession and let him go. If he had been wrong, there would have been hell to pay. Only fifteen years previously, in what is probably one of this country's most controversial murder cases, Walter Graham Rowland was executed for the murder of Manchester prostitute Olive Balchin on a wartime blitz site in Deansgate, Manchester, only after the Home Secretary had ordered a stay of execution whilst an enquiry was conducted into the confession made by David John Ware that it was he and not Rowland who had murdered Olive Balchin.

Of the three finger impressions found on the door at the sweet shop, only on the centre one of the sequence, the middle finger, was the ridge detail clear and easy to search. If the killer had previously been convicted of committing a burglary in Manchester, his prints would have been in our 'singles' index and three days' searching of that left, middle finger-print would have identified him. He had not. This meant that the three finger-prints were then compared by the Bureau staff with those kept in the main finger-print collection: hundreds of thousands of groups. It takes time. Naturally, copies of the prints had been sent to New Scotland Yard and direct to other bureaux. Three weeks after Mrs Cross's death the Finger-print Bureau in Edinburgh came up with the identific-ation. The print was on their files, in their singles index. A few days later and we would have traced the culprit ourselves, because his prints were contained in our main collection. We now knew the name of the man we were looking for, but still had to find him.

This did not take long, because his home was in Corfe Street, Beswick, Manchester, an area not only scheduled for demolition but within Cunningham's house-to-house finger-printing programme. A few discreet enquiries were made; not only was he about to move home but he had already sold some of his furniture. If he got wind that the police were on to him, he could slip through the net.

For nearly twelve months twenty-six-year-old James Smith had been employed as a rubber moulder by Fergu-son Shiers Limited in Cheetham Street, Failsworth, just outside the boundary of Manchester itself. His duties at the factory involved shift work, and when he was on the day shift he would normally finish at twelve noon on the Friday of that week. On Friday 4 May, he had been on the day shift and, when he had finished work as usual at noon, he went to a local pub for a drink with his workmates. His friend Edward Hunt, with whom he usually travelled part of the way home, left the pub at 2.45, leaving James Smith still drinking.

It was customary for both men to catch the bus home at Failsworth, going towards Manchester, where Smith would get off at the junction of Oldham Road and Hulme Hall Lane, less than half a mile from Mrs Cross's sweet shop.

From there Smith could get another bus to take him near to his home, or walk quite comfortably in a further twenty minutes. No matter the circumstances people tend to stick to routine, though it is quite often divergence from that routine which solves crime. On Sunday 6 May, Smith called at Hunt's home. He had a piece of sticking plaster on his right hand and said that he had cut it on a spike in his back yard.

So far in this account James Smith is something of an abstract figure. What did he look like? Nothing remarkable: six feet tall, slim, a bit hard looking. To kill for gain is evil; yet he did have something of a good side. He had brought up two children who were not his own but were his wife's before their marriage. Perhaps that would weigh in his favour.

After Mrs Cross's death, he had continued to go to work, trying to keep up appearances. Who knows what his thoughts were as his workmates discussed over and over again a local murder which had not yet been solved? This kind of event is of perpetual interest; people read the newspapers, which are always a source of speculation. The slightest rumour, repeated often enough, tends to become fact. Every man is an instant Hercule Poirot, Sherlock Holmes or Inspector Gideon. But the one person at Ferguson Shiers who knew the truth was not saying. It takes guts to carry through this kind of situation without a lapse; to continue the daily routine, to feign sleep at night, to eat normal meals, to behave in the customary way with one's family and at the same time share in the usual speculation about an unsolved murder, to wonder if the CID has any real idea of who has done it, to disguise apprehension and to contemplate flight.

Plans were carefully laid so that Smith had no idea of what the next few hours had in store for him. An attempt could have been made to arrest him on Saturday 26 May, at his home, but it could not be established whether he was actually in the house or not. As Saturday is a bad day to catch anyone at home, particularly a man who is a heavy drinker, and as an abortive attempt to capture him could have resulted in Smith being forewarned, Cunningham bided his time. Watch was kept; no one wanted the bird fleeing the nest. Detective Chief Superintendent Cunningham and Detective Inspector Tom Butcher knocked on the door of the Corfe Street house at eight o'clock the following morning, Sunday; churchgoing time.

A few questions for James Smith, Yes, he knew the shop at 162 Hulme Hall Lane, everybody round there knew that shop. It had been on television and in the papers. He denied that he had ever been in the shop, but said that on Friday 4 May, the day of the murder, he had walked past it on his way home from work.

Routine was followed, of course. Smith was officially cautioned by Inspector Butcher, told he was being arrested and would be charged with murder.

Next stop, Mill Street police station, a monstrously ugly, solid Victorian building not far away. A few more questions. Cunningham asked Smith if he had been drinking, and he replied that he had been drinking in the public house near his work. He said he had later gone home and at 4.30 P.M. on the day of the murder he was at home when the insurance collector called.

John Hamilton, the insurance agent, was much less certain. He did call regularly on Friday afternoons at 4

Corfe Street, but said he did not get there before a quarter to five and could not remember whether or not he saw Smith there on the 4th of May. Not much of an alibi, as the murder had occurred between 4.25 and 4.30 P.M.

A small matter of timing comes into the picture, and quick tests showed that at a brisk pace it was possible to walk from the sweet shop to Corfe Street in twelve minutes, and that it took sixteen minutes at a normal walking pace.

Following a few more questions, James Smith was charged with the murder of Isabella Cross. His reply was, 'Nothing so say whatever.' He meant that, of course, for the official record.

In some ways murders resemble each other, especially those of a domestic nature. Cases of murder in the course of theft resemble each other, too. Yet inevitably in every murder there is some particular thing which is what one might call a one-off, and this was no exception. It was something Tom Butcher will never forget.

When Smith had been cautioned and charged, and had made his reply, he turned to Tom Butcher and said, 'I'll bet you £5 I never hang.' The Inspector smiled rather grimly at Smith and replied, 'You're on.' It was a bizarre wager.

Smith's home then became the subject of an exceedingly thorough search, just as thorough as that of the murder scene. Great skill and experience goes into this kind of activity, because there are few second chances.

Not many people outside the forensic, medical or CID areas of investigation realize how even the slightest contact with another person can transfer evidence from one person to another, whether it is body cells, body moisture, blood, hair, fibres from clothing, dust, dirt and so on. We had the finger-prints, but they were not enough on their own. They said loud and clear that Smith had been at the back of the shop, but they did not say he had committed the murder. He was as entitled to hard, unshakeable proof as anybody else before being convicted. The scenes-of-crime team were determined to oblige him if they could.

An efficient, spotless vacuum-cleaner attachment was pushed down the side of the cushions of the settee in the Corfe Street livingroom. When the contents of the machine were checked, a tiny fragment of glass was found. Only just in time, too, because the settee was up for sale. This bit of glass was rushed to Chief Inspector Allen at the laboratory in Preston.

Chief Inspector Allen found that the fragment fitted perfectly into one of the reconstructed bottles. Good enough, and everyone breathed that little bit more easily. No one likes innocent shopkeepers losing their lives, whether for a little or a lot. Surprising how many burglars think the owners of corner shops have stacks of money at the back of the premises. It takes a lot to pay the bills and the profit of a small shop in those days was not great.

The trial, at Liverpool Assizes, hinged on the finger-prints and the glass fragment. James Smith insisted that he had never been in the shop. The finger-prints shouted their contradiction, but they alone did not prove he had committed the murder. The glass fragment from a bottle broken during the attack placed him firmly there at the relevant time and could not be denied.

The jury took only twenty minutes to find him guilty of capital murder. When 'time!' was called on James Smith it was not by the landlord of the pub near Ferguson Shiers, but by the judge.

During the period between sentence at court and its

execution, Smith was visited in prison by Harold Riley, the Salford artist, who gave him painting lessons. In that same time Smith's hair went from a mousey brown to pure white.

The death sentence was carried out at 8 A.M. on 28 November 1962, when Smith became the last Manchester criminal to be hanged – an odd sort of fame, not one to be envied.

Mary Smith remained loyal to the man who had married her and had brought up her two children. She kept a lonely vigil outside Strangeways Prison until the notice posted at the gate told her it was all over.

When Smith's body was cut down and taken on one side, Detective Inspector Tom Butcher had the unpleasant duty of formally identifying it. He did this and, as he turned away, he was heard to mutter, 'I should have taken his fiver.'

James Smith paid society with his life. Tom Butcher's still waiting.

7
Variety is the Spice of Life

Life is full of monotonous jobs. People, no matter what their background or education, can find work boring and stultifying because it does nothing for their personality and is only a means of obtaining sufficient money to stay alive. Those of us who have managed to get and stay in a job which has retained our interest and is reasonably well rewarded should be grateful. Mind you, I think that the pleasure we derive from our occupations often depends on how much we put into them. I therefore count myself lucky that I have had an extremely interesting job, which has supported my family comfortably and has given me much to look back upon with pleasure.

When I look back, I marvel how many times extremes of contrast have occurred in a single day. One morning, as soon as the fire brigade had gone, I was helping to remove six bodies from a fire-scarred pub in Back Piccadilly, Manchester, known as Mother Mac's. None of the dead were victims of the blaze: one had committed suicide and the other five had been murdered. Then I had to rush across to the Manchester Museum on Oxford Road to finger-print an Egyptian mummy for television newsreels – bodies to body, and a few thousand years between the two. Another day I had the pleasure of conducting HRH Princess Anne around police headquarters, Chester House, at its official opening, my task being to show her the workings of the Finger-print Bureau, and immediately she had moved to another part of the building I had to jump in the car and go out to the scene of a truly vicious murder. I can remember the thoughts that went through my mind one night when I got home in the small hours to realize that I had gone that previous twelve hours from dinner at the town hall to fish and chips in the mortuary!

The long road to becoming a finger-print expert has to be trodden by every trainee. It takes seven years in all and each stage has to be satisfactorily completed. Some get fed up and opt out; occasionally a trainee is found not to be suitable. One stage in the training process is the examination of vehicles which have been stolen and recovered. It is routine, but occasionally can be funny.

When I was a trainee, the finger-print examination of stolen vehicles was conducted in the yard of what was at that time the headquarters of the Manchester City Police. In Bootle Street and Jackson's Row, which bounded the station, there are large iron gates, which in those halcyon days were left open almost all the time, allowing the public to come and go. Security consciousness dictates otherwise nowadays. This yard has always been rather a cosy place, surrounded as it is on all four sides by tall police buildings. At the time there was a small garage portion in which the Chief Constable, Assistant Chief Constable and the Superintendent of the A Division had parking places. When you got a parking place there you had, as one might say, really arrived.

Another reason at the time for free public access was the presence of the Local Taxation Office on the Bootle Street side of the quadrangle. It used to be administered by the police and had for about twenty years been in the care of Chief Inspector Bees. From what I heard he was something of a tartar to work for: white was white, black was black and shades of grey did not exist. When the LTO moved out, the Summons and Warrants Department moved in.

Vehicles which had been stolen and recovered were brought into the yard by members of the Transport Department and, when this had been done, an officer would inform the A Division charge office clerk or the duty Sergeant. Their office was only a few yards away, down a short approach which was wide enough and no wider (give or take an inch or two) than the van which arrived every morning to take prisoners to court. The clerk's job was to enter all particulars of the vehicle in the appropriate journal, inform the owner that it had been recovered and arrange for its collection and, if it was thought necessary, also arrange for a forensic examination. When the latter, if required, had been completed, the vehicle would be handed over.

At about ten o'clock one bright spring morning I had a request to finger-print two vehicles in the yard. The clerk on that particular day was a friendly chap with a nice turn of phrase. He and I knew that it was my duty to go and attend to those vehicles, but nevertheless he gently put it that they were 'awaiting my pleasure'.

One of the vehicles, a Ford Consul, had been absent without leave for two days. The other, an old Bedford van, had been missing from home for a period of three weeks, which was quite a long time. With my box of finger-print equipment over my shoulder and particulars of the two vehicles in my notebook, I went down from my own department into the yard. I saw the Ford Consul right away and, encouraged by the fine spring morning, gave it a thorough examination. Then I cast around for the Bedford van. Now that yard was not very big and a Bedford van, or any van come to that, would have been difficult to hide, but it was not there. I nipped into the A Division charge office to tell them so. The friendly clerk assured me that it had not been collected by the owner and suggested that I had probably become prematurely blind through my then few years of searching in the finger-prints office.

I went into the yard again and examined the number plate of every vehicle there; there were not many, because of course room has to be left for driving in and out. Back in the charge office I suggested that the clerk, with his undoubted twenty-twenty vision, should walk by my side and point out the van he wished me to examine. As we went out there were a few more good-natured sallies from the charge office Inspector and Sergeant.

We looked again. The clerk was nonplussed and I gathered from the few unprintable words he uttered that he did not have a clue where it had gone. Arrive it certainly had, but its departure was shrouded in mystery.

We were joined in the centre of the yard by the Inspector and his Sergeant. After all, the A Division charge office had a certain amount of collective responsibility for truant vehicles which had been returned to the guardianship of the law. As we walked around looking here and there, it became obvious to other members of headquarters staff who, from time to time, gaze out of their windows upon the passing show, that something was amiss.

We were joined by a certain Chief Inspector. This man was always held in high regard and still is, even though he is long retired. He wanted to know what we were doing and, when he was told that we were looking for a Bedford van, he assured us that we had no cause to worry as he had been crossing the yard when the owner had been having considerable trouble in starting it and he, the Chief Inspector, had gone to his assistance. Using the starting handle, he had helped the driver to get the engine started and as the owner drove out and waved, the Chief Inspector had returned the wave, full of *bonhomie* and a deed well done.

Even though the paperwork had been bypassed, the charge office staff were much relieved – until the registered genuine owner of the vehicle was contacted that is. He told them that he knew his van had been recovered, but that he had not yet collected it and, what is more, he had not authorized anybody else to do so. The Chief Inspector, now rather red-faced, agreed that it must have been stolen from the enclosed police yard with his unwitting assistance.

Whilst there was a good deal of anxiety expressed, of course, because non-recovery could have led to several pairs of constabulary boots on the mat, at the same time there was an undercurrent of wry amusement that it had been re-stolen with the assistance of a Chief Inspector and not, thank God, of a similarly unwitting PC.

Particulars of the van were quickly recirculated and two days later members of the road patrol arrested the cheeky thief. He was driving the van through the city centre. He amiably told them that he had first taken the van some three weeks earlier and in that time had become very attached to it. He had left it parked in the centre of Manchester and, when he returned, was rather surprised to see it being towed away by police officers. He had followed the van on foot and had seen it taken the short distance to police headquarters, where they had left it in the yard. When all seemed quiet, he had entered through the large wrought-iron gates and was having difficulty in starting his new-found friend when he had been ably assisted by a kind police officer. He was fined for his misdeeds. And I am glad to say that the assisting Chief Inspector rose high in the police service.

A short time afterwards, the same amiable charge office

clerk rang through to the Finger-print Bureau to say that a bright, up-and-coming young comedian was at that moment in his office reporting the theft of some new, and to the comedian very valuable, scripts from his car whilst it had been left overnight at his hotel. Armed with the necessary finger-print equipment, I went into the yard, where I saw the comedian, a young man of my own age, standing next to a large American Oldsmobile, a very old Oldsmobile. He seemed a pleasant young man but, understandably, was not bubbling over with fun and merriment at that moment. He told me that the missing scripts were new material, and represented months of hard work. He and his partner had written them and, what was more, they were the only existing copies. He had to go back to London in a couple of days' time and his confidence in the Manchester Police was such that he was sure we would recover his property in quick time. I was pleased with the confidence he showed, but doubted whether we had the ability to live up to his expectations, especially when, after examining his car, I failed to find any finger-prints which could have been left by the thief.

However, God moves in a mysterious way, and by four o'clock that afternoon a member of the CID rang to say he had recovered the comedian's literary gems and was bringing them into the Bureau for finger-print examination.

It would be nice to report that the scripts had been recovered as the result of diligent police work; but, hand on heart, I have to admit they had been dumped by the thief in a Salford back street. The finder had handed them to a passing police officer, describing them as more of the 'bloody litter' which accumulated at her back door. It was getting towards the end of the day in the office, a time when a little light relief is welcome. One of the finger-print officers sat at his desk. The first of the scripts was put on the desk in front of him. Grouped behind him, and reading as best they could over his shoulder, were five other officers.

Taking care not to leave his own finger-prints on the manuscripts or to remove the thief's, the officer slowly flicked over the pages, allowing the discriminating group behind him to read and digest every word.

The first page was slowly read and digested; not a smile. Same with the second page; not even a titter. As each page was turned there was the occasional wry comment, but no display of mirth whatsoever. It soon became obvious that the script contained nothing at all to amuse those reading it. Reaching the end, as one voice we burst into spontaneous laughter: the thief had written, 'What a . . . !'

Over the years I have never ceased to be amazed at the physical agility certain burglars possess, at the luck some others seem to have, and the sheer ability that enabled a few of them to nose out and find money which had been well and truly hidden. Perhaps the most agile of the lot was a cat burglar nicknamed The Climber, who operated in Manchester city centre at the end of the 1950s and beginning of the 1960s. His *modus operandi* was to break into and enter office tower blocks, usually on a Friday or Saturday night. To achieve this he would climb up the fire escapes to the tops of the buildings and then, by means of downpipes and gutters, make his way to windows, which he would force open and enter. He would perform these hazardous acts in pitch darkness.

I recall examining the scene of one of his crimes early on a Saturday morning, standing at the top of a fire escape some hundred feet above the busy city streets.

From where I stood I was able to see that The Climber had gone a further nine or ten feet up a downpipe to reach the gutter, along which he had then swung, hand over hand, a further twelve feet until he reached a second fall pipe, down which he shinned to a small window. He had there stood on the outside of the window-sill whilst he broke the window to gain access to the building.

I have a reasonably good head for heights, but viewing all this made me very queasy; standing there and assessing what he had done brought home to me what a fantastic climber he undoubtedly was, and how brave he must be. However, he was not an accomplished burglar; not only were his pickings relatively small, he left his finger-prints behind at the scene of quite a lot of his crimes, and no burglar with any sense does that.

This climber operated over a two-year period, during which he was never caught. Then things went quiet. This quiet spell coincided with work being undertaken by British Rail to electrify the main railway line between Manchester and London. Whilst this work was in progress many miles of copper wire were stolen, because it is heavy and can be sold profitably at a scrap yard. Whilst attempting to steal some more of it, a man had climbed to the top of a pylon and tried to cut through the wire. Unfortunately for him, nobody had switched off the current. He was badly burned and crashed to the ground. For many days his life was in danger. Recovery was slow and, after leaving hospital, he was charged with attempted larceny. His finger-prints were, of course, taken and forwarded to the Bureau. When they were checked against the finger-prints left at the various office blocks we found we had at last caught up with The Climber.

Criminals do not necessarily take the statutory holidays, and one Boxing Day morning found me visiting a small, modern, semi-detached house in the Withington area, inside the Manchester city boundary. The house had been broken into on Christmas night, whilst the occupants were sound asleep. A quick examination showed that the point of entry into the house was via a pantry window, and the burglar had departed by the rear door with a modest amount of the occupants' property.

I could see that the window had been forced and was now gaping open with jemmy marks on the newly painted woodwork, and there were dirty glove impressions on the inside of the white window frame.

I stood inside the kitchen, looking into the pantry. It was like so many other pantries in the average semi-detached: a small, shelved cubicle about three feet wide, three feet deep with a small window on the outer wall. From the front of the house these windows are round the side and may indeed be out of sight of the road, especially after nightfall, when they are in the dark. This particular pantry had shelves on three sides, the door of course constituting the fourth. There were deep shelves on the outside wall and narrow ones on the side walls, with a space of about two feet between them.

Twenty-five years ago few families possessed a refrigerator and the occupants of this house were not one of the lucky ones. People made do, for the perishables, with a marble slab if they could get one, often the top of an old wash stand.

This was Christmas and the shelves were laden with the products of many hours' labour: mince pies, jellies, blancmanges, fruit cake, pudding, turkey, ham and so on. On the stone shelf in front of the open window, and over which the thief had to crawl, stood the remains of turkey, jelly and blancmanges and bowls of fruit plus some other leftovers. It seemed impossible, short of levitation and horizontal passage, that someone could squeeze through the window and go over all this food, open the pantry door and regain his feet without bringing the contents clattering around his ears. With a better disposition he would have made an ideal and thoroughly reliable Santa Claus!

For reasons of their own a certain number of people keep fairly large amounts of cash hidden in their homes. A few elderly people, who have not quite come to terms with inflation, and who do not trust the banks, believe that it is 'safer in th'ouse'. Also certain types of business people believe that it is advantageous to have a stock of ready cash available. Others feel that every pound earned is theirs and have reasons of their own for not wishing to reveal the exact extent of their estate. The hiding places range from the old lady's handbag hidden under the bed and cash hidden under the mattress or carpet, to the more sophisticated who prefer to hide their valuables under a loose floorboard or wrapped in a waterproof cover and hung in the toilet cistern.

Given time, the average burglar will find these hiding places and relieve owners of the worry of looking after their cash. A very few thieves seem to possess a sixth sense for detecting money which has been hidden in a most unlikely place. In the days before central heating became popular the home of a bookmaker was entered and the bookie was more than a little surprised when he discovered that a thief had found £500 hidden under the coal at the bottom of the coal scuttle. Another local businessman received a nasty shock when he awoke one morning to find a burglar had entered his home in the night and had found a quantity of bank notes which their owner had sellotaped underneath the bottom of a sideboard drawer.

The best find I can recall was by a thief who really must have possessed a radar especially tuned in to money. He broke into the home of a market trader and, in the trader's own words, 'found a wad of notes big enough to choke a horse' which he had hidden at the bottom of a two-pound bag of sugar which was on the top shelf of the kitchen cabinet.

I soon found out how lucky certain thieves can be when, early in my finger-print service, I was asked to attend the scene of a house-breaking in Openshaw, the home of an amusement-arcade proprietor. When I got there, I saw that the house was a large Victorian dwelling in a fairly poor working-class area. It had cellars and living accommodation on three floors; in the roof were were two large attics. The occupier was highly agitated and confided to me that someone had stolen £4,000 from a chest which he kept concealed under a blanket in the attic. That amount of money does not seem so much now, but in those days it would have bought two nice houses. He led the way up three flights of stairs to the top of the house. The door leading to the attic was padlocked and there was no sign of forcible entry.

As we got into the room all became clear. There was the empty, open chest and immediately above it in the roof was a gaping hole. The enterprising thief had taken off a few slates, broken through the laths and dropped straight on to the money. It was surely his lucky day. In some cases of theft I felt little sorrow for the loser and would occasionally recollect an old copper nicknamed The Vicar, who in similar circumstances would shake his head very sadly and murmur, 'Ill-gotten gains.'

Few of us, when looking back at our working life, will have no regrets; something we did which perhaps we should not have done or a chance we had and turned down. I still regret that during my police service I refused to tackle a job of work which was unique, would have proved most interesting and required but little time and effort. The request was for me to finger-print a ghost. I refused because I did not believe in ghosts and I considered at the time that the attempt would make me appear foolish. How I wish that opportunity would present itself again.

In the spring of 1961 I was working in the Bureau alongside a close friend whom I had known since my C Division days. There was a knock on the door and in came David Cohen, a middle-aged gentleman. He told us he was secretary of the Manchester branch of the Psychical Research Society.

Although this society has always taken itself and its work seriously, many people at the time did not. I believe that their purpose has always been to investigate phenomena which have no obvious explanation, to eliminate the possibility of trickery and to do this in as scientific a manner as possible, keeping careful records and statements of witnesses. The last twenty years or so have seen tremendous changes in the attitudes towards this kind of work by scientists and members of the public. Indeed, the late Arthur Koestler, scientist, philosopher, writer, indeed polymath, left sufficient money in his will for the funding of a Chair in Psychical Research at one of our universities.

Mr Cohen asked for the services of an expert to finger-print a pair of hands which were appearing during seances held in a small house in south Manchester, and to assist in enquiries he was making as the result of certain manifestations. He went on to explain that in his official position as secretary of the society he had been approached some two years previously by a woman who had an intriguing story to tell. She lived in a small terraced house on the southern side of the city. She had a teenage son, a younger daughter and had recently been widowed. She spoke of mysterious happenings in her home for which she could not find any logical explanation.

Her son was taking violin lessons, and shortly after the death of her husband she woke one night to the sound of a violin being played. She got out of bed and went to her son's bedroom, expecting to see him playing. The music stopped just before she reached his room. She opened the door only to find him peacefully asleep in his bed and nothing untoward to be seen.

She returned to her room somewhat troubled and tried to convinvce herself she had been dreaming. Over a period of time the incident was frequently repeated. Always there was the sound of a violin being played in her son's bedroom, and she always found her son fast asleep. The music was always the same, Ravel's Bolero.

Several months later, fearing she was on the edge of a nervous breakdown and believing the music to be part of her imagination, after yet another disturbed night, she asked her son if he had been awake during the night playing his violin, even though she knew the intricacies of such a piece were well beyond his ability. His answer astounded her: 'Oh, no, it was not me playing the violin, it was Nicholas.'

When she had recovered her composure she asked her son who Nicholas was. He said, 'Nicholas is the old man who plays the violin for me.' Somewhat reassured as to her sanity, despite great uncertainties about what had actually happened, she went to see Mr Cohen and asked if his society could help to lay the ghost, if that was what it was.

Mr Cohen set to work. He and other selected members held a number of seances at the small house in Fallowfield. The point had now been reached where contact with Nicholas had been established and during one part of the seance, held in a darkened room, a pair of hands had manifested themselves. This had become a regular occurrence, and the reason Mr Cohen was seeking our services was quite simple, and quite in accordance with the society's wish to eliminate all trickery: he wished the expert to come along and attend a seance. If the opportunity presented itself he was to finger-print the hands. If he was successful, the next step would be to finger-print every person present in the room. By comparing all these it was hoped to eliminate any suspicion and confirm that there was indeed another presence in the room.

Mr Cohen could see I was a doubting Thomas and was not in the least surprised when I refused my services. However, he appeared so genuine that I felt the least I could do would be to take his name and address and pass on his request to another member of the Bureau, Sergeant Rowland Mason, a close friend and finger-print expert of great ability.

A few words about Rowly Mason would not go amiss. He was an exceptional man in many ways, not least in the finger-print business. He often seemed to have had a sixth sense about a culprit even when we had so little to go on that we had almost given up. Perhaps his past experiences had to some extent honed his senses. Born in 1919, the son of a Manchester policeman, he had flown thirty-four missions as a rear gunner with the Royal Air Force during the war. That alone makes him special, because very few flew so many with Bomber Command.

The chances of surviving as Tail End Charlie in a Lancaster on a bombing raid were not good at their best; to survive ten trips was really going it; to survive the number Rowland did was bordering on the miraculous. The experience left him patient, philosophical, generally very cheerful and with a liking for life, a turn of wit and a wry attitude towards minor peccadilloes, but a burning dislike of real evil. We all liked him and he had many friends throughout the force. Better on your side than on the other fellow's!

Rowland eventually consented to meet Mr Cohen and attempt to finger-print the ghost. I remember the look on his face when he said, 'The difficult we do today; the impossible we'll try tomorrow.'

He met Mr Cohen and it was agreed he would attend a number of seances. He was to use the first two to assess the situation and any difficulties which lay ahead. In the office after each seance he gave a full report to the attentive audience, before work in the Bureau was allowed to commence. Not surprisingly, there was a certain amount of chaffing, but at the same time there was keen interest in deciding what the technical approach should be.

If my memory serves me well, the people attending the seances were the widow of the household, her son, and Mr Cohen; the only variation being whoever came from the society to act as observer and Sergeant Mason, the practised taker of genuine, earthly finger-prints.

At the first meeting Sergeant Mason was introduced to the other members of the party and it was explained to them that he had a plan of campaign. With the room in darkness and everybody sitting round a table, the 'spirit', Nicholas, confirmed his presence by a series of knocks. There was a fine example of levitation when the large table round which the people were sitting rose in the air to such a height that Rowland had to stand on tiptoe, with arm outstretched, before he could touch the top of it; and Rowland is a tall chap.

Later, a tambourine which had previously been painted with luminous paint flew about the room at incredible speeds, constantly changing direction as it did so and in a way which no human earthly agency could have achieved.

Next morning at the Bureau Rowland informed us all that he was completely mystified by the previous evening's events, and could not offer any logical explanation. Knowing him as we all did, respecting his professional abilities and his undoubted skill at sniffing out the less than obvious clue, we had to believe him.

A second visit to the Fallowfield house provided more mystery and suspense. Not only was there loud knocking on the table, accompanied by violent shaking and a degree of levitation, but after the tambourine had flown around the darkened sitting room a pair of hands manifested themselves. As the room was in total darkness it would not be right to say that the hands appeared, but Sergeant Mason said they were certainly there. Mr Cohen had described them as dry and scaly, and as having lace cuffs over the wrists.

What Rowland felt was touches on his shoulders and arms. He was absolutely sure that he was not being touched by any person present. Later he touched the hands himself.

During the course of a long career Sergeant Mason has, like every other finger-print expert, held hands in the nicest possible way with the quick and the dead, the guilty and the innocent, the young, the middle-aged and the elderly, the willing and the unwilling. He simply says that the hands were a little dry and fairly slim. When telling us this the following morning there was, of course, some good-humoured banter, but there was not one member of the department who was not intrigued by the happenings, and nobody for one moment thought that Sergeant Mason was imagining things.

He decided that on his third visit he would try to take the finger-prints of the ghost or the human being responsible for creating the illusion, and to accomplish this he was prepared to enter into a little legitimate deception. He would not do the obvious, which would be to grasp the hands and attempt to finger-print them, but would use the scenes-of-crime technique. He got to the house on the Friday evening well ahead of the others in order to prepare the scene. He was equipped with brushes, mercury powder (which is the best type of finger-print powder, only to be used with extreme care on special occasions) and a duster. He went into the living-room and, without telling anybody, removed the tambourine from its place on the sideboard. Using his duster, he carefully polished it to make sure that it was clean, shining and free of finger-prints, providing what he hoped would be an ideal surface. Then he put his duster by the side of the sideboard.

As soon as the other people had gathered, the seance began. The householder, acting as the medium, took charge of the proceedings. The room was darkened and all present were seated round the table. Suddenly Rowland was struck by a soft object. His hair stood on end on the back of his neck. He was rather shocked to find that the duster he had used to clean the tambourine had been flung in his face, but by whom? No human person knew what he had done, but something was letting him know he had been observed.

The events which followed were much as before –

violent knockings, levitation, being touched by hands and the tambourine flying wildly around the room; one difference was that the householder played a tape of Ravel's Bolero. After the meeting had ended and the lights were switched on every person appeared to be seated in his or her normal position. Rowland took immediate possession of the tambourine and carefully dusted it with finger-print powder, hoping to develop and recover a set of prints. The tambourine was as clean and free from finger-prints as when he had polished it an hour previously!

On a further visit the tambourine was powdered with the finger-print material before the seance began. The tambourine was seen to rise from the sideboard and circle the room; all observed this. Afterwards the powder which had been brushed on to it was found apparently undisturbed. The mystery deepened.

As the hands were now manifesting themselves on a regular basis it was decided to ascertain whether the spirit Nicholas would be agreeable to having his finger-prints taken. Through a series of questions answered by knocks, the answer was yes. Rowland decided to try using the clean print method. Whereas one normally rolls the fingers on a plate covered by a thin layer of printer's ink and then transfers the prints on to paper, the clean print method entails placing the fingers on to a chemically charged pad and, after removing them, touching them on sensitized paper. This ensures a reasonably good print without dirtying the hand. It was decided to do this the following week, and was to prove most difficult.

Rowland had to put the chemically charged pad and the sensitized paper on the table directly in front of him. In complete darkness he had to make contact with one of the ghostly hands; then he had to hold this hand in one of his own, and with the other find the finger-print pad, guide the spirit's hand to the pad and make sure that the tips of the fingers touched it, feel for the sensitized paper and complete the operation by putting the spirit's chemically treated fingers on to the paper – under the circumstances, not an easy task.

However, all went fairly well. In the course of the seance, with the agreement of Nicholas, Rowland caught hold of one of the hands; in the pitch darkness he could feel that it was dry. With his other hand he guided the hand to the finger-print pad and touched it. Now he had to seek the sensitized paper and bring the apparition's hand into contact with it. This he believed he had achieved.

Next morning he arrived at the bureau with the sensitized paper. The whole staff were agog. The paper was carefully examined. It revealed three one-inch long scratch marks, each parallel with the others. They could have been made by a bird's claw; they could equally have been made by three finger nails scratching the paper. There were no identifiable finger-prints.

More seances were held and the incidents re-enacted the following morning in the Bureau (to the accompaniment of Ravel's Bolero) for the benefit of a most receptive and expert audience. It was agreed that the police photographer should be approached to see if he could photograph the ghost or indeed any events connected with it. Constable John Cheetham, a photographer of great experience, confirmed the possibility of taking photographs using infra-red light, and what was more he would be prepared to try this if he could first attend a seance and check that the circumstances and events outlined by Rowland were indeed true.

On Rowland's next visit to the Fallowfield house he

was accompanied not only by John Cheetham but also by John's wife, Flo. Next morning at the office John confirmed that there certainly were mysterious happenings at the house. There had been loud knockings, levitation, and the tambourine had flown around the room; further, he and his wife had each been touched by what felt like two hands. Not only did he confirm everything Rowland had said, all of it defying logical explanation, but said that his wife was so frightened that she would never under any circumstances be prepared to enter the room again.

Before describing further events I must mention that whilst John Cheetham and his wife had been present a vase of flowers was standing well away from the table round which they were sitting; the flowers themselves were taken out of the vase and scattered around the room. Another point, and I gather the same condition has applied to hundreds of other such cases, is that the temperature often varied; these were fairly warm summer evenings and yet the temperature would drop to freezing. The music, too, was strange. It had been recorded on tape in a perfectly orthodox manner, but when it was played at these seances it would vary from very soft to deafeningly loud.

Rowland had always been a sort of elder brother figure in the Bureau, and of course no one could match either his Air Force or his working experience, or his instinct for the job. Nobody was bantering now after all these weeks of patient and serious investigation.

At the seance attended by John Cheetham and his wife, by the usual system of questions answered by knocks, Nicholas the ghost was asked whether he would be prepared to sit in an armchair and be photographed. Yes, he would.

Events the following Friday went exactly as planned. The camera was set, focused on the armchair which had been placed in position. The room was darkened, the medium contacted the spirit and requested it to occupy the chair. The photograph was taken.

Next morning found everybody eagerly awaiting the development of the negative. When the photographs arrived they showed a chair, resting against the back of which was a large creased cushion. Nothing else.

However, the older reader will recall the pastime of staring into a glowing coal fire and seeing an image, probably an image of what you wanted to see. Now, as each police officer present stared at that creased cushion he could see the image of a very old man, bearded and turned to the right, rather like the head of the old king on a coin. I could see it and I could describe it. So could the others. It was a remarkable coincidence that all present could see the same thing.

The experiment soon came to an abrupt end. Somehow, and I suppose it was inevitable, the story leaked out to the press. A full account of the events and the police involvement in them was printed in the *Daily Mail*. Although no police time was involved in the investigation, the Chief Superintendent in charge of the CID demanded that the two officers concerned should submit lengthy and comprehensive reports. They both did so, not withholding any of the details. Nothing further was heard and the events are but a memory.

If you were now to ask me if I believe in ghosts, I would reply that I do not readily disbelieve in the supernatural and that there are probably two reports still on file in police archives which bear witness to the events I have just related. Nobody was pulling anyone's leg about any of it, except perhaps Nicholas – and even he seemed to be perfectly serious. I am told that manifestations such as this often occur when there is a juvenile living in the house. Sometimes such juveniles have been found to be responsible for trickery. False or real, the phenomenon is known and recognized all over the world, particularly in Europe, and has been so for hundreds of years. I am sure that the teenage boy in this house in Fallowfield had nothing to do with the events which Rowland Mason described to us, that all concerned were perfectly serious in intent, and that no trickery was used. Mr Cohen also seemed satisfied in this respect, but of course could not give any explanation beyond, perhaps, the wish of the long-dead Nicholas to have a part in present life through the agency, somehow, of the boy. No more can be said by me, except that I fervently wish I had not turned down the opportunity when it was presented. There is so much we do not know, perhaps never will know and maybe never should know. There is an old saying that there is nothing new under the sun; true, I suppose. What is new is that scientists are now asking different questions and have much improved technology to help find the answers. It may be that the new Chair at Edinburgh, funded by the late Arthur Koestler, will provide some answers to such questions.

Somewhere around 1964 a colleague and I had to perform a most unusual job, and to my mind it was one of the saddest in my service. A surgeon at Manchester Royal Infirmary asked us to finger-print a patient of his who was seriously ill. This extraordinary request came about because the patient, a twenty-year-old girl who had a serious kidney disease, was one of triplets and, to ensure her recovery so far as the surgeon could do so, it was necessary for her to receive a kidney transplant. Both her sisters had volunteered to donate one kidney in this attempt to save her life.

The two sisters underwent a series of tests at the infirmary and the results indicated they were medically identical. There was now a dilemma. Each of the two sisters had offered a kidney; the three, obviously born from a single fertilized egg, had the same biological structure, so which one should he choose to give his patient the best possible chance? He wrote to the Chief Constable of Manchester seeking assistance from members of the Finger-print Bureau, asking if an expert could, as a matter of urgency, take the prints of the patient and her sisters, and then compare the results to see if any guidance could be given by the print patterns themselves. He appreciated that no two finger-prints are identical, even in identical twins and triplets, but hoped for some area of similarity.

Sergeant Mason and I went to the infirmary and met the surgeon, who took us along to see his patient. She was certainly a very sick young lady. We used the clean-print method described earlier in this chapter and gently took her finger-prints as she lay in bed. It was a poignant proceeding for all of us.

Returning to the Bureau, we quickly arranged for her two sisters also to be finger-printed and it was done that afternoon. We classified the triplets' prints and compared them. As expected, no one print was identical with any of the others, but two sets did have similar codes, those of the sick girl and one of her sisters; the other sister's prints were completely different in coding. We telephoned our findings through to the surgeon and later confirmed them by letter.

A short time later there came a letter from the surgeon. He thanked us for our efforts and had decided to perform the operation on the basis of our report. However, he was grieved to tell us that the patient had died before the operation could be performed.

Some crimes are solved by diligent routine and some by brilliant detection; others are settled as the result of information received and the occasional one as the result of a sheer fluke. Now, although I have always considered myself a rather sober type of individual there have been occasions, when I was younger, when I have had what one might call a drop too much, but always in my own time; being under the influence was not something which went well with working on finger-prints and I always knew my superior officers held the same view.

There was one time, though, when I could have been seen in a very different light by any interested observer. It was a New Year's Day. Being a family man, Christmas was a time for the children, but New Year's Eve was a time I spent taking my wife out, always presuming, of course, that urgent duty did not intervene. We would somehow get a baby-sitter, often my mother, and spend the evening at the home of a close Scottish friend, a native of Ayrshire and a former colleague from the C Division. His main object was to get me legless and then send me home in a taxi. I regret to say that, with my willing connivance and much to the amusement of my wife, he managed to achieve this on more than one occasion. New Year's Eve may well have been for pleasure, but in the police service New Year's Day was a normal working day and had to be treated as such.

The New Year's Day I wish to tell you about found me a recently qualified finger-print expert and promoted to the rank of Sergeant. I paraded for duty that morning in a state which did not reflect any credit on me or the

The author as a young PC

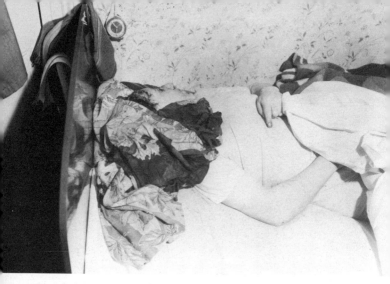

The victim at 1 Oakleigh Avenue, Burnage, Manchester

LEFT: At 162 Hulme Hall Lane, Manchester: broken bottles and the rifled till behind the shop counter

ABOVE: The reconstructed bottles – a missing fragment of one was found in the murderer's home

Harold, the orang-utan, was too intimidating

ABOVE: Finger-print of Jane, the orang-utan – the appendage at the top distinguishes it from a human print
RIGHT: Printing the baby chimp was much easier

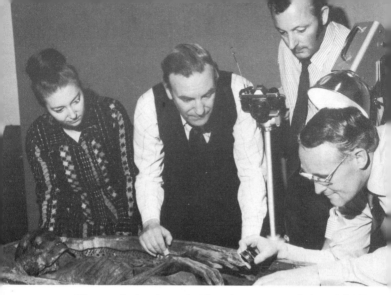

ABOVE: Finger-printing Asru, the Egyptian mummy: *(left to right)* Dr Rosalie David, Len Lloyd, Ken Caple and Tony Fletcher
BELOW: Asru's finger-print

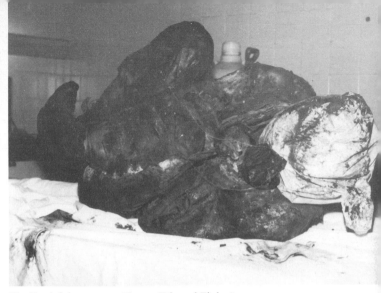

The Rochdale mummy (James Edward Finlay)

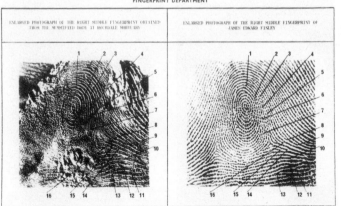

GREATER MANCHESTER POLICE
FINGERPRINT DEPARTMENT

| ENLARGED PHOTOGRAPH OF THE RIGHT MIDDLE FINGERPRINT OBTAINED FROM THE MUMMIFIED BODY AT ROCHDALE MORTUARY | ENLARGED PHOTOGRAPH OF THE RIGHT MIDDLE FINGERPRINT OF JAMES EDWARD FINLEY |

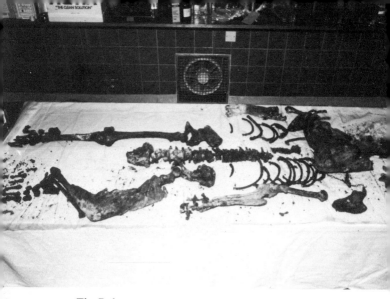

ABOVE: The Bolton mummy; BELOW: Reconstructing the head

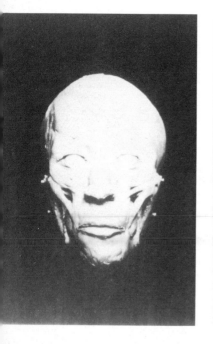

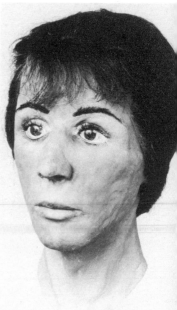

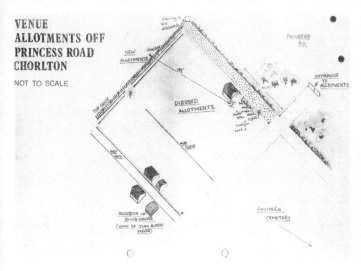

Police sketch plans for the Jean Jordan murder scene

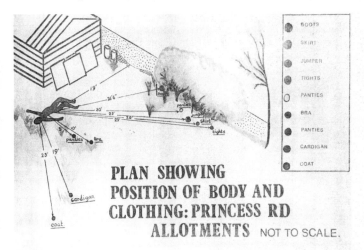

ABOVE: H.R.H. Princess Anne being shown round the Finger-print Bureau and Scenes of Crime Department by Tony Fletcher

LEFT: Author indicating the position of the thumb-print left by Michael Pinkney at the spot where he murdered William Hanlon

service. I was what is euphemistically described as 'under the weather'. Above all, I wanted to get out of the office and into the air, so I elected to visit the scenes of crimes which had been committed during the night. I am glad to say that I was driven by a colleague who was highly competent and in full possession of his faculties.

Our first call was to the place where the most serious crime had occurred over the holiday, a house in south Manchester which had been burgled and a large amount of jewellery stolen. My colleague took charge of the situation, introduced us both to the occupier and then started the examination. It soon became obvious to him that the intruder had been wearing gloves, as at the point of entry and on articles handled glove impressions were found. I had taken no part in the proceedings whatsoever, being content to stand on my feet – not too steadily, I admit – and say nothing for fear of making a bigger fool of myself than I already felt.

Suddenly I was aware that the lady of the house was staring at me. She may have felt that my semi-glazed look was not very helpful, I do not know, but whatever it was her look galvanized me into action. Making a supreme effort, I bent down, took up finger-print brush and powder, and staggered across to the nearest window. Once there I somehow regained my balance and started applying powder to the glass window pane. There was absolutely no earthly reason why I should have examined that pane; no indication whatever that the intruder had been anywhere near to it. With the application of the first brushful of powder, a large and obviously freshly made thumb print appeared. It was of a right thumb and the pattern revealed was the twin-loop type. After comparison with all the right thumbs of members of the household, it remained unaccounted for, the probability being that it had been placed there by the thief who, for reasons of his own, must have looked out of the window after taking off his right glove.

Back at the Bureau the thumb print was quickly searched and identified as that of an Italian gentleman named Rossi, who was arrested and committed for trial at Manchester Crown Court. On the day of his appearance there I attended the court and gave evidence of opinion as to the identification of the thumb print. By then I was, of course, perfectly sober, dressed in my best dark grey Crown Court suit and I made, I believe, a fully competent witness. Present in the court was the owner of the jewellery who had been staring at me in her home on New Year's morning. She came across to speak to me after the case had ended. In these altogether different circumstances she failed to recognize me. With her jewellery recovered and the thief safely behind bars, she stated her belief that the British police were wonderful. She did, however, confide that at the time of the burglary she had had her doubts: one of the police officers who came to investigate was as drunk as any person she had ever seen.

Should I admit my guilt? For a moment I wondered. They do say that confession is good for the soul. Regrettably, confession does not come easily to a police officer and I decided my soul could, for the time being at least, look after itself. 'Well, I am surprised,' was the only reply I could muster.

Sometimes one is asked to solve a problem normally considered to be outside one's field. When a solution is found to that problem, no matter how small the difficulty may be, success is sweet and lingers. Such an event occurred when I was requested by the Assistant Chief

Constable responsible for Crime Investigation in Manchester to find the tolerance of a watch spring!

As I sat in my office I could see that it had little to do with either finger-prints or scenes-of-crime work, but it could be quite an interesting challenge and a nice break from routine. The circumstances were unusual. Complaints had been received at Manchester police headquarters that the Orrell Rugby Club was breaking the law. Orrell is not far from Wigan in Lancashire. These complaints had come from several police forces, some of them in the South of England, alleging that Orrell Rugby Club, by organizing a certain prize competition, was acting in contravention of Section 47 of the Betting, Gaming and Lotteries Act of 1963.

Orrell Rugby Club has a high reputation within the Rugby world, and the ground lies to the west of Wigan. It is just within the boundary of Greater Manchester and, as the club came under the jurisdiction of Greater Manchester police, pressure was being applied by some of the other forces to induce them to take appropriate action.

The competition, which was organized by the club to raise much-needed funds, was to involve a new wristwatch, the make of which would be indicated to all contestants. At a given time the watch would be fully wound and then put into a safe, which would be locked. Tickets showing all the relevant information would then be sold and the contestants had to estimate the exact time at which the watch would stop. The person whose estimate or guess came nearest to the time shown on the watch face, would win the prize.

Now then, the provisions of Section 47 of the Betting, Gaming and Lotteries Act in relation to prize competitions seem to be extremely simple, in that:

It shall be unlawful to conduct in or through any newspaper, or in connection with any trade or business or the sale of any article to the public:

(a) any competition in which prizes are offered for forecasts of the result either:

    (i) of a future event,

    (ii) of a past event the result of which is not yet ascertained or not generally known;

(b) any other competition, success in which does not depend to a substantial degree upon the exercise of skill.

Put simply, was the competition a game of chance, which would be unlawful, or a competition where a contestant could be expected to exercise his skill, which would be lawful?

This particular prize competition had been a large one and hundreds of tickets had been sold in different parts of the country. Officers of several forces in whose areas the tickets had been sold were of the opinion that the competition was a game of chance with no element of skill involved and therefore unlawful. The hot potato was dropped firmly in my lap. The tolerance of a watch spring idea put forward was a good starting point, but after a full day of making enquiries at several Manchester watchmakers I found I was getting nowhere and yet everywhere. After talking to all these horological experts I found that I knew no more about the tolerance of a watch spring than when I had started, but knew a great deal more about the length of time a watch could be expected to run when it had been fully wound. So, sitting back quietly and thinking about the problem, it seemed to me that an intelligent person, by exercising his or her particular skills, would stand far more chance of winning the competition than a person without that knowledge.

I next spoke to the secretary of the British Horological

Society who, by coincidence, was staying overnight in Manchester. He agreed that if I obtained a new Seiko watch and wound it fully, by the application of his skill and knowledge of that particular watch, he would have more chance of estimating when it would stop than a person with no such knowledge.

The information he had given me, and an apparent solution, was relayed to the Assistant Chief Constable, who immediately instructed me to go to the headquarters of the British Horological Society and obtain a statement from the secretary to that effect. This was a bonus which provided me with one of my most enjoyable days in the service.

I spoke to this watch expert by telephone. He agreed readily enough to make a statement emphasizing the points he had made earlier; not only did we arrange a time for the meeting, but mutually decided that my visit would become more of a family outing. A leisurely drive on a lovely May morning took me to the headquarters of the society. It was a fine old manor house in the beautiful Nottinghamshire village of Upton. After an hour's work in which the necessary statement was obtained, we were conducted on a tour of the institute. It has a unique collection of timepieces, and is surrounded by lovely gardens. We took a stroll to the village, where lunch had been arranged at the pub. As we walked through the village street the publican, complete with white apron, was standing on the doorstep waiting for us. The meal was excellent, the company extremely convivial, the weather perfect, the drive home leisurely and uneventful. The pleasantest tour of duty I spent in thirty-five years of police work.

* * *

The work of terrorists in the 1970s brought hidden danger and fear to the streets of Manchester. First there were the threats and then the violent actions of the Angry Brigade, closely followed by the return to the city of the IRA, which kept the police of Manchester at full stretch. First officers had to learn how to deal with and then combat, effectively, the many acts of terrorism which occurred. It was at the scene of a bombing in the city centre in which I was directly involved which forcibly reminded me of the thin line which separates farce and tragedy. When an act of terrorism occurs, it is the duty of the Special Branch (the anti-terrorist squad) to spearhead the investigation, availing themselves of the resources of the police service or the armed forces as they see fit. When a bomb had been exploded, it was normally the duty of members of the Finger-print Bureau and Scenes-of-Crime Department, of which I was in charge, to examine the scene to find items of forensic interest: finger-prints left by terrorists, parts of the explosive device, timing device, wrappings or other items which may be of evidential value.

One of the early and most important lessons learned in the campaign was the need to be aware of a second bomb that might be timed to kill or maim the investigating officers. To counter this, the scene was cordoned off and no forensic examination done until the area had been officially searched and pronounced clear.

By Sunday 17 December 1978, which left just six more shopping days to Christmas, the seasonal trade was in full swing. I suppose all big cities present a similar picture

In the early hours of that Sunday morning I was woken to be told that two bombs had exploded in the centre of Manchester; would I organize a team of experts to be at the scene at 7 A.M. for a briefing? I was up at 5.30

telephoning colleagues and arranging the rendezvous. At seven I met the team at Barton Square, near Deansgate, the area which had been attacked. The morning was bitterly cold. Barton Square and adjoining streets were cordoned off. From information supplied by witnesses, it was thought that the bombs had each been put into holdalls and left in two shop doorways.

Normally a winter Sunday morning is not a time to find many people in a city centre. Not only were the police, fire brigade, and press there, but so were a large number of bystanders who had gathered from goodness knows where. There was no action either to film or to report, so people contented themselves with much stamping of feet, swinging of arms and talk of brass monkeys and pawnbrokers' signs. As the morning developed I received information that the area was now considered clear and that I was to take a team in and search through the debris for any items of forensic value. With four other officers in line abreast, I slowly made my way down a passageway near the seat of one of the explosions, eyes firmly on the ground, searching.

In the first passageway we had come across several objects of interest, and still walking in line we arrived at the entrance to a second passageway which branched off the right-hand side of the first at an angle of ninety degrees. Still abreast, we turned right into the entrance, slowly moving forward and scanning the ground in front of us. I was positioned at the extreme right of the line, my shoulder brushing along the wall of the passageway.

As I moved forward I could see that a piece of hardboard, about eight feet by four feet, was leaning against the wall directly in front of me. I reached forward with my right hand and moved the hardboard sheet away from the wall so that I could search behind it. As I did so, I was horror-stricken. Behind the hardboard, hidden from view, was a window-sill and on that window-sill was a holdall. As I moved the hardboard sheet, the holdall slipped and fell at my feet with a loud plop. The line froze. Four other pairs of eyes swivelled to the holdall. Expressions were taut. As quickly and as carefully as we could, we backed away. When we cleared the cordon, I informed the senior investigating officer. He crept down the first passageway, peeped round the corner into the second passageway and then immediately contacted the Army Bomb Disposal Unit at Liverpool. An hour later a team arrived, complete with a robot, expertly controlled by a member of the team. It was directed along the two passageways to within two feet of the holdall. Several shots from a loaded gun carried by the robot were then fired into the holdall. Wearing body armour, a sapper moved forward and opened the holdall, which he brought out for our inspection.

The panic was over. Some tramp or other had put his portable wash-and-brush-up outfit in that holdall and left it there. His soap, towel, shaving equipment and hair-brush were still in fair nick, and hopefully he would not mind too much about the bullet holes in a pair of his old underpants. The laughter was a little hysterical.

Finger-prints are normally formed on the human foetus at between five and six months after conception, and the patterns formed remain constant throughout our lifespan, though of course they can be damaged in accidents and so on. As finger prints do not alter, other than in size, and as all finger-prints differ, each individual is unique. This quality is true not only of humans but also of all primates, who have palm and finger-prints, sole and toe prints.

To demonstrate this for the purposes of a police exhibition being held at the annual Manchester show, I went along to Belle Vue Zoological Gardens, to finger-print a chimpanzee and an orang-utan. When I got there, I was fortunate in finding that the zoo possessed a baby chimp who was playful and easy to finger-print. I was then taken to the orang-utan compound where I was introduced to Harold, a giant male weighing some thirty stone, who, because of his mean disposition, had become known to his keepers as Harold the Bastard. His opinion of them may have been much the same, had he been able to express it.

I quickly realized that any attempt to finger-print Harold would prove disastrous and would end up with my being awarded a police disability pension, if I were lucky enough to survive. However, plans were saved when in the next compound I was introduced to Harold's mate, Jane. Where he was massive in build, she was relatively small. Where he was bad-tempered and introvert, she had a pleasant disposition and was an extrovert who loved to be the centre of attraction. With two oranges as a reward, not only did she enjoy having her finger-prints taken, giving her whole-hearted co-operation and posing delightfully for the camera, but when the time came for us to leave the compound she actually came to the gate and waved us off. What Harold the Bastard thought about his mate's behaviour only he knew, but if his looks and glares were any indication, Jane was due to get a certain amount of earache.

It was whilst doing this job that I also saw the bears, and reminded myself that, while the primates had finger- and toe prints, the bear, not being a primate, did not. So my thoughts turned to the Yeti or Abominable Snowman, and to the expeditions which have in the past gone to the

Himalayas to try to prove his existence. People who have seen a Yeti describe him as walking erect, between eight and ten feet tall, with the body of an ape, a pointed head and the face of a human. One popular theory is that he may be the missing link in proving man's descent from the apes.

Most scientists will say there is insufficient evidence to prove that such a character exists. What is known, however, is that before he was believed to have become extinct 500,000 years ago there lived in Asia a monstrous human-like primate named *Gigantopithecus*. Some people now believe the Yeti has descended from this source. Sightings of this giant primate have been reported in the Himalayas, where it is known as the Yeti, in the mountains of Russia, where it is known as Alma, and in the mountains of North America, where it is known as Sasquatch or Bigfoot. That sightings of the descendants of *Gigantopithecus* have been reported in Asia and America may be explained by the fact that, when he was roaming the Earth, these continents were not separated by water. Sceptics will say that (depending on where the sightings have occurred) what has been seen was either a Himalayan bear, a brown bear or a grizzly bear standing on its hind legs.

In the middle of this century there were several expeditions attempting to prove the existence of the Yeti. Each was led by an eminent anthropologist. Obviously, it would be far too difficult to disprove his existence, so the prime object of each expedition has been either to capture or photograph him, but so far without success. Many items have been photographed – remains of meals, faeces, footprints, all of which have generated a good deal of discussion, but so far no Yeti, live or dead.

Standing there in Belle Vue Gardens, I was considering

whether, in fact, if I were on such a mission, I would tackle it in that manner. After all, like the murderer or the burglar, the Yeti may not wish to be captured or photographed or even seen. It is far more difficult to record the comings and goings of life in the high Himalayas than it is to set an automatic camera and photograph a day's activities in a bank foyer. If the Yeti exists, it is a scientific fact that he will leave behind traces to prove that existence. The material already photographed may or may not have been part of the habitat of the Yeti; without much more confirmation nobody can be sure.

Perhaps a better approach would be for expedition members to consult scientists at a forensic science laboratory. They have greater skill in recovering foot impressions from all kinds of surfaces, difficult, moveable, changing and so on. Of course, the foot impressions of a primate will show toe prints or sole prints; the Himalayan bear will leave pad prints, which do not contain ridge detail and will, therefore, be blank.

If it were ever possible to find a known trail along which a Yeti had passed, even months previously, Sellotape 'lifts' will quickly recover hair. Animals rub against trees, rocks and shrubs, and hairs will adhere to stone and bark. Claw marks and bite marks can yield a lot to a properly trained gatherer of evidence, and saliva can be recovered and used to give blood groupings. So a bite mark or evidence left behind by an injured foot could give blood groupings. In the last twenty years so much work has been done on animal and plant genetics, such samples could prove very exciting. For most scientists the finding of a Yeti's lair is a pipe dream, but each scientist knows that chance comes into so many of the world's discoveries and the finding of such a lair could reveal sufficient evidence to solve the riddle.

However, these are merely thoughts. I have not been able to pursue them, of course. Whilst I know of policemen who, dependent upon their prowess, have been allowed time off duty to play football, cricket, rugby, box or wrestle, go fishing, play darts, bowls and golf, I have never known a scenes-of-crime officer be allowed time off duty to seek traces of the Abominable Snowman.

8

One Thing Leads to Another

Scientists and philosophers have theories about coincidence; it is asserted that there are many more coincidences than most of us are aware of. Not everybody is tuned in to what fate brings. And it often is not until later that we realize how coincidence has come into play and altered the course of events. The stories I am going to tell are clear illustrations of what I mean.

In 1976, I was given the job of trying to restore the King's signature. In his younger days, an ex-Lord Mayor of Manchester had been commissioned in the Royal Air Force and, like thousands of other young officers, had received the official document signed by King George VI. He was proud of this commission and kept it in the office he used in his normal occupation as a builder. Sad to say, when the fire brigade was called to put out a blaze, this commission had been well doused by their hoses and the signature apparently effaced. The former Lord Mayor had asked the Greater Manchester police if perhaps somebody could try to restore this signature. I was asked to see what I could do.

The document seemed to me in need of conservation, now an established science in the field of archaeology. So, off I went to Manchester Museum, where some highly technical work was done on the commission and a reasonable result achieved. It was on this visit that I first met Asru, the Egyptian mummy.

I knew that Dr Rosalie David, a member of the Department of Egyptology there, had assembled a team of experts to conduct a full scientific examination of their entire collection of Egyptian mummies. I examined Asru carefully and saw that it was possible to obtain both toe and finger-prints from her. I told Rosalie David of my findings and was immediately invited to join the team.

The unwrapping and finger-print examination of the mummies, and in particular of Asru, was of great interest to the police team involved. There is plenty of evidence to show that for many centuries man has been interested in the configurations formed by the skin ridges on his fingers and palms, and in many societies a thumb print has been accepted in place of signature: potters in Roman times left a print on the base of their work to show it was theirs.

As you read this, you are holding the book, and your prints will be left on the cover and on the pages as you turn over. If you look at the inner surface of your hand and touch the soles of your feet, you will find that the skin of these two areas is very different from the covering on the rest of your body. It is hornier skin, a system of minute skin ridges roughly parallel with each other, changing direction here and there, while forming clearly defined patterns, particularly on the last joints of the fingers and thumbs. The ridges are called 'friction ridges'. If you look again at your own fingers, you will see that these ridges are not continuous; there are frequent interruptions in their flow which are called 'ridge characteristics'. A ridge may end suddenly in any direction, or it can fork into two diverse ridges; short independent ridges which lie between two others are a regular occurrence, and there may also be formations resembling lakes. All these are the more common type of characteristics, although there are others. All along the summits of the ridges and characteristics are microscopic pores which, with others all over the body surface, discharge sweat. When an article capable of retaining a finger mark is touched, an impression of the ridge detail and the characteristics may be left on it, in sweat. We can make this visible by the application of a suitable developer.

Our knowledge and continual research show that the friction-ridge surfaces are there from birth and persist throughout life. Although the ridges, patterns and characteristics are common to all hands, no two impressions taken from different skin ridge surfaces, whether they be from the same hand or from different hands, have the same characteristics appearing in the same order relative to each other. Because of this, identity can be established by comparing finger-prints. While the task of the finger-print officer is normally to identify the criminal, it is often necessary to finger-print dead bodies in order to establish their identity. These bodies may have been dead over a long period of time, and have frequently been recovered from water; as a result, the flesh is putrefied and fragile. Nevertheless, there remains some amount of flexibility in the fingers, and prints can be obtained by conventional methods.

In certain circumstances, where the ridge surface is visible it is possible to record the prints with the use of photography. The technique involves the use of oblique lighting. This casts shadows from the ridges into the depressions, thereby highlighting the ridges in contrast. Similar effects were obtained when photographs were taken of craters on the surface of the moon. Nobody, of course, was trying to show that Asru had been a burglar, but nevertheless all the knowledge we have outlined was brought into use when we examined the mummy. Asru was not an ordinary dead body. This meant that we had to use extreme care, because of the delicate rigidity of the flesh. The position of the hands excluded the use of photography to record the prints, as there was not enough room to position and manipulate a camera.

Up to now we have been talking mainly about finger-prints. The palms, though, can also provide information about a person's activities during life: look at the hands of a man who does manual work, feel the callouses, the thickened skin; then look at the hands of, say, a clerk. He may have a small callous where he holds his pen to write, but the rest of his hand will be relatively soft and unmarked. A man who dresses poultry may have soft but strong hands; the softness will result from the fat of the birds' insides, but the physical strength used in preparing birds for the oven ensures a firm, well-used hand. Sole prints and toe prints can show not only deformity and fungal infections but also the damage which can arise from constantly walking barefoot. In the Western world few of us walk barefoot, but in the past it was not always so.

When it came to dealing with Asru there was a great difference between taking her prints and those of a living person. In the case of the latter, one finger at a time is inked and then rolled in a special place on a pre-printed form. However, because Asru's fingers could not be moved for fear of damaging the delicate tissue, another method was needed. Fortunately, there is a special and useful compound now in use in the dental profession. It combines at once a quick-setting quality with easy flexibility. We prepared small quantities of this com-pound, which looked much like the putty used by a glazier. Then, with one officer holding Asru's delicate but rigid hand from the top, another officer carefully applied the grey compound to the surface of each finger, passing it gently upwards in the narrow space available.

It was allowed a few moments to set, and was then carefully peeled away. The eight fingers and two thumbs were all treated in this way. Afterwards, several coats of black acrylic paint were applied to each of the moulds and then peeled away. These acrylic casts were inked and printed in the manner previously described.

These prints, as you will see if you compare them with your own, are not quite perfect because small fragments of the mummified flesh are damaged. Nevertheless, their ridge characteristics are clearly defined. A comparison of these shows that no fundamental change has occurred in the ridge system over the years. If Asru had been suspected of breaking into an Egyptian grocer's shop and had left tell-tale marks, we have no doubt that we could produce suitable evidence. However, there is no such imputation against the lady's character, so we can let her rest in peace.

For the most part, finger-print work involves comparing the prints of a suspect, taken in a police station, with the marks found at the scene of a crime. Sometimes the police have only the marks left at the scene of a crime and no trace of similar marks already on record. Then it is a matter of using years of experience to form a judgement. Frequently this judgement can be surprisingly accurate; for instance, experience can provide a reliable estimate of the age of a person. Although body cells are cast from the skin all the time and are replaced at the same rate, the texture of the ridges will be affected and the degree of wear and scarring will vary significantly. These features, if interpreted correctly, may lead to an estimation of age, a guide to the nature of occupation, and to general body structure.

One recent example was that of a finger impression left behind at the scene of a murder. The opinion of the experts was that it had been made by a man aged between thirty-five and forty years, who did not do hard manual work and was fairly tall. When interviewed he turned out to be a thirty-seven-year-old hairdresser, who was five feet eleven inches tall.

So, with a view to working on these lines, we examined Asru's finger-prints and came to the conclusion that at the time of her death she was in her early forties. This estimate was later supported by evidence from other sources. It was also fairly clear that she did not do hard manual work. Her fingers had not met with the small accidents commonly encountered by a housewife looking after her home, or by a woman working in the fields. This type of work tends to crease the skin, to lessen the depth of the ridges, and to affect adversely the general condition of the skin.

With the idea of finding out whatever we could to help delineate Asru's position in the world, we examined her toes. We took her toe prints in the same way that we had taken her finger-prints. When the cast was inked we were able to examine in detail the features of the toe prints. Asru had been associated with the Temple of Karnak and she was titled 'chantress of Amun'; that is, she was concerned with the chanting or singing of accompaniments to various temple rites. Some 3,000 years ago Egyptian temple dancers performed their ritual dances barefoot, the foot being used as part of the body's expression. The sole was in constant contact with the ground and even on the smoothest of floors there would be friction and consequent wearing of the ridges on the underside of the toes and ball of the foot. Asru's feet did not show any traces of this constant contact with the floor, and the depth of the furrows and the clarity of the characteristics did not indicate that her role as chantress had also included the performance of ritual dances.

Whilst the method used to obtain the toe and finger-prints is relatively simple, much thought had to be given to the actual manipulation of the materials needed, and to this end many experiments were made on spare mummified hands kept in the store-room of the Manchester Museum's Egyptology Department.

Close examination through a powerful magnifying glass showed that on one of the spare mummified fingers the epidermis – that is, the outer skin – had separated from the dermis, the under skin, during the period of mummification. The epidermis had deteriorated to such an extent that none of the papillary ridge system – which is what you can see on your own hand – remained. In his book *Mostly Murder*, the forensic scientist Sir Sydney Smith reminds us: 'It is from the dermis – the underlying, true skin – that the various ridges, loops and whorls that form the finger-prints develop. Dermal prints remain after the epidermis has been destroyed by putrefaction or other cause, and they are an equally certain form of identification.' He wrote this in 1959, basing part of his experience on a case in 1953, when Dectective Inspector Hammond of Glasgow City Police obtained a dermal print from the body of Mary Rogerson in the famous Buck Ruxton case, still vivid in popular memory. Sir Sydney said the Inspector had worked with great skill, providing identification of Mary, a servant in the home of the Parsee doctor Buck Ruxton in Lancaster, who had murdered both her and his common law wife, Isabella. The evidence was for some reason not given at the trial, thus denying the Inspector the credit he had earned.

On the spare finger we were examining, the ridge detail exposed on removal of the epidermis was extremely fine and somewhat damaged, but the use of the moulding and casting technique we were developing meant we could obtain a good dermal print, which we could readily have identified, if asked. Whilst we were engrossed in these experiments little did we expect that our work would be vital in the police investigation of the exceedingly bizarre case of the Rochdale Mummy.

On 15 March 1977 a man's partially decomposed body was found in the refuse area of a block of corporation dwellings in Ashfield Valley, Rochdale.

The room was dark, gloomy and badly lit. There had been no electric light since a fire in one of the five-foot-high bins (used to catch refuse coming down the chutes) had been put out by the fire brigade on 1 March. Because of the smoke, the firemen could not say whether the body had been there at the time.

On 8 March a lady and her two daughters had seen a wire shopping trolley in the refuse area and on it was a large bundle, which they did not examine. The smell was very bad. On 10 March a man saw the trolley in the room. On it was what he assumed was rubbish covered by a dirty sheet, and it smelt vile.

The caretaker was in the refuse room on 11 March, but did not notice anything unusual. On the 13th, his next visit, he saw the shopping trolley and what seemed to be a large old sack, which he touched. He thought it was a mixture of sand and cement.

On the 14th he asked the Cleansing Department to send a collection vehicle so that the rubbish could be moved. The two men who came gave the trolley a push. It struck a piece of wood and then tipped over. You can imagine how these men felt when they saw that the package was a partially mummified body, the hands and feet being bound and the head covered with a plastic shopping bag.

The forensic scientists had plenty of material to go on: the body's skin was dried and mummified, and examination of the liver showed that death was due to barbiturate poisoning. The plastic bag over the head had rendered facial identification impossible. Incidentally, the 'sand and cement' was not that at all, but millions upon millions of mites – not a comfortable thought for anybody. There were also thousands of maggots.

Using the technique developed from the work done at the museum, we examined the hands, which had been taken to the Finger-print Bureau after they had been removed from the body by Dr Garratt, a Home Office pathologist. On all fingers except one, the skin had deteriorated to such an extent that it was useless; the exception was the right middle finger.

On this, we could see that the epidermis had lifted, as in the case of the Egyptian mummified finger. With the greatest care we slowly removed it and found that the dermis was quite good enough for the application of the new technique. The illustrations, side by side in the illustration section, show how, following the rule that there should be not fewer than sixteen corresponding points of identification, we proved to the coroner that the body was that of James Edward Finlay, whose finger-prints were on file.

Cases of mummified bodies found in suspicious circumstances are fortunately fairly uncommon and the police were mindful of a much-publicized affair seventeen years earlier, when a similar body was found in a small terraced house in Rhyl, a popular holiday resort on the coast of

North Wales. For many years a Mrs Harvey had lived there, a widow in her sixties.

On 5 May 1960 the body of an elderly lady was discovered in a staircase landing cupboard by Mrs Harvey's son-in-law, who was decorating the house whilst she was in hospital. Shortly after the discovery, the Welsh police interviewed Mrs Harvey. She told them that the body her son-in-law had found was that of a Mrs Knight, a semi-invalid who had come to lodge with her twenty years previously, in the spring of 1940. Shortly after Mrs Knight had moved into Mrs Harvey's house, she had been taken ill and died, of natural causes, so Mrs Harvey said. She had panicked and concealed Mrs Knight's body in the landing cupboard; and, what is more, she had papered over the cupboard door so as to be able to keep her secret. I dare say there are already obvious questions in your mind. The body had lain there for twenty years – and during those twenty years Mrs Harvey had enterprisingly continued to draw monies due to the deceased as the result of a court order.

Mrs Harvey was adamant that her lodger had died of natural causes. Having regard to the evidence available to them, however, the police thought otherwise and she was charged with murder, the allegation being that she had strangled Mrs Knight with a silk stocking.

In the event, the evidence presented in court to prove that Mrs Knight's death had occurred as the result of violence fell far short of the required standard. On the fifth day of this sensational trial at Ruthin Assize Court the Solicitor General, with the consent of the Judge, withdrew the prosecution case and Mrs Harvey was formally acquitted. She was, however, convicted and sentenced to fifteen months' imprisonment for the offence of false pretences in respect of the weekly sum of money due to Mrs Knight.

With the identification of the Rochdale Mummy as James Edward Finlay enquiries could begin to ascertain the sequence of events which led to his death by barbiturate poisoning; and why his body should have been discovered in a supermarket shopping trolley left in the refuse area in the basement of a block of council flats.

It was soon established that Finlay had been born in Southport in 1943 and was a builder's labourer who had been known to enjoy reasonably good health. When he was twenty, he had married for the first time, but it ended in divorce six years later.

Eileen Willan was born in Dukinfield, Cheshire, in 1949 and at the age of eight years emigrated with the rest of her family to Australia. In 1968 she returned to England with her parents and they settled down to live in Southport. It was there that Eileen met James Finlay, who by this time was separated from his wife. After James's divorce was made absolute, Eileen went to live with him at his home. In 1971 she gave birth to a daughter and later in the year they moved to Rochdale, where James found work. In September 1974 they married at the registry office in Rochdale and shortly afterwards Eileen gave birth to a son.

After living at several addresses in the Rochdale area, they were granted the tenancy of a corporation flat at 28 Buttermere, which is in the Ashfield Valley area of Rochdale, in February 1975. Shortly after this move, Finlay became a 'regular' at his local pub, The Citizen, where he was known as an extremely good darts player and a member of the pub's darts team.

The previous year, in April, he had taken up employment as a labourer with R. & T. Howarth, a local firm of builders and civil engineers; he stayed with them up to 29 August 1975, and his wages had been paid up to that date. Eileen Finlay had taken possession of the council flat on 19 February 1975, but two years later, because she was so badly in arrears with the rent, an order was issued by Rochdale magistrates that she should be evicted from the home. Her last date of tenancy was to be 5 March 1977, but on 1 March she went to Rochdale housing office and handed in the house keys.

Eileen Finlay was interviewed. She was well aware that a man's body had been discovered in the refuse area of the flats adjacent to Buttermere. She said it was not her husband, because he had left her nearly two years previously. However, when she was told that the body had been positively identified as that of her husband, she admitted she had put the body in the refuse area after having it hidden in the airing cupboard of their home since the end of August 1975.

Naturally, she was questioned about the circumstances surrounding his death. She said he had committed suicide and she was much too frightened to report the matter to the police because they might have held her responsible. It had already been established that Finlay had died as the result of barbiturate poisoning, a quantity of Amilobarbitone having been found in his liver. This drug is commonly known as Amytal and their respective medical practitioners said that neither Mr nor Mrs Finlay had been prescribed that particular drug. Further enquiries, however, uncovered the fact that near to the time when James Finlay had last been seen alive a bottle containing some forty sodium amytal tablets had disappeared from the home of a female friend of Eileen Finlay.

Mrs Finlay at first denied all knowledge of the matter, but eventually admitted that she had taken them.

Her account of her husband's death and the events leading to the disposal of his body was as bizarre as the finding of the body itself. On the day her husband had died, which was, to the best of her recollection, towards the end of August 1975, they had been arguing. During the altercation he had assaulted her. In the final stages of the quarrel James had threatened to take his own life, at which point she had thrown at him the bottle containing the sodium amytal tablets, shouting, 'Bloody well get on with it, then.' After which, she stormed out of the flat and went to the pub for a drink, returning some three hours later, to find her husband dead.

There was, of course, the small matter of the corpse having been found bound hand and foot; it was pointed out to her that whilst he could perhaps have tied his own feet, to have tied his own hands in that particular fashion was just not possible. Her explanation was that, when she entered the flat, her husband was lying on the settee. He was quite dead and she then noticed that there were strips of cloth around both his hands and his legs. She had tightened the knots on these strips of cloth to enable her to drag the body and put it into the airing cupboard. She put the plastic shopping bag over his head so that she could not see his face. This is a not uncommon response in such a situation; it seems as if the dead visage still has the power to accuse or to cause alarm. Covered with old clothes, the body had stayed undisturbed in the airing cupboard until the eviction order arrived.

Arranging to vacate the flat, she removed her furniture on 23 February 1977, but kept the keys. On the evening of the 28th Eileen Finlay went back to the flat, took James out of the airing cupboard and put him into a wire shopping trolley which had been kept in the kitchen. Taking care not to be seen by anybody who might ask questions, she wheeled the trolley down to the refuse area of the adjacent block of flats. She had in mind that she would put the body in one of the waste disposal bins. These are five feet high, so it was not surprising that she found she did not have the physical strength to do this. So, faced with a dilemma, she left the body in the shopping trolley next to the waste disposal bins, hoping that it would be taken away.

The circumstances of the death and the attempt to dispose of the body did, of course, give rise to grave suspicion. Mrs Finlay was questioned carefully, because suspicion is not enough on which to base a firm charge, whatever the offence.

Eventually she was committed for trial on two seldom-used charges: the first was that she had intended to prevent the coroner of Rochdale from holding an inquest on the dead body of James Edward Finlay, who died an unnatural death or a sudden death of which the cause was unknown; or, intending to obstruct the coroner in the holding of such inquest, did conceal the said body. The second was that she had left unburied the dead body of James Edward Finlay, her husband, for whom she was bound to provide a Christian burial and had the means of so doing. Both these are offences against common law.

Without that vital dermal finger-print it would have been infinitely harder, perhaps impossible, to identify the body and discover the circumstances.

The woman was sentenced to two years' imprisonment on each charge, the terms to run concurrently. The sentence was later reduced to one of twelve months' imprisonment.

9

Name Unknown

The examination and finger-printing of the Egyptian mummy in Manchester Museum received world-wide publicity. There were articles and photographs in newspapers as far apart as America, Turkey and Japan. The success of the venture, followed by the identification of the Rochdale mummy and its ensuing publicity, meant that we in the Finger-print Bureau came to be regarded by other members of the Greater Manchester Police as a special authority on mummified remains. It therefore came as no great surprise when on a December morning in 1982 I received a telephone call from Detective Superintendent Barstow, head of the CID at Bolton, who had a most unusual tale to tell.

Bolton is yet another of the towns to the North-West of Manchester which employed vast numbers of people in the cotton industry until about thirty years ago, but which now has had to diversify in order to prosper. It is only some ten miles from the centre of Manchester by motorway, and although much of the town centre has changed, the splendid indoor market continues to be a vibrant source of trade, extended by the outdoor market on certain days of the week. Bolton is an adaptable place and its people are more unified than those of many towns of similar size. In the town itself stands a most interesting industrial museum which still houses the original spinning mule invented by one of Bolton's most famous sons, Samuel Crompton.

In the telephone conversation Mr Barstow said that a

Mr Baxendale, a native of Bolton, had recently bought a large Victorian house, 27 Bromwich Street, in the town. It needed some renovation and, with a view to this, he inspected one of the cellars, intending to build a kennel there for his Alsatian. As he looked at the site for the kennel he noticed that his dog had wandered into the next cellar, which had an exceedingly low ceiling. The dog was sniffing and acting in a most excited way in a rather dark corner. As the height of this cellar from floor to ceiling was rather less than four feet, it had never been used as a workplace and over the years a large amount of rubbish had been dumped there by previous occupants.

The actions of his dog caused Mr Baxendale to investigate further. There, in the gloomy corner of the cellar, he saw what he presumed to be an old tailor's dummy. As his eyes grew accustomed to the darkness, he could see that this 'dummy' was equipped with a full set of false teeth.

He touched the teeth, whereupon they fell into the back of a skull. No tailor's dummy, this; he had found human remains. Unfortunately, but perhaps understandably, he scooped up the head, put it into a carrier bag and set off for Castle Street police station, where he presented the head to a somewhat surprised duty officer.

Superintendent Barstow quickly assumed charge of the investigation; the removal of the head and disturbance of the remains constituted a problem for him right at the start. He was unable to establish whether the body had been in a sleeping position at the time of death or whether it had been placed in the cellar after death had taken place.

Access to the cellar was by a set of stone steps which led from the outside of the house. Was the body that of a vagrant who had used the cellar to sleep in, or was it the body of a murder victim dumped there by the killer? A full forensic examination was conducted and every scrap of evidence collected; it was not easy working in close and cramped conditions. For two days a team of detectives painstakingly searched the cellar. It was tedious and tiring, but they succeeded in collecting every bone bar one from the skeleton. A small neck bone was missing and was never recovered.

Of particular interest to me, and the cause of Mr Barstow's telephone call, was the fact that the searchers had recovered a mummified right hand and the remains of a mummified left hand which included the thumb and forefinger.

The skeletal remains were taken to the mortuary, where they were examined by a Home Office pathologist, who reported the body to be that of an unusually small woman between four feet eight inches and four feet ten inches. She had apparently been in reasonably good health at the time of her death and there was no sign of disease, deformity or injury. She was Caucasian and it was established that at the time of her death she had been approximately forty years old. A tuft of hair found near the body indicated that she had been a brunette and her hair was fairly short, curly or wavy.

Near the mummified hand, the one which included the left thumb and forefinger, were the bones from the remaining three fingers and on one of them was found a gold eternity ring, inset with small diamonds. When enquiries were made at the shops of local jewellers, it was found to be one of many thousands of such rings made in Birmingham and offered for sale in most towns in the north-west of England.

The body had been dressed in a turquoise roll-neck sweater, a mustard-coloured cardigan and brown 'trews'.

Her undergarments were pink. It was disturbing that no shoes were found. Recovered from the scene was evidence indicating the woman had been a Roman Catholic. Scattered around the body were several rosary beads and attached to part of the rosary was a small medallion showing the Madonna and Child. Near the shoulders was found a small copper crucifix.

The body was lying on top of a layer of cardboard, there were newspapers under the body and partly covering it. One of these was the *News of the World* dated 13 March 1966. From this evidence, and from the style of the clothing, particularly the trousers, it was concluded that the woman had died about that date.

Because so little of the body remained, apart from the bone structure, the pathologist could not establish the cause of death. Mr Barstow was now faced with a dilemma. Had she been one of those people who regularly sleep out? If so, where were her shoes? Had she been a murder victim? If so, where was the medical evidence? A vital clue appeared to be that the top set of her dentures was broken. Had she received a violent blow to cause the breakage?

The forensic science laboratory came up with the answer. Along the broken edge of the denture were traces of glue. She had tried to repair the dentures herself. It could not have worked well because adhesives were not as sophisticated as they are now. Enquiries were made to trace the maker of the dentures and the woman's dentist, but met with no success.

Enquiries were also made at Roman Catholic churches in the area. It was confidently expected that a priest or member of his congregation would be able to throw some light on the mystery, but the detectives could only report complete failure.

In the 1960s Bromwich Street, Bolton, was in the centre of the town's bed-sit land, heavily populated by Irish people and students. Was she Irish, with no relatives in this country? If so, would it be possible to trace her amongst such a migrant population some sixteen years after her death? Number 27 Bromwich Street had been a lodging house with many occupants. The landlord of the house for the period in queston had died and with him all hopes of tracing his tenants through records he may have kept.

If the enquiry was to make any progress, it was crucial to identify the body of this tiny woman. Mr Barstow asked if it would be possible, through examination of the human remains and the mummified fingers, to establish whether she had had a criminal record.

The system of printing mummified hands, developed during the examination of the Egyptian mummies, had now become standard procedure in the Manchester Finger-print Bureau; and a number of experts were both willing and eager to assist when, a few hours later, a detective arrived carrying a cardboard box in which we saw a mummified right hand and the mummified remains of the left hand.

An examination revealed that the epidermis was in a reasonably good condition. The fingers were quickly cleaned, and using the moulding and casting method previously described prints were obtained from the right thumb, forefinger, middle finger, and left thumb and forefinger. It was a neat bit of work which gave quiet satisfaction.

The finger-prints were then compared with those kept in the main collection at Manchester. Checks were made at the National Finger-print Bureau at New Scotland Yard and at other bureaux all over the country. These checks, coupled with those made in Belfast and Dublin, proved fruitless. Her finger-prints were not on record anywhere, forcing us to the conclusion that she had never been convicted of a criminal offence.

This impasse caused me to explore the possibilities of having the skeleton's face reconstructed. Six years earlier, as a member of the Manchester mummy investigation team, I had first come into contact with the process of facial reconstruction. The team had consisted of fourteen people, each of whom was eminent in a particular field. Collectively they were engaged in a wide range of scientific research, most members being attached either to the university or to one of Manchester's teaching hospitals. At the centre of the investigation lay the unwrapping and scientific examination of an Egyptian mummy, name unknown, but who at the Manchester Museum had been awarded the number 1770. The unwrapping of 1770 and the range of scientific techniques used in the examination became the focus of world-wide attention and provided a most interesting chapter in my life. It was perhaps a disappointment to most of the people concerned when, after the unwrapping was completed, it was found that the mummified body was in a poor state of preservation.

Apart from the hands, the item of particular interest to me was the skull, which had been broken into thirty pieces. It had been decided that the different pieces would be reassembled and the face of 1770 would be reconstructed. The team member elected to perform this task was Richard Neave, Assistant Director of the Manchester University Department of Medical Illustration at the Manchester Royal Infirmary.

The shape of a face is dictated by the shape of the skull, the face merely being a thin mask of flesh drawn over the skull. So, when the pieces of broken skull had been cast in plastic, an exact replica was modelled, and upon that replica Richard Neave reconstructed the face of 1770. When completed, it was the face of a teenage Egyptian girl. The work received national acclaim. It was a work of art based on scientific research.

As a member of the team I was delighted with the result Richard Neave had achieved, but as a detective I was far more interested in how this process could be used for the purpose of criminal investigation. By this time I had been a policeman for nearly thirty years, was head of the largest provincial finger-print bureau in the country, and for more than twenty years had been dealing with the identification of individuals. Yet I was very disappointed at how little I knew about a subject which could provide a useful contribution to the identification of certain murder victims.

I had no recollection of facial reconstruction having been used in this country for the purposes of criminal investigation. With this facility available at Manchester Medical School, virtually on my doorstep, the need to know more became pressing. Further, I realized it could be the basis of an interesting lecture to the CID.

All this prompted me to delve into the background of facial reconstruction and its previous history involving criminal cases. I was amazed how difficult it was to obtain information on this scientific discipline. Richard Neave was the obvious starting point. His assistance and advice proved invaluable. Not only did he point me in the right direction but also expressed a willingness to assist Greater Manchester Police in matters of facial reconstruction, should the occasion arise.

He informed me that a great deal of work had been done in Switzerland before the turn of the century, notably by the medico-legal expert Kollman and a sculptor named Buchly, which resulted in their publishing a paper in which they included a series of tables listing the thickness of soft tissue at twenty-six points in the human face. These measurements included the maximum and mimimum thicknesses in men and women of various ages.

This paper was published in 1898, and whilst Richard Neave used the tables supplied by Kollman and Buchly as the basis for his reconstruction work, he emphasized that little research had been done in the Western world on this particular topic, and that a great deal more, using modern technology not available to the two Swiss in 1898, needed to be done before the accuracy of their tables could be universally accepted.

As far as criminal matters were concerned some work had been done in Germany and America, but with little success, one notable exception being in New York where, as the result of the finding of skeletal remains, the head was reconstructed and identified as a person of Italian extraction who had been reported missing some months previously. However, it has long been believed that in this particular case the success came more by good luck than by good management.

Continued success is reported only from Russia, which has its own laboratory for plastic reconstruction, the Ethnographical Institute of the USSR Academy of Sciences. Here a great amount of work is done in the reconstruction of faces for use in the investigation of criminal cases and anthropological research. That Russia leads the world in this particular field can be attributed to the work of one man, Professor Mikhail Gerasimov, anthropologist, archaeologist and eminent forensic scientist. In the years between the two world wars this brilliant man devoted his time and energy to facial reconstruction, turning it into something approaching an exact science. Gerasimov was born in St Petersburg (now Leningrad) in 1907, less than a decade after Kollman and Buchly had published their famous paper. Later, as a university student, he became deeply interested in the morphology of the human skull.

Having moved at an early age from St Petersburg to Irkutsk in Siberia, he began his archaeological career with the discovery, at the age of twenty, of a most important Stone Age site in the neighbourhood village of Mal'Ta. As an anthropologist, much of his early life was involved with the reconstruction of the faces of prehistoric men. In his book, *The Face Finder*, Gerasimov recalls that the sensational results of three years' research at the palaeolithic man's hunting settlement at Mal'Ta led to his return to Leningrad, where he was offered a position in the Anthropological Department of the Academy of Material Culture. It was here that his work on the problem of facial reconstruction received a new impetus.

After being involved in this type of work for more than twenty years, turning it into a science, and satisfying many if not all of his critics, his skill was soon put to the supreme test. It began with the discovery in a cave in the Crimea of a double grave dating from the Late Upper Palaeolithic period in which the remains of an elderly man and a young woman were found. From the female skull Gerasimov reconstructed the face of an attractive young woman of classical Cro-Magnon type. This portrait received much publicity and resulted in the Head of Forensic Medicine at Moscow contacting Gerasimov and suggesting that if a large-scale experiment was successfully carried out then his method would be considered for use in criminological work.

With his reputation at stake, but with much to be

gained, Gerasimov agreed to the tests. From mortuaries in Moscow twelve heads were chosen. Each head was awarded a number, photographed in full face and profile, and after all of the flesh had been removed, the skulls, each bearing its number, were forwarded to Gerasimov at his laboratory in Leningrad. Apart from the number allocated to each skull, he was not allowed any further information as to the person's sex or nationality. After the reconstructions had been completed, he took the heads to Moscow, where he presented them to a panel of judges consisting of anthropologists, criminologists, and examining magistrates. The heads he had so carefully reconstructed were those of four Russian men, one Russian woman, three Ukrainian men, a Polish man, a Chinese man, a man of Baltic origin and a Caucasian man.

In his book Gerasimov states that the results exceeded even his own expectations, with all of the twelve heads so true to life that their identity could not be doubted. Through this success he became involved in the investigation of many criminal cases and later became the first director of the Laboratory for Plastic Reconstruction and was awarded the degree of Doctor of Facial Science.

Gerasimov was to reconstruct more than 140 heads for the purposes of criminal investigation; more than 200 faces of prehistoric man and many faces of historical figures, including Rudagi, the ninth-century Tadjik poet, Tamerlane, the fourteenth-century conqueror of Central Asia, Ivan the Terrible and the German poet Schiller.

As so little is known in this country of facial reconstruction for criminological purposes it is well worth mentioning three of the professor's many successes. His first involvement in a criminal case occurred in 1939, when a human skeleton was found in a wood on the outskirts of

Leningrad. As some of the bones showed traces of teeth marks, it was assumed by the police officers investigating the case that the remains were those of a person who had been attacked and killed by a pack of wolves. Upon examining the skull, the professor saw that it belonged to a boy about thirteen years old and immediately discounted the theory that he had been killed by wolves. He found that the skull had been fractured by a blow from a blunt instrument. Attached to the skull was part of the scalp, which showed that the young lad had short, reddish-blond hair. Gerasimov carefully reconstructed the boy's face on to the skull and, when finished, presented it to the investigators. Amongst the police files was the description of a boy reported missing from his home in Leningrad some months previously. When shown the model, the father of the missing boy recognized the face as that of his son.

Once identified, a murder investigation was begun. The boy's movements, and his associates, were traced and enquiries led to the arrest of the killer, who confessed to the crime.

In the spring of 1948 a thirty-two-year-old woman was reported missing from her home in the southern Ukraine, with no apparent reason for her disappearance. Eight months after this, the remains of an unknown woman were found in an old wartime trench a few miles away from the missing woman's home. There was a strong suspicion that the skeleton was hers. In 1950, in an attempt to verify these suspicions, the skull was sent to Gerasimov so that he could reconstruct the face. The skull had been so severely damaged that the professor diagnosed that the injuries must have been caused by a shell splinter and that the woman must have been a casualty in the Second World War. When informed of this fact, the examining magistrate concerned disagreed with the diagnoses and insisted that the skull must belong to the missing woman. Gerasimov, therefore, reconstructed the face on the skull and found that it apparently belonged to a young woman of about twenty-six. It was seen at once that the reconstruction and the photograph of the missing woman did not agree either in general appearance or in detail, and the professor was emphatic that such a divergence between the photograph and the reconstruction could not be the result of a mistake on his part, as the skull's shape would not permit of any variation.

As the skull and the face did not correspond, it was decided that the remains found in the trench did not belong to the missing woman and a two-pronged enquiry was begun: to find the missing woman and to establish the identity of the wartime remains. Photographs of the reconstructed head were published and a short time later the woman was identified by her relatives. She had been missing since the early years of the war and her relatives also identified a gold watch and an emerald earring found near the body. The missing woman was never found.

The third case involved the discovery of an unidentified and naked body in a haystack; the victim had apparently collapsed through exhaustion and then frozen to death. There were no marks of violence. The reconstruction revealed the head of a young man. Photographs were taken and then published with a view to identifying him. Three months later a woman identified the face as that of her son, who had been born twenty-five years earlier. Enquiries revealed that he had left his place of employment after suffering a mental breakdown and had stated his intention of travelling to a village near to where his body was eventually found. So this previously unknown man was identified.

Professor Gerasimov had many other successes and at the time of his death was regarded as the world's leading authority on this form of identification.

It soon became known in police circles that I had not only developed an interest in this particular subject but also had close contact with Manchester University and the Medical School. North Yorkshire Police were conducting a criminal investigation into the death of a young woman whose body – or, at least, her skeleton – had been found in suspicious circumstances beneath a hedgerow at the side of a lonely country road. The officers conducting the case had decided it would assist considerably if her face could be reconstructed in an effort to establish her identity and I agreed to act as liaison officer between North Yorkshire Police and the Manchester University Department of Medical Illustration.

The experience gained was to stand me in good stead when I had to perform the same function on behalf of my own force in the case of the small, mysterious lady from Bolton.

Having exhausted all the normal channels of enquiry, I realized that it was now going to be extremely difficult to identify a person who had been dead for sixteen years, had not been reported missing and apparently had no relatives living in the area. As the liaison officer, I made an assessment of the situation and decided that what was required was a good facial reconstruction, good realistic make-up to suit the type of individual we believed her to have been, and as much coverage from the television and press as we could possibly obtain.

Richard Neave agreed to do the reconstruction, and Ruth Quinn, deputy head of the make-up department at

Granada Television studios, agreed to put the finishing touches to the reconstruction. I was fortunate enough to be present when both these talented people did much of their work and I was constantly intrigued by the processes involved, curious to know how the finished result would appear and then was delighted as it neared completion.

When the head was taken to the Department of Medical Illustration, the first task was to remove all the flesh still adhering to the skull bones. The flesh was removed by human agency and not, as popular myth would have it, by introducing maggots to feed on whatever remained. The original skull was not used in the reconstruction, so, before any work could begin, a plaster cast had to be made.

The prepared skull and jaw were carefully wired together in their correct positions and the false teeth fitted into place. By using angles determined by the eye-sockets and the nasal apertures, the base for the nose was modelled in clay and fixed to the skull. Using plasticine, the blank eyes were fixed into a normal position, neither protruding nor sunken. Everything was now ready for a plaster cast to be made of the skull.

Using a technique developed at the Medical School, the assembled skull was carefully placed on its side in a plastic container into which a solution of algenate was gently poured until the skull was half covered. When the algenate had set, a further solution of algenate was poured into the plastic container until the skull was completely covered. When set, the algenate mould complete with embedded skull was removed from the container, the two halves of the mould split apart and the skull removed. The two halves of the mould were then carefully joined and secured in position.

Using a narrow tube pushed through the outer casing

of the algenate, a solution of plaster of Paris was introduced into the mould and allowed to set. When the mould was removed, the result was a perfectly cast plaster skull complete with jaw, teeth, eyes and the foundation of the nose. In the next important stages it was vital that Richard Neave should work to the table of measurements supplied by Kollman. To enable him to do this he had prepared a number of small wooden pegs which, when cut to precise length, he inserted into the plaster skull at specific points. Using a pair of callipers he measured each peg to see that it protruded from the skull at its required distance, according to the chart of measurements. All was now ready for the modelling work.

Richard started building up, in modelling clay, the soft structures of the face, starting with the most important masticatory muscles. These determine its shape. In a remarkably short time the muscles of the jaw had been finished and he was working on the buccinator muscles which fanned out across the cheekbones. When the muscles had been modelled into position, the shape of the head and face was built up to the level of the pegs. The lips and nose were modelled and the head and face smoothed off. The ears were the last feature to be added. This is where a little artistic licence is actually necessary. When they had been modelled and fitted into position, the clay head was complete and ready to be cast in plaster of Paris to allow make-up to be applied.

Using the technique previously described, the completed clay head was immersed in a solution of algenate, a mould was produced and from that mould a plaster cast obtained, on which Richard Neave painted the eyes.

I took the cast of the head to Granada Television studios in Manchester, where I handed it to Ruth Quinn, whose services were to prove invaluable. As a make-up artist, Ruth Quinn has duties other than making television personalities look young and beautiful, though doubtless she does improve faces from time to time. She has to prepare character actors and actresses for the varied parts they are required to play. She has learned what a person's actual nature can do to his or her face. Given two people very much alike, perhaps father and son, the pessimist has a set of lines very different from the thorough-going optimist.

Ruth was given a physical description of the body which had been found, the woman's estimated age at the time of her death and all the known circumstances of the case. She was shown the clothing from the body and told that it was felt the woman had been a vagrant and murder victim who had died in the middle part of 1966. What was positively known was that the lady had been a brunette with short, wavy hair. Through her training and experience Ruth knew the type of clothing and jewellery worn by most classes of women in the 1960s, together with the type of make-up used and the manner in which it was applied. Hair styles vary from year to year, and she knew what had been fashionable at any one time. However, it was likely that if the victim did have a wandering life-style she would not have been to the hairdresser very often, but would have adopted a shape which was simple and therefore one she could manage herself.

Having gathered all the information she could, Ruth began work. First she applied a heavy base foundation of a shade to suit the known details of the woman's colouring, eyes, hair, age, etc. This foundation was to give the cast life-like flesh tones and it really did have a natural appearance and texture. She then put some character into the face, the feeling that it had an expression. She

achieved this by shading in hollow areas – the jawline
and temples – and she followed this with the use of a
lighter foundation to highlight other areas – the cheekbones, chin, the brow and upper lip.

It is the eyes which impart to the face its immediacy and
expressiveness. Ruth delicately applied false eyebrows,
eyelashes and other eye make-up on top of the base,
having first rimmed the eyes with a thin brown eyeliner;
she also applied a pale fleshy pink cream to highlight the
fleshy part immediately underneath the brow. She had
chosen the colour of the eyebrows and eyelashes wisely.
The eyebrows, not too thick, appeared absolutely natural.
The artist reminded me that an important element to
bear in mind is that, while the woman is not intended to
have the appearance of wearing much, if any, cosmetics,
make-up has provided the only means of giving her a
natural appearance. Consequently the blusher she used
was an unobtrusive one, which she carefully blended into
the foundation on the cheeks, chin and tip of the nose.
Equally, the lipstick she used on the mouth was there
only to give the impression that this was warm flesh
rather than to convey the idea that this was a woman who
would have applied make-up to her own face. Great care
was taken with the selection of wigs from Granada's vast
wardrobe, and three different wigs were used to create
six different hair styles. At the completion of make-up,
six sets of photographs were produced, each showing the
modelled head with slightly different make-up and hair.

On the day following completion, a press conference
was called. As expected, it was well attended with representatives from the BBC and commercial television,
reporters and photographers from every national daily
newspaper and with good representation from the local
press. Within the next twenty-four hours millions of

people saw the reconstructed face staring at them from their television screens and daily papers.

I was hoping that an identification would be made, in view of the massive amount of publicity and the public interest aroused. You will understand, however, that even if such a suggested identification had been made Her Majesty's coroner would have wanted a great deal more to satisfy him with respect to the identity of the deceased than the opinion of somebody who may have formed a friendship some seventeen years earlier, especially when that recollection is based not upon the actual face of the dead person but upon an artistic reproduction of what that face may have looked like.

What the investigating officers were hoping for was that members of the public, upon seeing the facial reconstruction, would be able to suggest clues to her identity based on other known facts: that she was extremely small in stature, that she was about forty years old when she died, that she had short, dark, wavy hair, was probably a practising Roman Catholic, and that she had worn a particular type of clothing and jewellery. If a likely candidate had been produced, the services of the Fingerprint Bureau could have proven invaluable to the investigation. We had obtained good finger- and thumb prints from the body. There could still be in existence books which had either belonged to her or been used by her. In her parents' home there might be a personal diary, a prayer book, a Bible, a well-thumbed cookery book or a treasured school prize from childhood days. It is possible for finger-prints to lie on the pages of a book for many years and equally possible for an expert to develop such prints thirty years later. We had obtained both the woman's thumb prints, and thumb prints are those most commonly found on the pages of a book. Watch your own hands as you read a bound volume.

When photographs of the head reconstruction were shown to members of the public it was stressed that certain features were unknown. For instance, whether the eyes protruded or were deeply set; whether the hairline was well defined or not; the shape of the ears, large or small; whether the woman had a happy, miserable or tense expression on her face. All these are important facets of appearance. By careful arrangement of the wig it was possible to hide the ears and somewhat disguise the hairline, but with the eyes and the expression it was decided to adopt a middle line.

It must now be recorded that despite widespread publicity coupled with intensive enquiries by a team of dedicated detectives no identification was made.

Within twenty-four hours of the publicity given to the case seven couples came forward. They had lived in the house where the body was found at about the time death was believed to have occurred, that is during the mid-1960s.

The seven couples were all interviewed and eliminated from the enquiry. Most unusually, an old lady who was virtually blind recalled that in the mid-1960s she had befriended a vagrant named Martha and had given her some clothing identical with that found on the body – that is, a turquoise roll-neck sweater, a mustard-colour cardigan and brown trousers. Due to her near-blindness, the old lady was not able to examine the series of photographs carried by the interviewing detective, but it appeared to be a most interesting and useful lead.

Priority was given to finding Martha, who, in 1966, had been a vagrant wandering the streets of Bolton. Disappointment came when Martha was traced – to her burial place in the local cemetery. Had Martha given the clothing to another vagrant? Had she sold it to a second-hand clothes dealer? Or was it just another one of those coincidences which occur from time to time?

Many calls came from people who had seen the facial reconstruction and believed that they could identify her. Each person was visited by a member of the investigating team. One such call, which seemed later to be consistent with this bizarre and frustrating case, came from an elderly lady who had seen the news item on television and rang the police to say that she could positively identify the woman whose face had been shown. Arrangements were made for her to be visited by a detective the following morning. When the officer called at her home, he got no response to repeated knocking at the door. After further efforts to contact the old lady had failed and after neighbours had been interviewed, he decided to force his way into the house and check whether the old lady needed help. When he did get into the house, he found she had died before she had had a chance to pass on the information. Whether she did indeed hold the key to the mystery we shall never know.

If there is a lesson to be learned from the attempts to identify the mystery lady from Bolton then it is a simple one. If in future it is considered that facial reconstruction could be continuously and successfully used as a means of identification in criminal matters in this country, forensic scientists and police officers alike must learn to walk before they run. In the Bolton investigation we were trying to establish the identity of a person whose relatives probably did not live in this country, and who furthermore had not been reported missing from her home. She was possibly a spinster with no immediate family of her own, and a vagrant with no close friends and no settled address

– a person whose disappearance and death under suspicious circumstances some sixteen years previously had failed to rouse anybody sufficiently to comment on it.

When looking into a crime or suspicious circumstances, the investigating officers have to play the hand which they are dealt. In this particular instance the facts and circumstances available meant that the detectives could hardly have chosen a more difficult case in which to tread new ground. I believe that if facial reconstruction is to be considered a viable aid to crime detection here, then progress needs to be gradual and well researched, as in Russia. We must first start not with attempting to establish identification, but with confirming identification.

With no expensive equipment to purchase and no costly research to be done, facial reconstruction is quite inexpensive. If one is to do the type of work mentioned, it would provide a very useful service, would be a reassurance to both relatives and the coroner, would cost little and yet would provide the necessary foundation upon which to establish a new aid to criminal investigation.

The expertise developed would probably prove invaluable to future police officers when confronted with a similar set of circumstances and would reduce the number of people who, like the small lady from Bolton, are laid to rest in unmarked graves.

10

Kidnapped

To use the word 'kid' to refer to a child is common enough. Yet we use the word 'kidnapping' to describe the unlawful taking of any person, no matter how old. Curiosity led me to the Oxford English Dictionary. It seems the word originated amongst the class which followed the practice of kidnapping, the taking of children – or others – in order to provide servants or labourers for the American plantations. The first written reference to a kidnapper was in 1678, and in 1684 John Bunyan used the word in *The Pilgrim's Progress*. The word is now in universal use and refers to the illegal taking of any person. As a political crime it is, one might say, having a wave of popularity, however undesirable that might be, and getting full publicity in the media.

Lancastrian Danny Carr won over half a million pounds on the pools in 1975. There was a blaze of local publicity and a further spread in the national press. Two weeks later, when this big win was still a matter of comment, Danny's five-year-old daughter, Vanessa Claire Carr, was kidnapped. She was on her way home from school at 3.45 P.M. on Friday 16 May.

Later that day the kidnapper contacted Danny Carr and demanded £100,000 for the child's safe return.

The little girl's family and their neighbours immediately thought of the Black Panther, who had provided the newspapers with vast quantities of material over some eighteen months. Probably a fair number of police officers thought of him, too, though senior investigating officers always keep their options open. The publicity about the Black Panther had captured the public imagination strongly, but who was he?

Some five years before Vanessa was kidnapped, and before this agile burglar had received his famous name, he had been known as the 'brace and bit man', because it was thought this was how he broke into sub-post offices in the North of England. When committing his crimes, he was for the most part dressed in black, including a black hood (although on one occasion he dressed in red) and he armed himself either with a shot gun or a hand gun. He would bore holes in window-frames near the fastenings and then slip the catch to get in. What he used was not an orthodox brace and bit, but a sort of gimlet on a strong bit and, as he had strong hands, it worked well for him.

He always struck at night-time, usually in the winter months, when the longer night hours gave him more time to work with less chance of being seen. Once he had gained entry to a post office, he looked for the keys, usually searching in the bedroom where the postmaster was sleeping. He would empty garment pockets and, once he had found the keys, would leave the occupants undisturbed, go back downstairs, open the safe, steal the contents and make his getaway.

It was when he could not find the keys that he was at his most dangerous and terrifying. To be fast asleep and to be shaken awake by somebody holding a torch, the beam of which is directed down the barrels of a sawn-off shotgun and straight into your eyes, is something most of us would rather not experience. This masked intruder would then demand the keys to the safe, usually forcing the postmaster to accompany him to the safe, open it and hand him the money and valuables.

This brace-and-bit man was aggressive and dangerous. At times he had violently assaulted the sub-postmasters and on at least one occasion the shotgun had been fired during a fierce struggle.

Had all these raids taken place round the London area, in the West Country or over in East Anglia it is not likely that Vanessa's parents and neighbours would have connected them with whoever had taken the child, but many of the robberies had been in places surrounding Manchester. Only eighteen months prior to the kidnapping an attack had been made on the sub-post office at Radcliffe, just over a mile away from Danny Carr's home.

Early in February 1974 the man who had become known as the Black Panther entered a sub-post office in a Harrogate suburb and there shot and murdered the sub postmaster, Donald Skepper, in front of his wife and son. Seven months later, in September the same year, he crossed the Pennines and shot dead ex-Marine Derek Astin in his sub-post office in Accrington, Lancashire. At this time Joe Mounsey was head of Lancashire CID. Known for often trotting out a pithy and accurate phrase, he said, 'War has been declared on a cornerstone of English life, the sub-post office.'

Less than three months later the Black Panther killed again. On 11 November 1974, Sidney Grayland, the sub-postmaster of a West Midlands post office near Birmingham was shot dead. His wife was badly beaten. It was daytime and the premises were of the lock-up type. During the struggle Mrs Grayland ripped off part of the Black Panther's rubber glove. It is significant that, despite the most careful and thorough scenes-of-crime examination at all these dreadful incidents, not one fingerprint was found which did not belong to a person with legitimate access to the premises.

Ballistics tests later established that Mr Astin and Mr Grayland had been shot with the same gun, a .22 automatic pistol.

All forces are of course circulated with details of serious crime, whenever and wherever it takes place, and those police areas in which this man had committed a crime, or was believed to have committed it, deployed a particularly large number of officers and were in close contact with each other.

In the small hours of 14 January 1975, Lesley Whittle was kidnapped from the bedroom of her village home in Highley, Shropshire. She was seventeen years old, a student. At the time it was believed by many that Lesley was a wealthy young heiress who had inherited a considerable sum of money on the death of her father, George Whittle, who had been the owner of a successful coach business in the Midlands.

It was clear that the kidnapping had been well planned and carefully carried out. A ransom of £50,000 was demanded, to be paid in £5 and £1 notes.

Less than forty-eight hours after the kidnapping of Lesley, on 15 January, Gerald Smith was shot and badly wounded when he disturbed an intruder at the Dudley Freightliner depot, where he worked. He was the nightshift foreman. Dudley is about thirty miles from Lesley's home village of Highley. This event did not seem to have any connection with the kidnapping until, a short time after the shooting, a stolen Morris 1300 saloon with the false registration plates TTV 454H was found near the Dudley depot. It had been abandoned and, when examined, was found to contain a great many articles used in the Whittle kidnapping, also written instructions for the placing of the £50,000 ransom demand. It soon became apparent that Gerald Smith had disturbed the kidnapper whilst he was preparing the route the ransom carrier should follow.

But the real surprise was that ballistic tests showed Gerald Smith had been shot with the same .22 automatic pistol which had killed Derek Astin and Sidney Grayland at their sub-post offices the year before. The kidnapper of Lesley Whittle and the person who had so badly wounded Gerald Smith was the Black Panther.

Lesley Whittle's body was found on 7 March 1975 by a Staffordshire scenes-of-crime officer who was searching for her in a shaft which gave access to the underground drainage system in Bathpool Park, Kidsgrove, Staffordshire. In a culvert, a few feet from Lesley's body, was the first real clue as to the identity of the infamous attacker. On a Woolworth's Winfield reporter's notebook, which had been used by him, a partial finger-print was developed by means of a chemical process. Its quality was so poor that, when it was circulated for search to the regional bureaux, it was accompanied by an enlarged drawing of what Scotland Yard finger-print experts believed it looked like; this was the first artist's impression of a finger-print that I had ever known to be circulated. Near the top of the shaft was found a holdall containing a pair of good quality Zeiss binoculars, eventually traced to a Manchester retailer, who had sold them the previous year.

At the Finger-print Bureau in Manchester we had received a copy of the partial finger-print found on the Winfield notebook; the binoculars found near Lesley's body had been bought in Manchester by somebody who gave a false name and address, and of course it was known that the Black Panther had attacked several sub-post offices in the Greater Manchester area, so we were directly involved in the investigation. An immediate search began in the files. Early in April 1975 a finger-print conference was arranged at Stone, Staffordshire, and I attended. It was there that the co-operation between the various finger-print men involved became apparent and I formed several quite close friendships which have lasted to this day.

The general background of the case and the finding of Lesley's body received full coverage in the national and local press, though, of course, not all details were known to the newspapers. You will, however, realize that with all this publicity, available to anybody with a television set, radio or the price of a paper, it was quite reasonable for many people to think that the Black Panther had also taken little Vanessa Carr.

Two seemingly unconnected events also occurred, which at first sight seemed the work of petty criminals. On Tuesday 13 May 1975, three days before the kidnapping of Vanessa Carr, James Kerr Andrew left his car unattended for a few minutes in Byrom Street, Manchester. When he returned, he was upset to find somebody had broken into it and taken his wallet, which contained his driving licence, Barclaycard and other valuable documents. He reported the theft right away, but, realizing that this was a common event in a big city, did not really expect to see his documents again.

A few hours after James Andrew had missed his wallet, a Mr Karimi left his Morris Mini Clubman saloon car, registration NXJ 788H, parked in an official car park near Aytoun Street in the city centre, about half a mile away from Byrom Street on the other side of town. When he went to collect his vehicle at 2.30 the following morning he found that it was not there. Again, he reported the theft immediately and the police took all necessary particulars, circulating them appropriately.

Two isolated events out of many similar ones in Greater Manchester that day, many thousands in the country as a whole; they were not even interesting at this stage.

Back in Radcliffe, when Danny Carr had won his huge pools fortune, it had made little immediate impact on his life. He had been a chargehand in a paper mill and he gave up his job, but continued to live with his wife Irene and their three children in a small town house in Mount Pleasant Walk. His youngest daughter, Vanessa, was a bright, cheerful and confident little girl approaching her sixth birthday. She attended St Mary's Infants' School, no more than a hundred yards from her home. The neighbourhood was quiet, no major roads to cross, and because of this she walked the hundred or so yards along Lowton Street, which lies between her home and the school, together with her young friend Helen, without the supervision of adults.

Shortly after lunch, on Thursday 15 May, a pensioner living in Lowton Street, Mr Cubbage, was busy tidying his front garden before summer's lush growth made it more difficult. He noticed that a mini saloon car was being driven up and down Lowton Street from time to time. He was alert and saw the driver get out and walk up and down the street. The old chap was concerned, and kept car and man in view until the vehicle was driven away.

A little later, at 3 P.M., Janet Croft, a neighbour of Mr Cubbage, was standing in the garden of her home in the same street. It was a nice day, the sort to tempt anybody out. She, too, saw a mini saloon car, apparently the one Mr Cubbage had seen earlier, going up and down Lowton Street. It went away and came back again. Naturally, she was curious, because it was an unusual occurrence in this quiet backwater. She could see the driver clearly: he was about forty years of age, on the small side, and wearing a black leather jacket.

At teatime Mrs Croft, who was expecting a baby, saw Daniel and Irene Carr drive past her house in their car along Lowton Street to their home in Mount Pleasant Walk. She then saw the mini reverse in Lowton Street and follow the Carr couple until it went out of her sight. A few minutes later she saw this same mini being driven away along Lowton Street.

The next day was Friday the 16th, and at 3.45 P.M. Mr Cubbage was again in his front garden. He saw the same mini saloon parked close by and in it the man he had seen driving it the previous day. By this time he suspected, rightly as it turned out, that the driver's intentions were a long way from good. He took a cigar packet from his pocket and on it made a note of the number of the car, which proved to have been stolen earlier from Mr Karimi in Aytoun Street, Manchester.

About the same time Janet Croft saw the same car and driver parked at the end of Lowton Street. She recognized the driver as the one who had followed Mr and Mrs Carr the previous afternoon. As she was watching, Vanessa Carr walked along Lowton Street and got into the car, which was quickly driven off with the child in it, along Lowton Street and out of Mrs Croft's sight.

A little less than three-quarters of an hour after this startling but almost unremarked event, Carol Bugaja, a telephonist at the exchange, received a call from a public telephone box later traced to Chorley Road, Swinton, near Manchester, some miles from Radcliffe. A man asked to be connected with Daniel Carr at his home in Mount Pleasant Walk.

The Carr telephone number was ex-directory and the operator said she could not connect the caller unless the purpose was extremely urgent. He convinced her it was, and was put through.

That afternoon Vanessa's mother, Irene, had a hair-dressing appointment and was not at home. Danny and his mother-in-law, Mrs Kay, were there, waiting for Vanessa to come home from school. Her grandmother answered the telephone. She told the operator she was prepared to accept the call and then almost immediately heard a man's voice say, 'I have got Vanessa!' There was the click of the receiver being replaced.

Mrs Kay was deeply shocked and hardly able to believe what she had heard, but she felt instinctively that it was no practical joke. She was very alarmed and said so to Danny, who, fearing for the child's safety, immediately informed the police.

With the first police enquiries came the imparting of the news to a startled neighbourhood. Within minutes Mr Cubbage and Mrs Croft came forward, and gave detailed accounts of what they had seen that afternoon and the previous day. Obviously, the whole thing was desperately serious and a major incident control was established.

The fact that a description of the kidnapper and the number of the vehicle were known was indeed fortunate. Every officer in Greater Manchester Police was informed that five-year-old Vanessa Carr had been abducted by a white man, about forty years old, on the small side, wearing a black leather jacket, and had been taken away by him in a stolen Morris Mini Clubman saloon car. The number was broadcast over the police radio network every ten minutes. Observations were requested on public telephone call-boxes. The hunt was on and every police officer was alert. Doubtless, many of them had thoughts of the Black Panther.

In the Greyhound Motel in Warrington Road, Leigh,

several miles away, the assistant manager, Christopher Green, was busy discussing the day's events in the establishment with the receptionist, Mary Tasker. A man came in with a little girl. There was a brief exchange of courtesies and the man asked for accommodation for one night only. He was given room 116, paid for it in advance and was given its key.

Routine being followed, he was asked to complete a registration form, which he did in the name of James Kerr Andrew with an address in Blackpool, which he got, of course, from the documents he had stolen from James Andrew's car in Byrom Street, Manchester. The section of the form requiring his vehicle number was filled in with the number of Mr Karimi's car. Hr Hodgkins, the motel manager, saw a man and a little girl walking across the car park towards a grey mini saloon parked there. Naturally enough, no suspicion entered his mind. There was nothing unusual about it.

At 6.40 that evening Danny Carr was sitting, almost out of his mind with worry, beside his telephone. By his side was a police officer ready to record any conversation which might take place, and arrangements had already been made to have a trace placed on the telephone. Five houses away at number 26, Arthur Wall was going about his normal affairs when he received a telephone call. A man, who refused to say who he was, addressed him by name and instructed him to go to the Carr home and bring Danny to the phone. Arthur Wall did this. Danny answered the telephone, holding the receiver so that the accompanying police officer was able to listen in to the conversation.

Danny confirmed his identity and the caller told him that he had Vanessa, that she was safe, and demanded a ransom of £100,000 for her safe return. Danny asked if

Vanessa was there with him and was told she was. He persuaded the kidnapper to allow the little girl to speak to him. She was very excited, telling her father that she had been to London and that she was now waiting for him to come and take her home.

Danny Carr had never had any spare money until he won the £500,000, and was more than ready to part with a fifth of it to get his daughter back. He undertook to draw it out of the bank and asked the caller to give him the necessary time to do this and to ring him back at his own home within the hour. He gave the kidnapper his ex-directory telephone number to do this.

An hour later Arthur Wall's telephone rang again and Mrs Wall answered it. She heard a man say, 'The telephone at the Carrs' is engaged. Tell Danny Carr I'll ring again at half past eight.'

Unwittingly, the kidnapper had picked a significant time, for it was about then that Police Constable Michael Sheard was driving his panda car along Worsley Road, Swinton, some miles from Radcliffe, but not far from the Greyhound Motel. He was listening to the radio which, every ten minutes, had been requesting a sharp lookout for the grey mini saloon which had recently been stolen and used in the kidnapping.

As Sheard drove across the junction with the East Lancashire Road, a main trunk road connecting Manchester with Liverpool, he was elated to see this very car in the Manchester-bound carriageway, stopped at traffic lights. He turned his police car round quickly and set off in pursuit of the grey mini. He could see that the driver fitted the description, and in the car was a little girl.

He radioed Control, told them of the sighting and that he was pursuing the stolen vehicle in the direction of Manchester. After a chase of some three-quarters of a mile PC Sheard overtook the stolen mini and caused the driver to stop by the side of the East Lancashire Road. As he was getting out of his car, the stolen car mounted the pavement, passing the police car on its nearside, and sped away in the direction of Manchester.

PC Sheard was alone in his car, but was far from being alone in the area. PC David Russell, in another car, got word by radio of this latest incident and drove to the road island at the junction of the East Lancashire Road and Manchester Road at Swinton, parking his car so that it partially blocked the junction. He got out. Seconds later, the stolen car sped towards him. He stepped forward and signalled the driver to stop. This sort of action, in these circumstances, takes a certain amount of nerve. The driver did not stop. Maintaining his speed, he swerved to the nearside, mounting the grass verge as he did so, and drove along the pavement past the officer.

The kidnapper was undoubtedly reckless, but could not escape the net which was being drawn round him. The next sighting was by Police Constable Graham, who was driving his panda car along Bolton Road, Swinton, making for the junction with the East Lancashire Road. As the mini approached him, he turned his vehicle and gave chase.

He tailed it closely for a few miles, even going through road junctions against the red traffic signals. Proceeding along Agecroft Road, he turned right into Kersal Vale Road, Salford, where he momentarily lost sight of his quarry. Instinctively the officer turned left into Moor Lane, from where he saw the stolen mini abandoned in Castlewood Road. Its engine was still running and in the front passenger seat, distressed but unharmed, was Vanessa Carr. It was a welcome and heartening sight for the officer.

As PC Graham was standing by the stolen vehicle, taking stock of the situation, he was approached by a very excited lady, Mrs Brown. She was most anxious to tell him that she had been in her brother-in-law's home in Castlewood Road when she had seen the mini brake and swerve violently to a standstill. A man dressed in a black leather jacket had jumped out of the car, run through the garden of the house she was in, and climbed over the garden fence, which backed on to gardens in Littleton Road. Next he had run through one of the gardens, before disappearing from view on Littleton Road. As the man ran she could see that he was throwing away small items. A quick search brought to hand a pair of handcuffs, keys with a label saying '116 Greyhound Motel', and a wallet containing the driving licence and other documents belonging to James Andrew. The key to the handcuffs was found on the same key-ring as the ignition key which had been left in the stolen mini.

The northern end of Littleton Road is fronted on one side by large playing fields. As the kidnapper raced across these fields he discarded his black leather jacket and blue pullover. Some of his thinking, at least, was fairly quick. No doubt he thought he would be able to run more easily without these garments and would be less noticeable. In retrospect, one can see that by wearing a black leather jacket and driving a similar car up and down near the child's home, the kidnapper was trying to create the impression that she had been abducted by the Black Panther.

By the time the kidnapper was jogging in the playing fields many foot- and motor-patrol officers were engaged in the hunt. Two Constables, John Hynes and Tony Collier, drove their car down a cinder path which forms the southern boundary of these playing fields. They stopped their car near a footbridge which crosses the River Irwell, got out and stood on the river bank. Running towards them was a small group of people, dressed in running gear and obviously enjoying a training spell. A short distance behind them was another runner in ordinary shoes, ordinary trousers and a white vest, with a blue shirt tied round his waist – not exactly the right gear for a training run. The two officers stopped and questioned him; he claimed he was training, something he did most evenings. They did not believe him, told him so and arrested him.

At Bury police station he was interviewed by senior police officers. He denied he had been involved in the kidnapping, refused to say who he was or give his address, and took the attitude, not uncommon amongst suspects, that the police had made a serious mistake when they had arrested him, and that he would be taking legal action against them.

Later that Friday night I had a telephone call at home from one of the senior investigating officers: 'We've arrested a man whom we believe to be the Black Panther. He refuses to answer questions put to him and has declined to identify himself. I have made arrangements for his finger-prints to be taken. Will you please compare his finger-prints with those on file in the Bureau and see if you can identify him for me? Will you also check his finger-prints against the finger impression found on the notebook at the scene of the Lesley Whittle murder?'

In view of the nature of the crime, and the events over the previous twelve months, these were reasonable requests. The finger-prints were quickly found in the main print collection and identified as those of Brian Anderton, thirty-nine years old, with an address in Whitefield, Manchester, but his prints did not match the

one on the Winfield reporter's notebook. This Brian
Anderton was not the Black Panther, however much we
all would have liked him to be.

Back at Bury police station Anderton was still being
questioned. Whilst this was going on, one of the officers
present noticed that he kept rubbing the back of his left
hand. A closer look showed he was trying to erase a
number printed in ink on the back of it: number 116.
When he was asked by the officer to account for it,
Anderton stated it was £1.16, an amount he had paid
earlier in the day for something he had bought. The
significance of the key to room 116 at the Greyhound
Motel was pointed out to him. He remained unmoved
and denied all knowledge of the kidnapping of Vanessa
Carr.

A few enquiries proved that he owned a fish and chip
restaurant in the centre of Manchester, which appeared
to provide a good standard of living for his wife and
family. The mini saloon and documents had been stolen
from points less than half a mile from Anderton's business
premises.

After doing the Bureau check and identifying Anderton, I went to Bury police station to examine the car. On
it I found three finger impressions, which I identified as
belonging to Brian Anderton and three belonging to
Vanessa Carr. A piece of paper was found in the car. On
it were written the names of a number of people who
lived in Mount Pleasant Walk, including that of Arthur
Wall, Danny Carr's neighbour. It was found that these
compared with those on the electoral register for the
Borough of Bury. I checked the paper for possible finger-
prints and on it developed eight impressions, each of
which had been made by Anderton. Under the driver's
seat was a sheath knife and a hand-operated spray. When

this stray was examined, it was found to contain a strong solution of aqueous ammonia. This can cause burns to the skin and it emits fumes which greatly irritate the eyes and the respiratory system.

I next went to the Greyhound Motel, where I conducted a thorough examination of room 116. On furniture in the room I found eight of Anderton's finger-prints. On the dressing-table top was a large writing pad. On its front page I found five finger impressions, all belonging to Anderton. On the back of the pad were five finger or palm impressions, all from little Vanessa Carr.

To make even more sure, an identification parade was held at the station on 17 May 1975. Three people picked out Brian Anderton: Mr Cubbage, Mrs Croft, both of Lowton Street, and Mr Green, the assistant manager of the motel.

In all its forms, political and private, the crime of kidnapping remains comparatively rare here and thank goodness for that. Nevertheless, it is not a legal term and the charge against Anderton was that he 'stole and unlawfully carried away Vanessa Carr against her will', and that he made 'an unwarranted demand for £100,000 from Daniel Carr, with menaces.'

He pleaded not guilty and was tried at Manchester Crown Court. It was a long trial. He was found guilty as charged and sentenced to a term of twelve years' imprisonment. He later appealed against the severity of the sentence, but the judge, in dismissing Anderton's application, said, 'It is well known that kidnapping is now a fashionable crime and is being indulged in increasingly.'

The possession of a large amount of money can and does bring vulnerability. No doubt Mr and Mrs Carr have had to come to terms with a situation for which their earlier years had certainly not prepared them. In retrospect, they were probably relieved that the misguided man who took their daughter was not the Black Panther.

What of the Black Panther, then? In December 1975, two perfectly ordinary, yet very brave, members of Nottinghamshire Constabulary, Constables Tony White and Stuart McKenzie, overpowered and arrested the Black Panther after he had held them at gunpoint whilst they were checking his activities late at night in a village near Mansfield. He was later identified as Donald Neilson, with an address in Bradford, Yorkshire.

A check on the Winfield reporter's notebook print showed it was his, and the artist's impression so expertly compiled was found to be accurate. The .22 automatic pistol used to kill the two sub-postmasters had been stolen from a house in Cheadle Hulme, a commuter village on the outskirts of south Manchester.

Neilson was tried and found guilty of the murders of Lesley Whittle, Donald Skepper, Derek Astin and Sidney Grayland. He was sentenced to a series of terms of life imprisonment. Gerald Smith died fourteen months after receiving his injuries, beyond the legal requirement of a year and a day for it to be considered as murder.

It still horrifies me to think how many people are affected in one violent crime, let alone the number committed by Neilson. Families, friends, neighbours alike can never be quite the same again.

11
Widespread Alarm

The finding of the naked and mutilated body of a twenty-year-old woman in an allotment garden near Princess Road, Chorlton, Manchester, sparked off the biggest murder hunt in the history of the Greater Manchester Police and brought terror to the red-light districts of the city.

This allotment plot, disused and overgrown, adjoined Manchester's huge Southern Cemetery, and it was on the morning of Monday 10 October 1977 that the body of Jean Bernadette Jordon, also known as Jean Royle, was found there. She was a part-time prostitute and it soon became evident that she was the sixth victim of the Yorkshire Ripper, who had, until then, confined his murderous activities to the eastern side of the Pennines. Detectives from Greater Manchester Police combined with their colleagues from West Yorkshire to work on one of the most complex murder investigations ever tackled in Great Britain. This massive enquiry was to last until 2 January 1981, when Peter William Sutcliffe, a lorry driver from Bradford, Yorkshire, was arrested by uniformed police officers in Sheffield as he was about to commit his fourteenth murder.

Journalistic exaggeration, allied to the shortness of public memory, produces at least once in every decade the 'crime of the century'. Really serious crime, especially multiple and unsolved murder, is a gift to the media.

In the last twenty years Manchester police officers have investigated two 'crimes of the century'. The Yorkshire

Ripper case was one and the other was the Moors Murders by Ian Brady and Myra Hindley, whose infamy will never be forgotten.

The enquiry into the Moors Murders began with the arrest of Ian Brady and Myra Hindley, the object of the exercise being to establish what they had done, and then to prove they had done it. The Yorkshire Ripper case differed in that it soon became apparent to everybody what he had done, the difficult part being to identify and capture him. However much the objects of these investigations differed, the procedures adopted were almost identical, as indeed they are for most murder enquiries.

When a body has been discovered in circumstances which indicate that a murder may have occurred, the first police officer or officers to arrive must ensure, as far as possible, that life is extinct. To do so they may on occasions have to cut through a ligature tied round the victim's throat. In doing this the cut must be as far away as possible from the knot; the way in which the knot has been tied may prove valuable to the enquiry. If there are persons present at the scene who are suspected of committing the offence, as in the case of Brady and Hindley, they must be detained. Officers may be required to call either ambulance or fire brigade, and will notify the duty officer based in the Force Control Room who, in turn, will notify the senior investigating officer. Pending his arrival, it will be the duty of the officer or officers present to preserve the scene from contamination, seek out witnesses in the immediate vicinity and provide radio facility.

Looking back, I realize how often these tasks have been the lot of a young officer out on a beat on his own, perhaps for the first time. What is more, he is required to identify the body as the one he has seen, not only to the senior investigating officer but also to the mortuary staff and the pathologist.

When the senior investigating officer, usually a Detective Chief Superintendent, arrives, he takes immediate command of the enquiry and checks that all the initial work has been done. His is not an enviable position. Knowing full well that he will, in the modern phrase, be carrying the can, he will automatically assert his authority to ensure the smooth running of the operation. If the investigation is a protracted affair, he knows that his officers will be dealing with unknown factors and that, inevitably, mistakes will be made. He hopes that these mistakes will be small ones and will not adversely affect the outcome of the enquiry.

As the person responsible for all releases to the press, radio and television, he soon becomes the focal point of attention. When things go wrong, often through no fault of his own, he is soon aware that, 'A man must serve his time to every trade save censure – critics all are ready made.' If any senior police officer (or SIO) was unaware of Byron's words before the Yorkshire Ripper case started, he was well aware of the truth of them when it had finished. Before people criticize the SIO engaged on a murder hunt they should first have some knowledge of what his duties entail, and his approach to them. If afterwards they still wish to criticize him then that is, of course, their right.

After checking that all the initial work has been done by those first on the scene, he will appoint an exhibits officer, usually of the rank of Detective Sergeant, who will be responsible for the collection, documentation, labelling and safe custody of all property and exhibits;

their transfer between forensic laboratories and the incident room; their display to witnesses; the production of exhibits at the trial in sequence with those witnesses testifying to them, and the subsequent disposal of all items.

Staff must be deployed urgently to identify the name of the deceased; once the deceased has been identified the task is simplified to some degree. The attendance of the pathologist is requested. All pathologists now like to visit the scene and see the body *in situ* before performing their main task of establishing the cause of death at the mortuary.

The SIO will then consider the examination of the murder scene. The body will have been photographed from many angles, as will the surroundings in which the body was found, together with any clothing or weapons which may be near.

The important thing is to follow the routine. This is not as rigid as one might think, because no two cases are alike, but following a set procedure does minimize the chance of missing something which later is irrecoverable: scent, explosion, food, sweat, drugs, contamination, dirt – all leave odours which can evaporate. One cannot bottle and label such things, but if they are detected then confirmation must be made and a note taken.

There are many types of specialist officers and you have to decide which ones are needed for a particular enquiry. The photographer will be needed not only at the scene of the murder but also at the mortuary to record the appearance of particular injuries both on the surface of the skin and after its removal, for instance in the case of skull fracture. Small wonder that jury members, unused to such things, can become distressed.

Certainly the finger-print expert will be busy, as will

members of the forensic science laboratory staff and the scenes-of-crime man. Each one will be briefed as to all the circumstances of the case. After this, the SIO will arrange with his deputy to set up a murder control, which in Manchester consists of a suite of offices set aside at Longsight police station. These offices are fully stocked with all materials likely to be needed including specialized stationery, chalk, board, lamps, ropes, tents, batteries, spare clothing, Wellington boots, rubber gloves, dustbins, small tools, big tools, long-handled rakes – a veritable hardware shop.

The control room will be the nerve centre of the operation and will be staffed by a Detective Chief Inspector, two Detective Inspectors, a Detective Sergeant (usually the exhibits officer), two Detective Constables who will perform clerical duties, two telephonists and a police-woman. Often, the seconding of a cadet or two is helpful; errands have to be run, the tea-urn has to be kept up to the mark, papers have to be sorted, visitors to the control have to be ushered in and assisted. Many a cadet has expected instant excitement and been very disappointed at the sheer volume of routine and hard slog. The occasional cadet has seen more than he or she bargained for, felt a bit queasy, learned an unforgettable lesson, and later, perhaps, has remembered with quiet satisfaction, 'Oh, yes, I worked on that one.'

Much of the material stocked by the murder control at Longsight police station is portable so that, if it is more helpful to establish a control room elsewhere, it can be done with a minimum of delay, often not longer than an hour.

The SIO will go to the mortuary to be present whilst the pathologist conducts the post-mortem examination. The first officer to see the body will also be there. The forensic scientists will be patiently collecting all sorts of samples such as sellotape 'lifts', fibres from clothing, finger nails, toe nails, hair, swabs, and blood. All must be labelled with exactitude. The finger-print officer will take palm and finger-prints of the deceased.

After leaving the mortuary, the officer in charge will drive back to the murder control suite confident that all is going according to plan. There will be a conference with his senior officers to decide on the number of men required in the murder squad, and then he has to go out and meet the media.

This contact with the media is another area in which the requirements of the job have changed. The police have always spoken to newspaper reporters, but it is the inclusion of television encounters which is new. The senior officer has to become used to this. It is no good being too reserved, yet he cannot be too forthcoming; a balance has to be struck.

Having made sure that the examination of the scene of the crime is being conducted in a satisfactory manner and that murder control is fully operational, he will divide his squad into four groups, with a senior officer in charge of each one.

The first group, usually comprising only a small number of officers, will conduct enquiries into the background of the deceased, establish identity if it is not known, interview relatives, friends, neighbours, work associates and so on, and build as complete a picture as is possible of the victim's background and life-style. A second squad will be detailed for general enquiries stemming from information received at murder control. The third group, known as the 'MO suspect squad', will interview all criminals residing in the area whose records show that their way of working is similar to that demonstrated in the crime under enquiry; this may relate to sexual crime, violence in the form of stabbing or battering, robbery, etc. Last but certainly not least is the house-to-house enquiry squad. It is the least popular of the duties allocated and known to detectives involved as being 'on the knocker'. A draft form is prepared and in this particular respect an experienced clerical worker can be of great assistance if willing to be called out at odd hours so that the draft can be ready for printing at the first opportunity. Attempts have been made to produce a standard form, but it simply does not work.

The house-to-house squad usually operates from the mobile police station (a caravan) near the murder scene. The staff will visit every house in the area asking the series of questions on the form, and filling in the answers alongside. They will very likely ask occupants about where they were between certain times, any vehicles owned, occupations, how many people in the house and so on. Occasionally people lie, usually to protect somebody whom they may think is involved in the crime.

To set the ball rolling the SIO will avail himself of the services of the Criminal Record Office, the staff of which will give him details of crimes similar to the one he is investigating and also a list of people convicted of similar offences. They will arrange for the despatch of express messages, and publication of the details of the crime being investigated on national and local crime informations. Assistance will be requested of the Criminal Intelligence Department and the SIO will also arrange for question-naires and posters to be printed. The services of a police artist may also be needed to draw a likeness based on witnesses' statements.

By virtue of his experience and long training, the SIO knows what equipment is available to him. First there is the mobile command vehicle, then mobile lighting systems, video recording equipment, portable radios, portable tape-recorders, metal detectors, listening and recording devices, infra-red equipment for night-time observations and photography, and the provision of special services such as helicopters for large-scale searches.

At lunch time on Monday 10 October 1977, I received a call from the SIO, the Detective Chief Superintendent of the Greater Manchester Police Central Crime Area, to go to a disused allotment near Princess Road, Chorlton, Manchester, where the body of a young woman had been found. I was there to examine the scene of the crime.

It is a fundamental assumption that, when a person commits a crime, he alters both himself and the scene of that crime. Examination of the scene can be divided into four basic operations and calls for an integrated approach by different specialists.

Firstly, the scene will be photographed and a video recording made before anything is further disturbed. Secondly, the various specialists need access to the intelligence material of the crime. The investigating officer supplies this. Thirdly, there will be a search for fingerprints, footprints, glove prints, tyre impressions, instrument marks etc. This search will be combined with the fourth operation, which is to search for other materials such as hairs, fibres, blood, glass, paint or things which have been accidentally dropped or discarded by the offender; these could be cigarette ends, weapons, bloodstained clothing or personal effects. Samples are taken for comparison with the suspect's clothing.

The allotments I was asked to go to were owned by Manchester Corporation and rented off to private individuals. Earlier in the year a section of these allotments had been fenced off and fallen into disuse. There was no gate and the allotments were entered by a driveway leading from Princess Road. People exercised their dogs there and it was known to the police that prostitutes took their clients there, both by day and night. A narrow pathway and a fence separated the old allotments from those in current use.

I was informed by the SIO that two of the allotment holders, Mr Jones and Mr Morrissey, whilst searching for house bricks in the old allotments at 10.30 that morning had found the body near a wooden shed, less than twenty feet from a well-used pathway.

The naked body was that of a young woman. She was lying face downwards and her arms were spread wide apart, She had been badly mutilated and there was a coil of intestine wrapped round her waist. It was later established that death had been caused by head injuries consistent with having been struck a number of times with a hammer. An attempt had been made to sever the head, a fact which was never revealed to the press.

It was obvious to the experienced eye that the incised wounds on the trunk had been inflicted a considerable time after death. As the allotments were quite close to Manchester's huge Southern Cemetery my first thought was that someone had violated a recent grave and had mutilated the corpse. This idea was soon dispelled, because scattered in long grass around the area of the body I found articles of a woman's clothing: boots, coat, cardigan, skirt, jumper, panties, bra and tights. Most of the top clothing was badly blood-stained and crawling with fully developed maggots. Under the privet hedge which separated the allotment from the pathway was a depression which was absolutely teeming with maggots, and leaning next to the adjacent wooden shed was a wooden, interior house door. It was deduced that the victim had been murdered some days before; that her body had been put into the depression near the hedge and covered with the wooden door; that the murderer had returned to the scene on the night prior to the body being found and had removed it from its place of concealment, stripped away the clothing and then had mutilated it before attempting to cut off the head.

Samples of the maggots found on the body and the clothing were taken to Manchester University. The entomologist there was able to establish, by observation of the various stages of development of the life-cycle of maggots to blow-flies, that the eggs had been laid on the body eight or nine days previously. This kind of specialist service is available whenever needed and can prove invaluable.

The discovery of the body was given widespread publicity. As a result, Alan Royle came forward the following day to report that his common-law wife Jean had been missing from their home since Saturday 1 October 1977. After Alan Royle had been interviewed and had been shown articles of clothing found near the body, it was concluded that the dead woman was Jean Bernadette Jordon, alias Royle. The decomposed state of the body precluded its being shown to him for the purposes of identification.

I took Jean Jordon's finger-prints, obtained the previous day, to her home and searched it with a view to finding a corroborative print on an article of furniture or household equipment. I arrived there at 7.30 P.M., accompanied by another finger-print expert, quite confident that within twenty minutes we would find plenty of other prints with which to establish identification for the benefit of the coroner. Incidentally, I should mention that her finger-prints were not on file at the Criminal Record Office.

I chose to start my examination in the kitchen and my colleague examined the lounge. After two hours, with every article of furniture examined, we had drawn a blank. By midnight we had examined every likely object, every piece of crockery and cutlery, all pans, dishes, tins of food, almost everything including the kitchen sink, but without success.

I then ordered tea chests to be sent for. Each item which had not been finger-printed was packed and taken to the Bureau for examination the following day.

At 8.30 the following morning, I organized a team of six experts to examine the remaining articles. Five minutes later we found the mark we had been searching for. On a lemonade bottle which I had taken from under the kitchen sink one of the experts found a left thumb impression which was identical with the left thumb print of the victim.

After the lengthy examination of the previous night, this identification had only taken five minutes. In an effort to provide further evidence of identification and to satisfy my curiosity every other article was examined, but no other finger-prints found had been made by Jean Jordon. The only print she had left in her own home was the left thumb print on the lemonade bottle. It was later established that her common-law husband did all the cooking and most of the housework.

When Alan Royle had examined the clothing of the dead woman and identified it, he said that her handbag was missing. Now that we had a positive identification, posters were printed showing a coloured photograph of her. They were put up in public places in an attempt to trace her movements, and the wording on the posters drew attention to the missing handbag. All the allotment holders were traced and interviewed.

At 10 A.M. on Saturday 15 October, a Mr Cox went to his allotment on the new section situated near Princess Road. Underneath the fence separating the old area from the new, concealed in the long grass, he found a green leather-type handbag. He reported this to the police, and Alan Royle later identified it as belonging to Jean Jordon. This handbag had been found 189 feet from where the body was discovered. It was lying open and in the main compartment there were cigarettes, matches and make-up. In a small side pocket on the outside were a £5 and a £1 note.

It appeared that the handbag had been searched, but whoever had done so had missed these two notes. The investigating officers knew that a few years earlier, in the Manchester 'Di Giorgio' case, a sequence of three new £1 notes had been found in the possession of a dead prostitute and they had led to the arrest and eventual conviction of her killer. Naturally, they felt that the £5 note in Jean's handbag was likely to provide a valuable clue to the identity of her killer. It was a new note and the indication was that it may have been given to her as payment for sexual favours on the night of her murder. This belief was strengthened by the fact that the killer had returned to the scene, obviously to renew his search for the £5 note, which he himself suspected could be traced back to him.

The handbag and its contents had been exposed to the weather and no finger-prints were found there. The method of bank-note manufacture in this country makes recovery of finger-prints from a note's surface a difficult task and, despite the utmost care, we drew a blank. However, enquiries at the Bank of England in London were more productive. Millions and millions of new notes are issued each year. When the Bank of England issues new notes, a record is made of first and last serial numbers in particular groups, and to which district central bank they go. A chain of number-checking persists until the issuing bank breaks the paper seal round a certain number of new notes and they are dispersed to the public; indeed, it may go further than that, because wrapped bundles are issued to firms still paying wages in cash. The £5 note in Jean Jordon's handbag bore the number AW 51 121565 and it had been issued in Leeds on Tuesday 27 September 1977. It was one of five thousand £5 notes which had gone to the Midland Bank, Shipley, Yorkshire, and from there to four local firms, where the notes had been paid out in wages.

Detectives from Greater Manchester Police were sent to join their colleagues in the West Yorkshire force operating from the murder control at Leeds police station. Within days seventy detectives, half of them from Manchester, began the task of interviewing 5,943 people in an effort to trace the man to whom the £5 had originally been given.

Bank notes are not the most interesting items, except perhaps to an engraver, and their numbers are merely numbers after all. Few people note the numbers of the bank notes which pass through their hands, and these days a £5 note is of no more moment than a shilling was fifty years ago.

Once Jean Jordon had become the sixth murder victim of the Yorkshire Ripper, and as each of the six enquiries had one ultimate objective, it was both necessary and desirable that all enquiries should stem from one murder control. Collectively, the murder control staff is responsible for maintaining the following:

The murder log, in which every scrap of information, no matter the source, no matter how trivial it is thought to be, is recorded.

The daily job sheet, which contains entries taken from the daily log and shows the nature of each enquiry to be made, the officer to whom it is allocated and brief particulars of the outcome. Every job entered results in a report, statement or questionnaire being completed and filed.

The time book, which shows hours worked by the individual officers, and their duties.

The daily duty lists showing the duties allocated to each officer.

The property book showing details of all property received or recovered and details of property forwarded for forensic examination. The recording of the 'chain of possession' of property is very important.

The correspondence diary with details of all letters received and sent.

The teleprinter message book with details of all teleprinter messages received and sent.

The photograph book contains details of photographs shown by members of the murder squad to witnesses, and also names of witnesses or possible witnesses who attend the Criminal Record Office to view photographs, and the result.

Lists of persons brought to murder control, which notes the reason for attending and duration of stay.

Files for original statements, control copy reports, original reports, questionnaires, telephone messages, correspondence, press cuttings, etc.

An alphabetical card index, which is as comprehensive as possible. As soon as information is received it is carded with reference to a place where it is recorded in the control room. Included are names, aliases, nicknames and other details of interest, e.g., man carrying window-cleaner's ladders seen at the time, prostitute in blue coat seen getting into van, victim seen with young scruffy man two hours before the murder. The index will also contain details of reports, questionnaires and statements cross-referenced against each other.

The card index is difficult to maintain and update under normal circumstances, but at the time of the Jordon murder it was proving almost impossible and as a result was ineffective. The enquiry into the murder of Jean Jordon was interrupted four months later, when the Ripper struck again.

On 31 January 1978, the body of Elena Rytka, a nineteen-year-old prostitute, was found in a disused timber yard in Huddersfield. At the time it was thought that she was his seventh murder victim, but, in fact, she was the eighth. Just ten days earlier he had murdered another prostitute, Yvonne Pearson, in Bradford. Her body, which had been concealed under a settee on waste land, was not discovered until two months later.

On the morning of Wednesday 17 May 1978, I received a telephone call requesting me to go to a small compound at the rear of the private wards at Manchester Royal Infirmary. I was told that the body of a woman had been found in circumstances which left little doubt that she was the ninth victim of the Yorkshire Ripper.

The compound measured about 170 feet by 60 feet and was formed by brick walls on the north and west, and a wire mesh fence to the south and east. A section of the wall on the western side near its junction with the north wall had fallen down and had been temporarily replaced by a length of wire mesh fence. Access to the compound was by an opening in the fence at the southern end.

I was told that shortly after eight o'clock that morning a party of six workers had arrived to do gardening jobs at the Manchester Royal Infirmary. They had parked their two vehicles in the compound and were removing their tools from the back of one of the vans when they saw what they first thought to be a tailor's dummy lying near the temporary fence. One of the men walked over for a closer inspection and was horrified to see that it was the body of a dead woman. A nurse on her way to work appeared almost at the same time and she too could see the woman was dead. A doctor from the Infirmary quickly appeared and certified the death. The police arrived soon after and immediately preserved the scene for forensic examination.

The post-mortem proceedings at the mortuary established that death had been caused by severe head injuries, apparently inflicted with a blunt instrument similar to a hammer. The body was severely mutilated.

A plain-clothes police officer working on the Vice Squad was at the mortuary and he identified the deceased as a prostitute whom he knew as Vivienne Brown. It demonstrates the near infallibility of the finger-print system of identification to record that, when the prints of the dead woman were taken at the mortuary and checked at the Bureau just over a mile away, they were found to be not identical with those of Vivienne Brown.

After classification, they were searched in the main finger-print collection and identified in minutes as those of Vera Evelyn Millward, a forty-one-year-old prostitute. She had seven children, and was in exceedingly poor health. She had been missing from her home since ten o'clock the previous night, when she had said she was going to Manchester Royal Infirmary because she had severe stomach pains.

When girls first become prostitutes they are probably in reasonable health, but few remain so. It is an irregular life, and if their means of meeting clients is by standing on street corners the worst of the weather is often theirs. The men they come into contact with can be suffering from any one of a number of transmissible diseases. Meals tend to be irregular and probably far from wisely chosen. More than likely the girls smoke and drink too much. Small wonder that they can look old before their time and have more than their fair share of ailments.

A close examination of the Millward scene was made. From the position of tyre tracks, footprints, blood and the spot where the body was found it was assumed that the murderer had driven through the opening in the wire mesh at the southern end of the compound and had veered sharply to the right; he had then reversed his vehicle until the bonnet was pointing towards the exit, ready for a quick getaway. Whilst not a particularly difficult task, recovering tyre impressions is quite a long process. First the tracks have to be examined to determine the direction in which the vehicle was travelling; then sketches are made showing the direction of travel, the width and position of each track in relation to a fixed point, and which wheel the impression had been made by. Once the sketch has been made, a ruler is placed by the side of each tyre impression and close-up photographs are taken, usually with the flash gun held at an oblique angle. This highlights the ridges and throws the furrows or depressions into shadow. When the photographs have been taken, plaster casts are made. How effective these are depends on the ground surface.

To make the casts a small retaining fence is built around the impression. Then on to the surface of the impression is sprayed a fine coat of shellac (hair spray) to seal and stop the plaster running through the surface of the soil. A pint of water is mixed with one pound of dental plaster, and the mixture is poured gently into the impression.

We were fortunate to find and cast the impressions made by all four tyres of the suspect vehicle. From these casts and the measurements obtained, the scientists at the North-West Forensic Science Laboratory were able to prepare a list of only eleven vehicles within the suspect range, one of which was the Ford Corsair that the murderer was eventually known to be using at the time of the attack.

The information was supplied to the murder control room, where things were rather chaotic, with up to twenty-seven officers controlling a murder squad of more than 1,000 detectives, and with a nine-month backlog of reports containing information waiting to be cross-indexed. This can be better understood if we appreciate that the telephones rang 1,200 times each day with information being offered, and all that information was recorded in duplicate on a miscellaneous information report form, known to detectives as a 'misk'.

The telephone officer enters all information in duplicate on the misk form and then hands both copies to the Detective Inspector in the control room, who puts all details into the murder log, allocates to it the next consecutive report number and puts that number in the murder log and on the report. He then decides the action to be taken, notes it on the report and enters it on the job sheet. Both copies of the report go to the clerk who prepares and files a temporary index card and pins an index card to one copy of the report, which goes back to the Inspector. The report is then ready for allocation to a detective for action. He gets one copy of the report and the index card, and his name and number are entered on the job sheet. The remaining copy is retained at control and put in the jobs-out file. At any given time the SIO can check the file to see how many jobs are outstanding.

When the detective has finished his enquiry, he will complete the miscellaneous report form showing the result of his enquiries and hand in both the form and index card to the murder control, where a senior officer will check what has been done. If he is satisfied, he will mark it 'file' and hand form and card to the clerk, who enters a summary of the information on the card, files the report, cross-references and then removes the temporary index card from the alphabetical card index and replaces it with the completed one.

The system should ensure that all information is recorded and its importance appreciated at an early stage, that there is no duplication of enquiries and that all information received is indexed and cross-referenced. It works well enough in normal circumstances, though in cases of multiple murder the sheer volume can be a great handicap. As the murder control at Leeds was hopelessly bogged down with paperwork, it will be appreciated that, although masses of information was being collected, only a small proportion of it was being effectively collated.

The now notorious, so-called Ripper letters and the tape addressed particularly to Assistant Chief Constable George Oldfield must be mentioned. Three letters, each one taunting the police investigating the murders and signed 'Yours Respectfully, Jack the Ripper', were immediately linked with a cassette tape sent to the West Yorkshire Police. Few of the millions of people who heard the tape being played on radio and television will ever forget the mocking tone of the man with the Geordie accent who claimed to be Jack the Ripper. Unfortunately, the bogus letters and cassette tape were accepted as genuine. The recorded voice indicated that the murderer was a person born in the North-East of England, who spoke with a pronounced Geordie accent.

The trouble was that they were relied upon far too heavily by some people, though not by all, and when in one of the letters written to a newspaper in March 1978 the writer indicated his next victim would be a low-class woman in Manchester, the death of Vera Millward, the prostitute, at the back of Manchester Royal Infirmary two months later only served to give them credibility. It was understandable, but unfortunate.

It is traditional throughout the Western world to refer to 'red-light' districts, meaning those in which prostitutes ply their trade. Acceptance of this stratum of society varies according to country. Each big city in the British Isles has its own prostitute area or areas, often recognized by name amongst people who have never visited that particular city. The policing of such areas by members of the Vice Squad is a fairly routine thing, understood by both sides, the resultant fines perhaps being regarded as a form of income tax. In monetary terms the rewards are quite high, but it is the rare bird who saves her money and 'sends her son to Eton College' – the fanciful idea expressed in novelettes in which the woman of the streets has a heart of pure gold and only sells her wares because she is forced to do so by unfortunate circumstances.

Moss Side, Manchester, is and has been for many years notorious in this respect, along with its neighbour Whalley Range. As I have said in another chapter, it is not such a long time since both places were residential, the degeneration only occurring between the two world wars. It was in Moss Side that Vera Millward had plied her trade, and her body was found only a few minutes' run by car from wherever she had been picked up. What a risk every prostitute takes when she gets into a vehicle driven by a man she does not know: he may be a reckless driver, he may be suffering from infection, even if it is only flu, or he may have intentions of murder or theft – not chances that most of us would take.

By the year A.D. 200 the Romans had laid out a well-used road between Manchester and York, over the moors in the direction of Leeds. It later became a well-established stage-coach route. Up until the advent of the motorways it was still a well-used road, which could become hazardous in bad weather; much of the journey is high and very exposed, suffering cross-winds, snowdrifts and the like. The advent of the motorway system altered all this. Some special engineering was done on the motorway between Manchester and Leeds, the M62, so that it would not have to be closed even in the vilest of weather. This promise has been kept and it is an excellent route; a vehicle can without difficulty get from Leeds to Manchester in three-quarters of an hour.

A little-known operation on this motorway, allied to one within several of the northern cities' red-light districts, kept a check on every vehicle which travelled along it in either direction between certain hours. This operation did not achieve its main aim but there were the usual side benefits in finding people who had been sought for other matters. In the red-light districts many people who are household names or eminent in their professions found themselves being stopped in the small hours well away from their own homes. Some very strange and unbelievable excuses were put forward, many indeed providing welcome relief to tired officers.

The reign of terror continued for a further two years with the Ripper committing another four brutal murders in Yorkshire. The widespread alarm now felt by all members of the community rose to fresh heights. Questions about the efficiency of the police were being asked in Parliament and senior officers drove themselves to the point of exhaustion.

The close checks kept upon the red-light districts in the North of England were fully justified when late on Friday 2 January 1981, Peter William Sutcliffe was arrested in Melbourne Avenue near the red-light district of Sheffield as he was preparing to commit his fourteenth murder.

Sutcliffe had just reversed his car into the darkened forecourt of the Light Trades Building and was speaking to his passenger, a coloured prostitute named Olivia Reivers, when he was spotted by the crew of a cruising police car, Sergeant Ring and PC Hydes, who decided to interview the pair. As the two officers left their car and walked towards the suspicious vehicle, they noted that it was a Rover. They quickly made a note of its number, and using their personal radio immediately checked it against the police national computer; they were instantly informed that the registration plates displayed by the Rover had been allocated to a Skoda vehicle, so the Rover was being used with false plates.

Before the officers had finished interviewing Sutcliffe, they knew they were going to arrest him on the basis of this information. When questioned, Sutcliffe admitted stealing the number plates from a scrapyard. He was taken into custody and charged with that offence.

He was also interviewed by a member of the Ripper murder squad, but even a day and a half later it was still not realized that he was the murderer they were seeking. Yet, over the years, enough information had been collected by the squad to make him a major suspect; he had, in fact, been interviewed by members of the squad on nine different occasions. Now, if all the information then available had been put on a computer at murder control, these interviewing detectives would have had a facility similar to that simple car registration check carried out by the arresting officers. The squad would have known, at a slightly later stage, that Sutcliffe had been one of the 5,000 or so people interviewed about the suspect £5 note; that he answered the general description given by survivors of his attacks; that he took size eight and a half in shoes, corresponding with those left at the scene; that he had driven one of the makes of car listed, a Corsair, and that he had been spotted thirty-nine times in the red-light districts. Without computerized help, the amount of paper work was overwhelming and the likelihood of quick coordination that much less possible.

Although the Ripper enquiry was closed with Sutcliffe's conviction, the matter has not rested. The writer of the letters and the evil orator on the tape are still sought. They may be one and the same man or they may not. Somebody knows. All forces recognized that there were many lessons to be learned and to this end much detailed work has been going on at high level. What had in the past been a good system, serving us well, was found disastrously wanting.

Computerization has been implemented and co-ordinated throughout all the big forces in this country. It is adaptable and can be updated as required. Enormous sums of money have had to be spent, but the saving in manpower and greater efficiency will make it all worth the trouble. The presence of even a small computer from the beginning would have made an enormous difference to the whole Ripper enquiry. It would have saved manpower, time and materials, and might also have saved life.

Very few officers join the force after having a first-class education, though the number who do is increasing. However, most have received education in the university of life. They can profit from mistakes, and I have no doubt that the next generation of bobbies will become accustomed to using computers. A further thought occurs to me: if you were now to ask the officers who laboured on that vital, but boring, £5 note enquiry, I bet quite a lot of them could still quote its number!

Mass murderers surface regularly all over the world,

though of course this kind of killer is not as common as those who cause but a single death. Most multiple killers are psychopaths, which is not mental deficiency in the way most people understand it. The law in relation to abnormality is complex. A brief explanation of psychopathy is that the person is morally defective. He or she knows that what is being done is wrong, but is simply not interested in that aspect. Pursuance of will is the most important thing to the psychopath, and quite often a crusade of a supposedly moral kind is being carried out, such as a hatred of prostitutes and a desire to rid the world of them. There can be a fixation on girls with long hair, redheads or nurses, or anything equally insubstantial or irrational to the normal mind can provide the impetus. Sadly, the Yorkshire Ripper epitomized this kind of killer.

12

Extensive Enquiries

Manchester City Police Force has existed since 1839. There was policing long before that, of course, and over the decades the matters with which the police have had to deal have been very different from those they deal with now.

The police do not now have responsibility for the collection and disposal of night soil, for street cleansing, gas lighting and other public utilities; nor do they have to accommodate public meetings within their office; and, generally speaking, if a soup kitchen is needed somebody else does it. They still police the markets, but no longer do they have to make arrangements for police processions conveying convicted people to the scene of their hanging. Indeed, we do not hang anybody nowadays, though whether we should again do so will always be a subject for lively debate.

As populations have grown and towns extended, so has the necessity for the wider policing of roads, traffic and the pursuit of criminals. Shortage of accommodation and the proliferation of paper work, plus new developments in technology and the emergence of additional responsibilities have always caused problems.

In its formative years Manchester force headquarters was in the town hall, then situated in King Street. The entrance to the police office was in what is now Police Street at the back of Kendal Milne's old building. In 1877 it was transferred to the new town hall in Albert Square, designed by Alfred Waterhouse. It was there for some sixty years, when in 1937 it moved into a new, purpose-built edifice in South Street, on the other side of the square. This building has a flat roof on two levels, and its purpose was to permit the building of extra floors should it become necessary. It certainly did become necessary, but never came about for reasons of cost and, I am told, some doubt about the strength of the foundation. Incidentally, this flat roof was something of a liability during the war years; incendiary bombs did not roll off it!

It was to this friendly building in South Street that I was transferred in 1956. Even then, office space was at a premium. Because of this the Criminal Record Office and the Finger-print Bureau moved, in 1961, to Longsight police station, which lies between Stockport Road and Plymouth Grove. This building had formerly been an industrial school for Roman Catholic boys, not criminal but in danger of being so if uncared for; most were without parents or had parents unable to look after them. The building is very interesting, despite the changes which have been made to it, and it is nowadays referred to as Colditz.

The accommodation it offered was reasonable enough, but, when Greater Manchester Police was created in 1974, other plans had to be put into action; the need for more space for the greater territorial area to be catered for became even more pressing. Early in 1979 police headquarters was moved to its present site at Chester House, an eleven-storey office block near Old Trafford cricket ground.

On Tuesday 29 May 1979, the building was to be officially opened by HRH Princess Anne and, as the Finger-print Bureau and Scenes-of-Crime Department were considered to be operational, it had been arranged that the Princess should spend at least twenty minutes there talking to members of staff. It was in the midst of last-minute preparations that a telephone call informed me of a vicious murder which had occurred at Radcliffe, and requested my attendance there.

In most countries of the Western world householders receive regular callers. In Britain the milkman is almost a social worker, keeping in regular touch with his customers, many of whom are housebound and elderly. Then there's the young paper girl or boy, the person who pushes leaflets through doors, the window-cleaner, the postman or postwoman, numerous salesmen, and the gas- and electricity-meter readers. Few of us remain unvisited by *bona fide* callers. Therefore, it is likely that, if illness or a worse disaster has befallen somebody in a house, the fact may be discovered by a regular caller. So it was in the case I am about to relate.

In Unsworth Street, Radcliffe, Lancashire, there is a small bungalow in a complex of old people's homes. At about 7.40 on the morning of 29 May 1979, twelve-year-old Rachel Tatton was delivering newspapers and, as she reached the door of number 51, she saw it was open. Many people might be up and about on a bright May morning at this early hour, but Mrs Griffiths, whose house it was, was not one of them and the child was naturally curious. She was also resourceful. She opened the door wider, threw in a magazine and shouted, 'Paper!' There was no reply, so she called out, 'Are you all right?' There was no answer to this either. She moved to the front window of the bungalow, but could not see inside because the curtains were closed. She went back to the front door and then opened the inner door. There, lying on the floor of the living room, the youngster saw Mrs Griffiths; she was dead.

Rachel Tatton saw enough to be able to say that Mrs

Griffiths was lying on her back, appeared to be partially undressed, had a cushion over her face and on this cushion was a knife. Naturally, the girl was frightened and she ran to get help.

People are drawn into the net of a murder investigation in curious ways. Two men, Edward Ronald Davison and David Arthur McAngus, were meeting nearby with the intention of travelling to work together. Rachel attracted their attention and both men went with her, entering the house far enough to confirm what the girl had said to them. They did not touch anything, but merely looked into the room. They went to call the police and were fortunate enough to flag down a passing police car, driven by Police Constable Frank Lucas, who went to the scene, made sure nothing further was disturbed and called senior officers.

Mrs Griffiths was an eighty-six-year-old widow who lived alone in this small community for elderly people. About eighteen months previously a stroke had left her handicapped and she could move about only with the aid of a Zimmer walking frame. She was the kind of old lady it is hard not to admire, being of independent spirit and managing to do most of her own housework. She had a home help, and her family visited weekly and assisted with shopping. However, she remained housebound unless somebody could give her a lift in a car.

She had held on to the religious habits of a lifetime, supporting her local church. Other members of the congregation called fairly often and a clergyman called occasionally to give her Holy Communion. Others helped her by reading items from the newspapers and the like. Each Saturday her son, Alan, called in his car and took her to his home for the day. Whilst Mrs Griffiths was old and infirm, she was certainly not abandoned and, as so many people kept in touch with her, one imagines she was a jolly nice old lady who still had something to contribute to those younger around her.

At the age of eighty-six it is not surprising the old lady was a creature of habit. To save herself undue effort she would leave her front door open during the hours of daylight, enabling friends to get in easily. She would close her door when darkness fell, or by about eight o'clock each evening, whichever came earliest. Having closed her front door on the Yale-type lock, she would then protect herself doubly by fixing a chain in a retaining hold.

The back door of the house was secured with a mortice lock. To reinforce this she would put a broom, with its head under the door lock and the end of the handle in the well provided for the door mat. This is an old local custom and can prove quite effective in resisting entry from outside. If the brush does eventually fall it can make something of a clatter, perhaps a deterrent in itself.

Once she had locked herself in for the night, she was extremely reluctant to open the door, and even relatives had to shout to persuade her to open the front door for them. In all this she showed a fair amount of good sense for an old lady living alone, and it seems unlikely that she would have admitted anyone after she had locked her home up on the Monday night.

Mrs Griffiths had last been seen alive about 2.30 P.M. on Sunday 27 May, when her son, Alan, and his wife had been to see her. They had stayed about half an hour and, having satisfied themselves that she was in her usual good health and spirits, they went. Alan Griffiths does not smoke and his wife may have smoked one cigarette whilst she was there. I mention this because the fact later became important. The old lady was not seen at all after this time, until young Rachel, the newspaper girl, found her body.

Rachel's sister, Victoria Tatton, was fifteen years old in 1979 and she delivered the evening papers in Unsworth Street, Radcliffe. On Monday 28 May, which was a public holiday, at about 4.20 P.M. she delivered the *Manchester Evening News* to Mrs Griffiths's home. She says the front door was open as usual, but that the inner door was closed; she threw the paper inside the vestibule and says she heard a shuffling noise inside, which almost certainly was Mrs Griffiths making her way to the door to collect the paper.

It therefore seems that the old lady met her death between 4.20 P.M. on 28 May and the time when she was found, which was 7.40 A.M. on Tuesday 29 May. The medical evidence indicated she actually died at about 10 P.M. on the Monday night.

So far little has been said about Mrs Griffiths's actual injuries. A murdered body is usually a pretty pathetic sight, that of an old person or a child even more so. This was no exception.

She was clothed and lying with a pillow beneath her bottom and a cushion over her head. On top of this cushion was the blood-stained breadknife seen by the paper girl. Her throat had been cut, there were lacerations to her face, bruises on her forehead and chin, and later forensic examination confirmed police opinion that she had been subjected to sexual intercourse. The house had been completely ransacked, suggesting an initial motive of robbery. You will recall that the front door was open, but the back door was firmly locked on the inside; entrance and exit had clearly been by the front door.

Mrs Griffiths's family and friends did not pry much into her affairs, because they respected her privacy.

Consequently it was not possible to establish what, if anything, had been stolen from the house. Hidden in different parts of the house and quite near to the body in some instances, various sums of money totalling about £250 were recovered. Whilst the murderer had not found this, there was evidence which indicated that he had probably exercised reasonable care when ransacking the house, for not only was a man's glove found but also the matching glove was found some distance from the house, wrapped in a tea towel which had clearly come from the murder scene.

Also wrapped in this tea towel was a woman's glove which could not be identified as having belonged to Mrs Griffiths. Near the house was found a partly burned candle and a large box of matches. There was clear evidence in the house of a search by means of a lighted candle, because traces of candle wax were found on the body. Importantly, a number of cigarette ends were also found in the house.

Later, the post-mortem examination revealed more than was evident at first sight. The old lady had died because of the wounds to her throat, and asphyxiation. The doctor said twenty separate cuts had been made. This was not the whole of her suffering. Her forehead and chin bruises seemed to have been caused by blows, perhaps from a fist, and it is likely that the fracture of two ribs had been caused when rape was taking place. That was not all. A gag had been pushed down her throat to such an extent that it reached the area where the cuts had been made. She would not have been able to breathe in any event because of this gag, but if, as seems likely, the throat wound was inflicted immediately after, this may have provided her with the means of getting air, though not enough to sustain life in view of her injuries.

This was a foul, horrible crime without mitigating circumstances. To say the killer behaved like an animal is to be unfair to the animal kingdom. He left her for dead, and she probably lived out her last few minutes around 10 P.M. on 28 May.

Extensive police enquiries resulted in a rough description of a man who might have been involved in the murder. He seemed to be between twenty-five and thirty years old, five feet six or seven inches tall, of slim build, with dark shoulder-length hair, and a thin face with a blemish on the right cheek. He was dressed in a dark anorak and trousers.

Considerable publicity was given to this word-picture in Bury, Radcliffe and Bolton, and no fewer than five possible sightings emerged, all adding to a more complete pattern of movement. Our man had been careful enough to wear gloves at the murder scene, but from the sightings, which I will detail in a moment, it is clear that the pressure of guilt was becoming too much for him, and he was behaving as human beings do under pressure, irrationally.

The first sighting was at 4.45 P.M. on Monday the 28th, when a man answering the description called at the home of a verger of St Thomas's Church, Radcliffe. The verger sensed he was a scrounger and, when the caller asked if he could see the vicar, he was directed to the home of the curate. The direction of the curate's house was down Pilkington Road and Unsworth Street, where Mrs Griffiths lived.

The second sighting was some forty minutes later, when Peter John Holden was driving past the Unsworth Street houses and saw a man of this description standing nearby. Mr Holden thought the man looked rather suspicious, but, as he was on his way to work, he dismissed the matter from his mind until publicity revived it.

The next sighting was at 12.10 A.M. on Tuesday 29 May, by which time Mrs Griffiths was dead. A man fitting the description called at 25 Unsworth Street, the home of Norman Slingsby, who was in bed. His younger brother was watching television and the light was on in the living room. You will appreciate that this house is in the same street as Mrs Griffiths's.

The caller said he was working in the area and had just had a message that his wife had been taken to hospital to have a baby; needing a taxi rather urgently, he asked to use the telephone. Slingsby tried several taxi firms, but could not find anybody prepared to turn out and himself refused an offer of £2 to take the man to Farnworth. Eventually Bank Street Taxis of Bolton was contacted. The caller gave the name Alan Thompson and asked to be taken to Manchester Royal Infirmary, which normally does not accept maternity cases.

The younger Mr Slingsby wisely refused to allow the caller to wait for the taxi in his home and suggested that he should walk to the bottom of the road and wait outside the Turf Hotel on Bolton Road, where a taxi driver had been asked to pick him up. Brian Woolfall was the taxi driver.

About 12.20 the same morning a young man, Ralph Lowe, was walking home past the Turf Hotel, when he was approached by the man described, who asked him if he knew any local taxi firms. Ralph walked from the Turf Hotel into Radcliffe with this man, but became somewhat apprehensive, and was relieved to part company with him in the vicinity of Radcliffe town hall, where he directed the man to a taxi office.

In the meantime, Brian Woolfall of Bank Street Taxis

drove along Bolton Road towards Radcliffe town centre
and passed the Turf Hotel without realizing he had
actually done so. He saw the man described walking
along the main road towards Manchester. He slowed
down and, before he could speak to the man and ask him
where the Turf Hotel was, the man said, 'Bank Street?'
Woolfall relied, 'Thompson?' and the man said, 'Yes',
and climbed into the front passenger seat.

Woolfall says the man asked to be taken to Piccadilly
in Manchester. Clearly, he was the man who had used
the telephone at 25 Unsworth Street. There was some
desultory conversation, during which the man said he had
been a shot blaster in a foundry, his wife was having a
baby, he had another child aged two whom his mother
was looking after – and his wife was in Townleys Hospital.

The mention of Townleys Hospital is significant. It
indicates someone accustomed to living in the Bolton
area, because outside Bolton the hospital is known by its
proper name, the Bolton and District General. Only local
people still refer to it as Townleys. Brian Woolfall thought
it strange the man should ask to be taken to Manchester,
if his wife was in Townleys. The man also told Brian that
he smoked forty-five cigarettes a day.

Woolfall eventually dropped his customer in the centre
of Piccadilly, Manchester, and by this time it was 1 A.M.
on Tuesday. You will now understand that the suspect
had been directed by the verger past Mrs Griffiths's
home, and had, presumably after killing her, called on
Slingsby in the same street to get a taxi to take him into
Manchester. This likely string of events was given wide
press publicity.

Our man was seen again, this time at 5.40 A.M. on the
same Tuesday, not a time, even in May, when many
people are up and about. David Hughes and William

Dudson were standing at a bus stop in Rochdale Road, Blackley, some miles from Radcliffe, when they were approached by a man who asked them the way to Bolton. They told him as best they could, whilst they were doing so, a taxi which had apparently dropped a fare nearby came back into the main Rochdale Road. The man flagged down the taxi, got in and was driven away. The driver, subsequently traced, said the man asked to be taken to Bolton and said he had come from Bradford, an inner suburb of industrial Manchester. He directed the driver to a part of Bolton and paid £5 for the journey.

A few hours after this sighting, the investigating officers were joined at Mrs Griffiths's house by Dr Abendstern, Bury divisional police surgeon, along with Home Office pathologist, Dr Woodcock, and a team from the North-West Forensic Science Laboratory at Euxton, near Chorley, headed by Dr Briggs. A finger-print team also attended, though I was not with them at first, because I was conducting Princess Anne on her visit to the Fingerprint Bureau.

It is somewhat disheartening to find at an early stage in an enquiry that the culprit has been wearing gloves. The surfaces touched by the killer in Mrs Griffiths's home showed glove impressions only, no finger-prints.

However, as the old lady had been subjected to sexual assault, the experienced scenes-of-crime man knows that during such an assault the assailant is more than likely to remove his gloves. You will appreciate, therefore, that the best chance of finding finger-prints is close to the body. A few inches to the right of Mrs Griffiths's body was a leatherette armchair and on the arm of it was a portion of a right palm print. Near her head was a tiled fire-place; on both bottom and top tiles of this, right and left palm prints were found. The positions of the palm impressions on the fireplace and the armchair made us believe the murderer had put his hands on them when rising from the floor. The palm prints on the fireplace were powdered and photographed. The chair was later removed to the photographic department at police headquarters for the best possible photograph to be produced.

After an examination of the murder scene, I accompanied the finger-print team to the home of Mr Slingsby, where enquiries had turned up the fact that a man, suspected of having been involved in the killing, had called in the early hours of that morning to use the phone to call a taxi. No outstanding finger-prints were found, but on the telephone handset itself was a small bloodstain, later found to be of the same blood group as Mrs Griffiths.

It was now time for patient searching to begin in the Bureau. It was vital to trace the owner of the palm prints. At the Manchester Bureau finger-prints are filed according to a classification system which allows for the easiest possible search, but in 1979 palm prints, for the most part those of people convicted of breaking offences, were filed according to the surname of the person concerned. It was the task of the Bureau staff to check the palm prints found at the scene of the murder with those of people named as possible suspects.

This naming of suspects is done on the basis of personal knowledge, a criminal's likely habits and personality, and his possible presence in the area. The quality of the plam prints were not good from the experts' point of view and, because of the large number of suspects given to the Bureau staff, the checking was a long and difficult exercise. Then came the break one always hopes for.

On the 19th of June there came a call from a new direction. A vicar's wife in a vicarage on Chorley New

Road, Bolton, reported that at some time during the day a thief had entered her home through an unlocked door and had stolen cash and hi-fi equipment. As she was in another part of the vicarage at the time she had not seen or heard anything. As things turned out, she was possibly very lucky. Had she seen the intruder, she might well have been violently attacked.

Detective Constable Wilkinson, an experienced scenes-of-crime officer attached to Bolton division, went out to the vicarage to conduct a routine examination. On a cash box he found a left-middle finger-print which he forwarded to the Bureau for identification. At that point nobody realized its significance.

Then came another link, though we did not realize it at the time. In the early hours of Wednesday 20 June 1979, a twenty-two-year-old nurse was asleep in her room at the Nurses' Home, Bolton Royal Infirmary. The infirmary is close to the burgled vicarage and at the time there were alterations and repairs in progress, for which a certain amount of scaffolding had been erected. The nurse's bedroom window was near the scaffolding and she had left it open. She woke to find a man standing by her bed. He was naked and armed with a knife with which he threatened her. She was raped twice. The rapist stayed with this young nurse until daybreak. He talked, and smoked cigarette after cigarette. He walked about, stealing property from the room and removing his finger-prints with a cloth as he did so. Indeed, he took the greatest care to wipe any and every surface which he may have touched. As daylight came, he held the knife close to the girl and forced her to show him the way out of the building, which she was very thankful to do.

Immediately the police were informed and a thorough examination of the nurse's bedroom was conducted by

Detective Sergeant Blackburn and by Detective Constable Wilkinson, who had attended the vicarage a few hours previously.

Rape is a nasty crime and one which gets a fair amount of publicity, not only when it is committed but also as an emotive subject of discussion. It is a difficult incident to deal with. Victims are often acutely distressed, and searching personal questions have to be asked. In this case the rapist seemed to have done just about everything he could think of to remove from the scene any print he might have left.

However, he had not been vigilant enough. On the outside window ledge, at the point of entry, the detectives found the finger-prints they were looking for. A few more enquiries revealed that an empty room near the nurse's bedroom had been entered. It, too, contained finger impressions left by the intruder. These prints were photographed and the results were examined at the Bureau. This last attack on the nurse proved one too many.

The finger-prints from the infirmary were compared with the one from the vicarage; they belonged to the same person. Fortunately these prints were of good quality. Even if only part of a finger-print is available, we still need, for court purposes, not fewer than sixteen points of identification. Another bonus was that these prints were of an unusual pattern, enabling the search to be quick. They were identified as belonging to Derek Pendlebury, a twenty-eight-year-old labourer living in Bolton.

A number of things began to tie up. We had identified a violent man, with a Bolton connection, who was known to visit the homes of vicars, and was a heavy smoker; he could be the man we were searching for in connection with the murder of Mrs Griffiths. The palm prints of

Pendlebury, a known 'breaker', were taken from the files and compared with the palm prints at the murder scene. They were the same: we had found our man.

Derek Pendlebury was arrested at 7.50 P.M. on 21 June 1979 at his brother-in-law's home, and told he was being arrested on suspicion of burglary. He did not raise any objection to going with the arresting officers, but, when he realized he was not going to a police station in Bolton, he asked where he was being taken. When told Bury, he said, 'Murder? Bury? I've never been in Bury!'

Apart from being violent and something of a con-man, what sort of man was he really? An evil man, of low intelligence, although cunning, who had numerous convictions for crime. He had formed an association with a girl and had married her three months before the commission of this crime. A child of this association was six months old at the time and placed in care. Pendlebury and his young wife had been leading a stormy existence and had no properly settled address. He gave as his home address a house only recently allocated to them, and there was no furniture in it. It was a strange and trammelled life.

The bus station in Bolton town centre provided shelter, and it was there that these two met people from whom they hoped to scrounge meals and overnight accommodation if possible. Pendlebury often visited clergymen in their rectories, vicarages and presbyteries, and was a dab hand with a sob story, though in the Bolton area he had more than outstayed his welcome, because he had not hesitated to steal from vicarages when the opportunity arose.

Being known to local detectives, his name had been thrown up, with many others, in the first few days of the enquiry. He was interviewed on Wednesday 13 June, by two detective officers. Naturally, there are tactics in dealing with suspects. Even if the police know that a person was murdered at a certain moment, a suspect is not asked to say where he was at that particular time; several hours, or even days, might be covered in the questioning. That way discrepancies come to light, and lies and evasions are more easily detected.

You will remember that Mrs Griffiths's body was discovered by the girl delivering morning papers on 29 May, and it was two weeks after this when he was being questioned about his movements on the 28th and 29th. Yes, he knew where he had been on Monday the 28th. He had visited Pioneer Mill, Radcliffe, to collect wages for a half day he had worked there. He had returned to Bolton and in the evening had been drinking in a couple of pubs. He was asked for the names of witnesses who could support his alibi.

Great care has to be taken in checking alibis. Sometimes witnesses lie deliberately to protect an accused person. Sometimes what they have to say is what they believe to be true, but is not in fact so. In this case Pendlebury distinctly recalled where he had been on the night of the 28th. Somewhat colourfully he remembered he and his wife had had a fight outside the Trotters public house. He said his wife would confirm this.

The alibi evidence of relatives and interested parties has to be treated with caution. On the face of it Pendlebury could not have been in Radcliffe on the Monday evening if he was fighting with his wife outside a Bolton hotel. Pendlebury's name had been forwarded to the Bureau by the interviewing detectives, but, as the result of his apparent alibi, had been given low priority as a possible suspect and his name had been put to the bottom of the list of persons to be checked against the palm prints found at the murder scene.

At Bury police station he was interviewed at some length by Detective Superintendent Drury, an experienced and capable investigator, who already knew that the arrested man's palm impressions had been identified at Mrs Griffiths's home and his finger-prints in Bolton, where the nurse had been raped.

Whilst the interview was taking place, Pendlebury's nineteen-year-old wife was traced and brought to the police station. She quickly retracted any support she had until then given to her husband's alibi. She said she had agreed to say what Pendlebury had asked her to because he had already told her he was worried and could not remember where he was on the 28th – a classic case of *qui s'excuse, s'accuse*.

June Pendlebury was co-operative when her husband was arrested and made a statement saying he was not with her during this fatal Monday evening. Indeed, she went further than that, describing how, when she next saw him, he had minor injuries to his face and that his left arm appeared to be troubling him. He had explained this away by saying he had been attacked by a group of young lads.

Pendlebury's interrogation did not bring any admissions. He emphatically denied having been to Mrs Griffiths's home and was equally sure he had not raped the young nurse. But, having now realized that his wife had ruined his original alibi, he came up with a second. He said he had been in Manchester during the evening of Monday the 28th, in Papa's Club.

In his new alibi he involved a married couple who, to say the least, were extremely odd. They knew Derek Pendlebury well enough, because he had stayed at their house on several occasions. Their oddities were not a part of the enquiry and need not be detailed here, but

Derek Pendlebury was well aware that the woman had some strange ways and was completely unreliable, so that if he said he was with her at a particular time she would be quite likely to confirm it, because her ideas of time were somewhat elastic. However, the husband's evidence was a little more sensible and, in the event, did Derek Pendlebury more harm than good.

It was decided that an identification parade should be held. Most people imagine that a number of people of the same sex are stopped in the street and asked to join, and that the suspect is put somewhere along the line and the witnesses are brought in. Not so, there are strict procedures to be followed. Efforts have to be made to get eight people of similar age, height and general way of life. In other words, if we are looking for a scruffy twenty-one-year-old, the manager of the local bank would not be invited to join. Strict arrangements are made so that no witness can see the parade beforehand, speak to another witness, or go back and have a second look. Witnesses are asked to go up and touch any person they identify. Sometimes, in cases of assault, witnesses are reluctant to do this. The suspect can stand anywhere in the line he wishes, and change position between the visits of the witnesses, who come in one at a time. All these changes, if they occur, are noted on the official form, and all actions and comments a witness may make are noted also. Those in the line-up may be asked to make certain movements or repeat phrases, according to the nature of the case. A correctly carried out identification parade takes careful organization and the attention of several uniformed officers.

The identification parade in which Pendlebury was present did not have entirely satisfactory results. He was not picked out by the church verger or by the man who allowed him to telephone from his home. The witness who saw a man outside Mrs Griffiths's house did not pick him out, nor did the taxi driver who took him to Manchester. The man who met him outside the Turf Hotel and accompanied him towards a taxi office picked him out without hesitation. One of the two men who had been waiting at the bus stop on the Tuesday morning picked out Pendlebury without hesitation; however, the other did not pick him out at all. The second taxi driver, who took him from Blackley to Bolton, picked him out. The nurse who had been raped was sure, absolutely sure. So, five did not identify him, and four did. Not ideal, but good enough.

For some time Pendlebury went on telling lies and trying to justify his actions, to the extent that his solicitor became acutely embarrassed.

Significant throughout the conduct of the case was Pendlebury's constant need to smoke, in particular Chesterfields. He was unwilling to talk even to his solicitor without a packet of cigarettes for comfort. There were Chesterfield stubs in Mrs Griffiths's house, and forensic tests showed that Pendlebury could have been the one who smoked them. Medical tests on the nurse and Pendlebury were equally convincing.

Even awaiting trial, he did not give up. He tried all sorts of tricks to fix the blame on somebody else, but of course none of this worked.

Pendlebury was later found guilty of the offences with which he was charged and sentenced to life imprisonment.

13

A Year and a Day

Television shows, literature and films from the United States have made us familiar with the term 'homicide squad'. In Britain the term is 'murder squad'. Nevertheless, in this country homicide is legally defined as the killing of a human being by a human being. Such killing can be lawful or unlawful.

Lawful or justifiable homicide occur, for example, when a person is sentenced to death and is duly executed, or when an officer of the peace kills someone whilst in the lawful execution of his duty, for instance in a riot. Homicide can also be lawful when a person is killed at sport or when a surgical operation, carefully performed though it was, has gone wrong.

Unlawful homicide can be further classified as murder, manslaughter, infanticide or causing death by dangerous driving.

To murder is to kill a person unlawfully, under the Queen's Peace, with malice aforethought, the death to occur within a year and a day. This time factor is most important. Under English law, if a person is wounded and death occurs beyond this period of a year and a day, it will be presumed that the death was due to some cause other than the act of the person accused of the wounding. Application of this particular point can sometimes appear to be unfair, and the following case is an example of this. It is of such a nature that it will remain a long time in the memories of those who were concerned.

The south side of Manchester within five miles of the

city centre was an area of landed gentry in the seventeenth, eighteenth and nineteenth centuries. In 1764 Platt Hall, Rusholme, was built at a cost of £10,000. It is an elegant, though plain, structure, still new-looking because the bricks were soaked in oil before use. It now houses the lovely gallery of English costume and is surrounded by what was earlier a private park, which became a public park in the early part of the twentieth century. It acquired three lakes (to provide work for the unemployed), one for boating, one for model yachts and a paddling pool. Like all public parks, it became important for the local people, although in the last twenty years its use has changed somewhat as greater numbers of families have acquired cars and have sought recreation further afield. The park is now used for an annual show, which has become famous nationwide, and in recent years Manchester's Ideal Home Exhibition has been held in Platt Fields.

In 1980 the Ideal Home Exhibition was held towards the end of April. Josef Rauter, an Austrian, and Josef Eckert, a German national, were visitors to England, employees of a Munich-based catering company. There were plenty of local catering services, of course, but nowadays, following the expansion of continental travel, novelty and variety are demanded and so it was thought that a Bavarian beer garden would encourage attendance.

With other members of their team, the two Josefs were booked in at the Elton Bank Hotel in Platt Lane, across the road from the Fields. Josef Rauter was a chef and Josef Eckert, the son of a country farmer, had trained as a master butcher. The whole team were quite young and probably much enjoying this trip abroad.

Perhaps it is not strange that having worked hard all day catering for others, they chose to spend their recreational time going round a few clubs in the city on the Saturday night, sampling Manchester's various ales, night-life, and no doubt weighing up the activities of its citizens. They had probably had quite a lot to drink by the time they left the New Pigalle Club in Whitworth Street at 1 A.M. on Sunday, when they got a taxi and went straight back to the Elton Bank Hotel, where they shared a ground-floor bedroom. Their two single beds were along one wall, with the two footends together. They went to bed and, probably because of the liquor they had drunk, were soon sound asleep and no trouble to anyone.

These two young men were not, of course, the only ones who had spent their Saturday night enjoying themselves. About half a mile away from Platt Fields and the Elton Bank Hotel is Genevieve's Club. This has for many years been the haunt of teenagers and people in their early twenties, providing disco music and a bar. At Genevieve's on Saturday 26 April 1980 were Paul Gerrard Burns, a twenty-one-year-old postman, and his friend Simon Charles, a nineteen-year-old boy who lived with his mother. Simon Charles was well known to local police as a burglar and a young man of some violence.

At the club they each had drunk several pints of beer. On leaving, they decided to walk to Charles's home, which was not far from Burns's home. The route took them along Platt Lane. As they passed the Elton Bank Hotel Charles stopped and said, 'Let's do this flat.' That simple decision to burgle what was not in fact a flat, but a hotel bedroom, led to the tragedy.

It is as well to note that the large amount of beer each of those young men drank in Genevieve's was not their first alcoholic drink that day. Earlier in the evening both had been drinking in the Parkside Hotel in Fallowfield, quite near their homes, only going to Genevieve's at closing time with friends.

When an unlawful act results in tragedy it is common for those involved to become desperate and cover their tracks with a myriad of lies. The account of this night's events was no different, and it became a matter of weighing up likely truth against likely lies.

Having suggested to Burns that they should burgle what he thought was a flat, Charles then went down a side street and round to the back of the hotel, where he climbed over the rear wall. Burns went up the garden path to the front of the hotel and waited for Charles to come through and open the door, evidently having complete confidence in his companion's ability to get in. When Charles opened the front door, in went Burns.

First they went into the television lounge, on the right of the hallway as one enters. After spending some time searching this room and finding little which interested them beyond the television itself, which of course was bulky and heavy, they went into the bedroom nearby in which the two Bavarian caterers were fast asleep.

For the moment unconcerned about the two sleeping men, they searched the room. Burns looked under the beds, whilst Charles was going through their clothes. Charles, the experienced burglar, realized that Burns's plastic anorak was making swishing noises as he moved. Aware that this could waken somebody not heavily asleep, he told Burns to get out of the bedroom, which he did, standing at the door to receive various items of clothing and two suitcases which Charles passed out to him.

They both spent some time looking at what was in the suitcases and Charles produced from one of them a knife, which he handed to Burns. Burns said he put this knife down in the television room a few moments later; it was one of a set of chef's equipment which Josef Rauter had put in his suitcase under his bed when he had finished work, before he and Eckert had set out for their night on the town.

The two intruders stole several items of value, small and easy to carry, some English, German and Austrian currency, and some papers. Their stories as to what happened at this point differ considerably and it is just as well that evidence for charging was not dependent upon their instincts of self-preservaton. It is certain that Charles took hold of the knife which had been put in the television room; Burns said he was going, and his evidence that Charles then said, 'No, let's do it proper,' may well be true. Charles went back into the bedroom and plunged the knife into the head of the sleeping Josef Eckert. Burns says that, whilst he was waiting at the front door, Charles joined him and said, 'I've stabbed him. Let's go.'

Josef Rauter woke, disturbed by voices in the bedroom. He turned over in bed and saw that the bedroom door was open. He thought Eckert had gone to the bathroom. He got out of bed to close it and could see, by the light from the hallway, Eckert lying in bed. A knife was sticking out of his head.

This was the sort of shock for which human beings are not prepared. He ran from the room to raise the alarm, quite unable to say what had happened and not at that point knowing it was his own knife which had been used to maim his workmate.

His natural terror and his lack of knowledge of the English language made the next few hours a horrifying experience for him.

He roused other guests and one of them opened and shut the front door several times to activate a buzzer in the bedroom of the resident manager. When Mr Knowles, the manager, heard the buzzer, he came quickly into the hallway and saw a number of guests, including Rauter, who was wearing only his underpants. Josef was highly distressed and continually pointing to his bedroom. Mr Knowles went into the bedroom and saw Josef Eckert lying there with the knife protruding from his head. He asked a guest to awaken the hotel proprietor, Mr Young. Mr Young came, and with Mr Knowles he witnessed Josef Eckert trying to raise himself from the bed, making guttural sounds as he did so.

The police were called. At 3.17 A.M. Constable Vesey arrived. He saw Eckert raising his hands as though trying to withdraw the knife from his head; he was trying to tell people something in his own language. Other officers arrived and Eckert was taken by ambulance to Manchester Royal Infirmary not far away.

Dr Bamford, house surgeon at the infirmary, immediately alerted Mr Strang, consultant neurosurgeon, on account of the extreme gravity of Eckert's injuries. The end of the knife was lodged on the opposite side of the skull, though the actual tip was never found, despite thorough searching by forensic specialists. Josef was unconscious, but still breathing unaided at this point.

His condition stabilized a little in the coming days, and although full consciousness never returned he did respond a little to speech. He could move his limbs slightly and open his eyes, though normal eye movements were much affected. His speech centre was close to the entry point of the knife and before long he had to be assisted by life-support equipment.

Mr Strang's view was that Josef Eckert would have a serious neurological handicap for the rest of his life; his life expectancy would be severely reduced and he would very likely require long-term institutional care. Events proved this to be an accurate prognosis.

The whole process of a CID major incident investigation had begun immediately. My own part in this began at 8.30 A.M. on the Sunday morning, some five hours after the discovery of the crime, when I went to Elton Bank Hotel to conduct a finger-print examination.

I saw that the bathroom transom window at the rear of the building was open and the security bar hanging loose outside the window. Such windows tend to be forgotten when locking up for the night, and it was particularly unfortunate in this case. It seemed to me that someone had gained access via the window, climbing up a soil pipe to reach the window-sill. On the soil pipe, ten feet from the ground, was a perfect thumb print. It seemed to be freshly made and had probably been carelessly put there by the intruder. Had it been made earlier, perhaps by a house painter or a window cleaner, it would have not been in such pristine condition; wind and weather dry and erode the perspiration which causes most prints.

We cut out this section of the pipe and took it back to headquarters to be examined at the Finger-print Bureau. This precautionary measure was justified when rain started falling almost immediately; had the pipe not been removed the finger-print could have been ruined and lost as evidence.

On the inside of the transom window, at the point of entry, I found a sequence of finger impressions and on the inside of the bathroom door was another sequence made by somebody with dirty hands. These were all treated and photographed.

Detective Chief Inspector Dampier had meanwhile been examining the scene of the attack. Close to the bedroom door were two open suitcases with their contents scattered on the floor, and there amongst the general untidiness were two large knives.

Other members of the Bureau staff took elimination finger-prints of all people who had, at some time, had legitimate reasons for entering the bedroom and the bathroom. Josef Eckert's bed was heavily blood-stained as was the carpet nearby. Many forensic samples were taken by Dr Briggs of the Home Office Forensic Science Laboratory at Chorley, Lancashire, the same day.

In the meantime I was more than a little surprised when, within eight hours of leaving Elton Bank Hotel, I was summoned at 4 A.M. on Monday 28 April, to the scene of a murder outside Jerralea Hotel, Anson Road, Victoria Park. Although in a different police division, it was less than a mile away from Elton Bank Hotel and, in fact, not many yards away from Genevieve's Club, though that did not mean anything at the time. We slowly began to consider the possibility that the two hotel incidents were the work of one person. The CID staffs of the E and D Divisions were being kept busy, and naturally there was complete liaison between senior officers of the two divisional stations.

After Simon Charles had plunged the knife into Josef Eckert's head, he and Paul Burns had collected their stolen property and walked to Charles's home, where Burns stayed a little while and was then taken home in a car by Vincent Charles, Simon's younger brother. This was some time before daylight on Sunday 27 April.

At 2.30 in the afternoon that day two young men, Joseph Lyons and his friend Michael Gregory, were trying to hail a taxi on Princess Road, when the Charles brothers drove up in a car. Vincent was driving. Lyons and Gregory said they wanted to visit the Russell Club in Royce Road, Hulme, and both were given a lift there.

Lyons, Gregory and Simon Charles spent the afternoon drinking in the club. When the senses are clouded by alcohol the truth is apt to come out, and so it was with Simon Charles, who told Lyons that he was responsible for the incident at Elton Bank Hotel.

During that afternoon, still in the club, Charles chatted to a woman. During the conversation he produced an Austrian 100-schilling bank note and claimed to be responsible for the attack at Elton Bank Hotel. The woman was wary of him, but naturally curious, and Simon Charles went on at some length about how it had all happened, saying that delivering the blow was 'like stabbing a melon'. This incident came to police notice on 29 April, shortly after the thought that the two hotel cases were possibly related had occurred to someone else whose actions were to prove crucial.

For the Elton Bank enquiry the incident caravan had been set up in Platt Fields, and at 1.15 on the morning of the 29th, Policewoman Jayne Bond was on duty in the caravan when two men walked in. They were Paul Gerrard Burns and his brother Anthony. Paul immediately admitted being involved in the incident at Elton Bank Hotel. He had heard over the radio about the killing at Jerralea Hotel and knew it was nothing to do with him, but did not know whether Charles was concerned in it. Thinking that Charles was, he began to be afraid for his own sake. Policewoman Bond called other officers and Paul Burns repeated the story of his involvement at Elton Bank Hotel. He was cautioned and arrested on suspicion of wounding and burglary.

The Serious Crime Squad, already heavily involved with both enquiries, took up this part of the affair, and to Detective Inspector Smith and Detective Sergeant Sutton Paul Burns admitted being involved in the burglary, but not in the attack. Property from the caterers' bedroom which had been his part of the share-out was recovered from the home of his brother Anthony.

It was now time to interview Simon Charles. The same two officers went to his home, arrested him on suspicion of involvement and took him to Longsight police station to the Serious Crime Squad offices.

He was questioned, but at first only admitted being involved in the break-in at Elton Bank Hotel. Thieves do fall out and it seemed natural enough for him to blame Burns for the killing, but this façade was soon demolished and he eventually admitted attacking the sleeping Eckert, saying, 'It was like a melon. It made a squelchy sound.' This curious and probably accurate description by Charles is as damning as any one expression could be. His defence for having the knife at all was, 'Just in case someone came down. We could scare them and get away.'

I will remind you that after a certain point Burns's and Charles's stories diverged, each in his own favour. Charles could not say why he had struck Josef Eckert at all; the sleeping man did not pose any threat. He demonstrated how he had done it and again made reference to the thrusting of a knife into a melon. He said Burns was with him when he did it and that they left the bedroom together, but as they reached the front door Burns went back into the bedroom, coming out in a few moments to say, 'I've just wiped the prints off it.'

Charles admitted taking the property and said they shared it out at his home; he burnt some German currency and Eurocheques, leaving the remainder of the stuff in his home, from where it disappeared. He assumed that his mother had heard about the Elton Bank incident and had disposed of the property, protecting her son as mothers will.

Burns was reinterviewed about the discrepancies in the two tales, but little further came of it, though he insisted the share-out of the spoils had been done at the hotel. He denied having wiped any prints off the knife, but nevertheless a finger-print examination of all the knives proved negative.

Over the last ten years co-operation between police forces has grown considerably. Methods of working in serious incidents – be they murder, riots, or hijackings – have been discussed in great detail. One result of this is a certain standardization in procedure. From the outset of such a case, an exhibits officer is appointed. He or she will record, send out, recover and release all exhibits from whatever source. Their comings and goings, whether to laboratory, court, or for submission to witnesses, are written down. In the Greater Manchester Police Force exhibits are usually tagged with the initials of the person, be it a civilian witness or an officer, who first raises the item, and if it should happen that two people have the same initials then an adjustment is made. Each label is signed by the witness who will testify to it in court if required.

Inevitably, the finger-prints taken from Simon Charles on the official form, signed by him as required, matched with those found on the soil pipe, on the unlocked bathroom window and on the bathroom door. All were eventually produced along with other exhibits at the trial, and the individual finger-print officers testified to their evidence.

The innocent people caught up in the events at Jerralea Hotel in the early hours of Monday 28 April 1980 must have been just as appalled as those at Elton Bank Hotel.

The Jerralea and the New Jerralea are two hotels near

each other and run by two partners. Each hotelier adjusts to his trade and in one area there is a greater need for bedrooms during the week and in the other greater need at weekends. At weekends the New Jerralea is closed on Fridays, Saturdays and Sundays. On Sunday 27 April there were six guests in the Jerralea. At least one of them had come from London specially for a conference which was to be held there on the 28th.

One guest, Mr Crook, had experienced a hiccup in his travel arrangements and during the evening of Sunday, the 27th, he telephoned from London to say he would not be at the hotel until after 2 A.M. on Monday, the 28th. He spoke to a man who identified himself as the night porter. This night porter was William Hanlon, fifty-four years old, separated from his wife and living with his son in Gorton, Manchester. He had been employed at the hotel since April 1979, at first as a kitchen porter and then as night porter three months later. He was of good character and his employer regarded him as reliable. In build he was somewhat stocky, tending to portliness, and was about five feet eight inches tall.

William Hanlon had duties at both hotels, though they were relatively simple. He had to secure both sets of premises after 11 P.M., tidy the lounge area and pay particular attention to each building's general security. On the Sunday night in question his duties were only at the Jerralea, the New Jerralea being closed for the weekend. This particular evening he was due to begin work at 9 P.M., but arrived before half past eight to relieve the weekend manager, Mr Hitchen, who then locked up the beer cellar and bar, locked the keys in a metal cabinet inside the hotel and took the cabinet keys home with him.

Mr Crook's train was late arriving in Manchester, so he

caught a taxi right away and arrived at the Jerralea about
2.45 in the morning. He saw only one other vehicle in
Anson Road, on which the hotel is situated, and he did
not see anybody walking about. The main front doors of
the hotel consist of two sets of double glass doors at the
top of a flight of four steps. He found the outer doors
unlocked and within a doorbell, which he rang. In a short
while a man came to the inner door and opened it. Mr
Crook realized this was the man he had spoken to on the
phone from London, because the fact that he had no
teeth made his voice distinctive. This was William Hanlon.
Once inside, the inner doors were immediately locked.
Mr Crook registered and was directed to room fourteen.
He went up, leaving Mr Hanlon at the reception desk. In
his room Mr Crook made himself a cup of tea, then
retired to bed. He took off his wrist watch and put it on a
bedside table, noting that it was 2.58 A.M..

He went to sleep and was not disturbed, waking naturally at 7.50 the following morning. His evidence thus
confirms that Mr Hanlon was alive and well at 2.45 that
morning.

Another guest, Mr Martin, had stayed there many
times before. He arrived at 6.15 on the Sunday evening.
He had room one on the ground floor, on the left-hand
side of the building looking from Anson Road. The
window in the room overlooks the car park at the side of
the hotel. Before going to bed Mr Martin had a glass of
milk and a single brandy. He opened the window of the
room, climbed into bed and was asleep by about 11.30.

During the night the sound of voices wakened him. He
could not hear exactly what was being said, but realized
that the voices came from outside. He sat up in bed and
clearly heard one voice shout, 'Clear off, clear off! Help,
help! Police!' The shouting was loud and distinct. He

switched on a small fluorescent tube light on the bed head and got out of bed. He went to the window and looked out, being able to see clearly, because the street lighting is good on Anson Road. He could not spot anything untoward and left the window after half a minute or so, sat on the edge of the bed and lit a cigarette. It was shortly after 3 A.M., certainly not more than five minutes past. He got back into bed, switched off the light and settled down again to sleep.

Within minutes he heard more voices coming from outside the hotel. He went again to the window and looked out, seeing, this time, a man standing in the car park. The man shouted something to him. Mr Martin put on a coat and went through the hotel foyer, where he saw the doors were open. On the forecourt was a police officer and near him an ambulance. Lying there on the floor, in a pool of blood, was the night porter Mr Hanlon.

The few minutes between Mr Crook's arrival at 2.45 A.M., and his departure to bed, and 3.10 A.M., when Mr Martin was disturbed for the second time, had been full of dreadful happenings. This next part of the story comes from Mr and Mrs Elliott, who live at 4 Milverton Road, and, in fact, it was Mr Elliott who had called to Mr Martin from the car park.

The garden at the rear of the Elliotts' house is separated from the car park at the rear of the Jerralea Hotel by a low wall. They sleep in a first-floor bedroom at the back of their house and the window of this room faces on to the car park at the back and left-hand side of the hotel. They had gone to bed at about 11.30 P.M. and fallen asleep in half an hour or so.

Mrs Elliott awoke some time later to the sound of a man's voice and she thinks she heard the word 'money'. She could hear only one voice and got the impression that the speaker was pleading. Then the tone of the voice changed and she heard the words, 'Help, help, police, police!' shouted urgently. She got out of bed and went to the window. In the car park near the front of the Jerralea Hotel she could see two men. One appeared to be attempting to restrain the other who was advancing slowly towards him. Mrs Elliott was joined at the window by her husband.

The two men moved to the front of the hotel and out of sight of the Elliotts, who heard more shouting. Mrs Elliott heard what she described as a short grunt and then the shouting stopped, but she could hear some heavy snoring.

One of the men then returned into the view of the watching couple. Mrs Elliott continued to watch from the window and her husband went downstairs. She saw the man kicking at something which was on the ground at the front corner of the hotel building. He stood away from the corner and then began kicking at the same place. He stood away from the corner again and soon afterwards walked across the car park towards the rear of the Elliotts' house. He climbed a low wall and trellis fence at the end of the garden of another house, and then disappeared out of sight.

In the meantime, Mr Elliott had dressed and driven his car from the front of his house round to the front of the Jerralea Hotel. He saw Mr Hanlon lying on the ground near the front left corner of the hotel, badly injured. He tried to clear thick blood away from his face; he was still alive. The police were called.

When Sergeant Cochrane arrived it was still only nine minutes past three. Mrs Elliott shouted from her bedroom window to tell her husband that the man she had seen had jumped into the garden of 10 Milverton Road.

The police officers searched. Mr Hanlon was taken to Manchester Royal Infirmary nearby, but was certified dead at 3.35 A.M.

A police dog handler, Constable Clifford, had also arrived. His dog led him directly to 8 Milverton Road, the home of the man eventually charged with the killing, Michael Anthony Pinkney, who was twenty-eight years old. The officer spoke to members of this rather assorted household, though not to the accused.

The well-oiled investigative machinery moved into action and, as I said earlier, I was there at 4 A.M.

A careful search of the scene revealed that on a fall pipe at the rear of the hotel there were smudges and scuff marks consistent with someone having climbed up the pipe to gain access to a bathroom window. Another investigator pointed out to me footprints which had been found in the garden of 10 Milverton Road, into which Mrs Elliott had seen the man disappear. These footprints were protected and later cast in plaster.

On a low, painted stone window-ledge directly over the spot where Mr Hanlon was found dying, I discovered a left thumb print which I treated with powder. Its position was consistent with someone having held the window-ledge to steady himself whilst kicking someone or something on the floor.

You will remember that only some hours earlier I had removed a portion of soil pipe from the rear of Elton Bank Hotel, shortly before rain had begun to fall. The rain had continued, but this beautiful, unmarked thumb print on the window-sill at the Jerralea Hotel had not been spoiled in any way, and I was convinced it had come from the person who had killed the night porter. I instructed that this portion of the stone window-ledge with the thumb print should be cut away so that it could be presented as evidence if the occasion arose. It did and I was relieved that I had had the foresight to make this arrangement.

The portion of stone sill was taken to the Finger-print Bureau at Chester House and the print was photographed. Tracing a single print can take time, but luck was with us. The following day, during the morning, Detective Constable Byford, a finger-print expert, recalled having interviewed a youth from the Milverton Road area some years previously. It was the matter of a few moments to retrieve the relevant finger-print form from the collection and identify this left thumb prints as that of Michael Anthony Pinkney.

Michael Pinkney was arrested on Tuesday 29 April, at the home of his sister in Salford. When interviewed at Longsight police station near Jerralea Hotel, he said he knew why he had been arrested.

His story was that he had walked through the grounds of the hotel, as he had done many times before. It was nearly three o'clock in the morning. A man had sworn at him and grabbed hold of his shoulder. Being very drunk at the time, he took exception to this and struck him in the face with his fist, knocking him to the ground. The man then grabbed his leg, so he kicked him about the head several times. He did not have any other reason for assaulting him and put forward his drunkenness in mitigation of a sort, as his drink had been a mixture of cider and a bottle and a half of Pernod, according to his statement.

The police view was that he was not half as drunk as he wished them to believe, and other witnesses of his evening's activities confirmed this. Also, he had climbed the wall and trellis fence, then jumped into the garden of 10 Milverton Road, easily enough. What is more, he had disposed of all the clothing he was wearing, hiding it in a plastic bag. A big search was carried out around the area where he said he had put it, and much further afield, but it was never found. Not altogether the actions of a very drunken man.

The scuff marks on the fall pipe at the rear of the hotel were unconnected with this incident and were the result of a previous burglary.

Dr Woodcock, the Home Office pathologist, conducted a post-mortem examination. Mr Hanlon had severe head injuries, including a fractured skull and bruising of the brain. Photographs of such injuries are always taken and now that they are done on colour film a much more vivid record is obtained than was possible before.

Pinkney's defence solicitors engaged Dr Julius Grant as a forensic expert. Certainly he had some expertise in paper manufacture and had been used by the Government in the interesting field of false propaganda put out by the German High Command during the Second World War. He was present during the trial. When he heard the evidence from the Manchester Weather Centre about rain on the Sunday afternoon and the unspotted state of that thumb print on the stone window-sill, which was painted, he wisely did not contest it. Without that weather evidence it might have been possible to say that the thumb print could have been made by Pinkney on one of his many previous trips through the hotel grounds. But no, it was a beautifully clear print, unspoiled by weather and atmosphere.

Although an arrest was made quickly in each case, given the coincidence of violent crime at two hotels not far from each other, and the marks on the two vertical pipes, it is no wonder that I thought for a time that both crimes had been committed by one man. Educated guesswork can be a help, but hard facts are needed and in each case we had them through finger-prints and the subsequent gathering of other evidence and admissions of guilt. It was most gratifying that each case was detected within a day or two.

Mr Hanlon had died a short time after being attacked. Pinkney was charged with murder, tried, found guilty and sentenced to life imprisonment.

In the Elton Bank Hotel case Simon Charles was sentenced to ten years' imprisonment on the charge that he 'did unlawfully and maliciously wound Josef Eckert with intent to do him grievous bodily harm'. Paul Gerrard Burns was sentenced to nine months' imprisonment for burglary.

And what of Josef Eckert? The unfortunate man never regained full consciousness; when it was possible to move him, he was returned to his own country, where he died on 16 November 1981, well beyond the legal requirement of a year and a day for his death to be considered as murder. Yet murder it undoubtedly was. Perhaps it can be regarded as one of the exceptions which emphasize the application of the general rule.

Obviously, when severe injury may or may not lead to death, the trial of an accused person cannot be delayed indefinitely, awaiting the outcome. Dividing lines have to be drawn, and in England that line is set at a year and a day.

14

To Err is Human

I often take comfort from the old saying that 'To err is human,' and rather than appear foolish, even to myself, an inclined to ignore the other, which says, 'Wise men learn by other men's mistakes, fools by their own.' In my experience most policemen and probably most criminals learn by a combination of their own and other people's mistakes, and regard this process as valuable experience. When committing crime, many criminals blunder, as can the investigating police officers. Sometimes the errors, if trivial, can be rather amusing, though they may have very serious consequences.

A mistake which assisted the police to convict a killer happened during the Christmas holiday period of 1976. At 4.30 P.M. on Thursday 23 December 1976, Patricia O'Flynn left her place of employment, intending to do some late Christmas shopping on her way home to Eileen Grove West, Rusholme, where she lived with her elder brother, Gerrald. Patricia, who was twenty-nine years old, was of good character and quiet disposition, and she worked as a packer for a Manchester-based mail order firm. Shortly after getting off the bus on Wilmslow Road, Rusholme, she went into a nearby butcher's shop, where she bought the Christmas turkey. She often went to this particular butcher's and it was less than quarter of a mile from her home. At 5.15 that evening Gerrald returned home from work to find the house lights switched on, as was normal for that time of the year. It indicated to Gerrald that Patricia had, as usual, arrived home first and would be getting the evening meal ready, which they always shared.

He walked through the back garden to let himself in by the French window. As he was unlocking the window, he looked into the living-room and saw a man standing by the Christmas tree. As Gerrald was expecting an electrician to call at the house to mend a broken fuse-box, he was not in the least perturbed at seeing this man, but as he opened the French window the man saw him, turned away and ran into the hall. Gerrald started to chase him and was then shocked to see his sister lying in the hall, her face and clothing covered in blood. He chased the intruder out of the house, but almost immediately returned to help his sister, only to find that she was dead. Grief-stricken, he went to a neighbour for help; the police and the ambulance service was summoned. Patricia had been stabbed to death.

At seven that evening I was contacted at home and asked to visit the scene and conduct a finger-print examination. When I got there, I saw Patricia's body lying in the hallway, near the open living-room door. In the living room I could see the Christmas tree with its twinkling lights. Near the tree was a chair and on it were two carrier bags, in one of which was the turkey and in the other Christmas presents.

After the premises had been thoroughly examined and following a discussion with the senior detective who had been conducting the preliminary enquiries, I formed the opinion that Patricia had barely had time to take off her coat after arriving home when she had been summoned to the front door. She had opened the door to her murderer, who had immediately started to attack her. From the evidence of bloodstains and scuff marks it was apparent that the attack had begun at the front door, with Patricia being driven back along the hall by the man, who was repeatedly stabbing at her with a knife. Before he had a chance to search the house and steal anything he had been disturbed by her brother's arrival home. Along the walls on both sides of this narrow passageway, on the door leading to the living room and on the front door through which he had made his escape, the killer had left a trail of bloody glove impressions.

At nine o'clock that evening a neighbour from an adjacent avenue found an anorak hanging from a strand of barbed wire which ran along the top of her fence. She lifted the anorak from the fence and, as she did so, a glove fell out of one of the pockets. Not connecting her discovery with the crime which had occurred, she threw both anorak and glove on to a nearby croft, where they were found the following morning by searching police officers.

The matching glove was found in a pocket of the anorak and, when examined, the anorak and both gloves were found to be badly blood-stained. Enquiries continued and on Christmas morning I was at the incident room which had been established at Longsight police station. An hour earlier, shortly before 10 o'clock that morning, a man and his son, visiting a building site near Claremont Road, Rusholme, had found a knife and sheath which had apparently been thrown over the high perimeter fence of the site. Being aware of the importande of such a find, they had immediately contacted the police. I was asked to look at these articles.

The badly blood-stained knife did not have any fingerprints on it, but after my lack of success at the murder scene my eyes lit up when I looked at the leather sheath because on the back of it was a blood-stained print made by the top of someone's finger. The murderer had made a mistake.

Having taken the precaution of wearing gloves whilst breaking in and killing the woman, he had nevertheless panicked when being chased from the house and had discarded his gloves before throwing away the knife and its sheath. In the process of taking off his anorak and gloves his fingers had become smeared in blood, and later, running past the building site, he had thrown both knife and sheath over the high fence, leaving on the sheath a valuable clue to his identity.

The murder weapon was a deerstalker knife of German manufacture, difficult to trace because 20,000 such knives had been imported into this country. Extensive enquiries were made over the Christmas holiday period to try and trace the brutal killer, and a team of finger-print experts was kept busy endeavouring to identify the blood-stained finger-print. The efforts of the squad came to fruition when, on 29 December, six days after the vicious killing, information was received which implicated Hughie Osborne, a thirty-two-year-old married man living on a council estate to the north-east of Manchester. Osborne was seen by detectives at his home. He denied being involved in the murder and was taken to the murder control room for further questioning. He persisted in his denial. His finger-prints were taken and rushed to the Bureau, where a quick comparison was made. I was able to establish that the blood-stained finger-print left on the sheath of the murder weapon had been left there by Hughie Osborne. Later that day, when confronted with this and other evidence, he finally confessed to the killing.

In crime novels it is not unusual for the murderer to return to the scene of his crime and this, of course, sometimes happens in real life too. However, not even in crime fiction have I read of an occasion when the victim returns to the scene.

In the mid-1950s, in a town not too far from the centre of Manchester, the police photographic section had indented for and received a most expensive new camera which, if advertising can be believed, was the finest that money could buy and a most essential piece of equipment for modern police photographic work. The camera arrived complete with instructions which unfortunately were not fully read. The photographers of the unit, extremely experienced, may perhaps be forgiven for thinking that a leaflet of instructions was intended more for the inexperienced amateur than the professional man. They firmly believed that one camera was much like another and that all that was needed was a little time to familiarize themselves with their latest acquisition. Unfortunately, on this one occasion, time was not on their side. On the day the camera arrived it was given a full inspection and then, before the photographers retired from duty, was left loaded with film, ready for instant use should one of them be recalled to duty to deal with an emergency.

An emergency arose in the early hours of the following morning. The body of a prostitute was found in premises she was temporarily using; she had been quite brutally murdered. In such circumstances, under normal police procedure, after death has been certified and before the body is removed to the mortuary for a full forensic examination, a complete photographic record is made of the scene. Not only can photographs prove of value to investigators, it is essential that they are available for inspection by the coroner, and by judge and jury if the case comes to trial.

When the photographer was turned out of his bed that

morning he was, very likely, not at his best. Having dressed, he quickly went to the photographic department at his police headquarters, collected all necessary equipment, including the wonderful new camera, and made his way to the murder scene. Working in close collaboration with the senior detective, he photographed the body, the scene and items of evidential value, to their mutual satisfaction. Years of experience had made this a routine matter, nothing whatever to get excited about.

When all this was done, he returned to the department to develop the film. The senior investigating officer, after ensuring that the preliminary medical examination had been concluded, ordered that the body be removed to the mortuary. When the photographer returned to the studio, he had, as usual, to develop his film before returning to bed. The developed film would then be printed later in the morning by other members of staff.

He unloaded the film from the new camera, developed it and was shocked to see that it was blank. Not one of the photographs had come out. Panic stations!

So many different stories were told, so many excuses put forward and so much blame was allocated to individuals and equipment that it is now difficult to establish just where the fault lay. The situation called for immediate thought, careful but rapid action and a certain amount of secrecy. In a cloak-and-dagger action, reminiscent of the days of Burke and Hare, a small group of detectives, including the photographer, returned in a police van to the mortuary, where they retrieved the body of the murdered prostitute. After dressing it, they returned to the scene of the crime, where they arranged her body exactly as it had been found. The police photographer, now using his old and trusted camera, rephotographed the scene. Not prepared to take any chances, he sped away to the studio to develop the film before sanctioning the return of the body to the mortuary. Although sworn to secrecy (how on earth does one keep such a secret in the police service?) the officers concerned had to do what thousands of police officers before them have had to do when things have gone wrong: sweat it out. I must agree with Sir William Gilbert, 'When constabulary duty's to be done, a policeman's lot is not a happy one.'

Gloves can present more than the obvious problems to a finger-print expert. When they have been worn by criminals in an attempt to evade detection, the expert has to use diligence, science and probably more than his fair share of luck to tackle the problem. A less than obvious problem is that caused by a few, sometimes quite experienced, police officers. Wearing gloves at the scene of a crime, they will deliberately touch articles and surfaces, and not exercise sufficient care when examining the point of entry used by a thief. They mistakenly believe that by wearing gloves they are preserving the scene for forensic examination, whereas in fact their actions may cause the intruder's finger-prints to be rubbed off articles, or to be obliterated by having gloved fingers placed over them.

Luck and diligence were combined when police officers investigated yet another 'crime of the century.' The Great Train Robbery was a most carefully planned criminal operation. Despite meticulous attention to detail and the constant use of gloves and masks, most of the criminals involved were identified by New Scotland Yard finger-print experts after they had inadvertently left their finger-prints at the farm where they had taken refuge.

Within the Finger-print Bureau at New Scotland Yard is a small section which deals exclusively with the examination and comparison of glove prints. If one produces a glove impression for inspection, not only can they identify the type of glove that made the print but in certain cases can also name the manufacturer. There have been occasions when experts have presented evidence of identification of a particular glove, the print of which has been left at the scene of a crime. Whilst this is extremely useful evidence, it is merely corroborative as it falls short of naming the person who was wearing the glove at the time the crime was committed.

Quite often criminals have been unfortunate when gloves have split, allowing a finger to poke through and leave a tell-tale print. One criminal was similarly unfortunate when he chose to wear a pair of leather gloves which buttoned at the wrist. While committing a burglary, he pushed a drawer shut with the palm of his gloved hand and left behind a small V-shaped portion of his palm print from the uncovered area beneath where the glove buttoned. Small, yes, but enough to identify and convict him.

Many thieves make mistakes when, for a brief moment, possibly to handle a small object or to perform a delicate operation, they remove their gloves. This is where the diligent and experienced finger-print officer can score.

A few years ago, along with another expert, I attended the scene of a burglary. During the night a lock-up post office in one of Manchester's inner suburbs had been broken into, the safe had been blown and its valuable contents stolen. The thief had entered the post office by means of its blue slate roof. Once inside, he had found the safe, which contained a large amount of cash and postal orders. To blow the safe he had inserted into its keyhold a small amount of gelignite, which he had then tamped in position with half a pound of butter. A detonator was then pushed through the butter and into the explosive. Once in position, the detonator had been wired up and the wires attached to the light switch on the post office wall. A carpet had been placed over the safe to baffle the sound of the explosion; it was then blown in quite a professional manner. When we arrived at the scene, it was all rather chaotic. A rope was hanging through a gaping hole in the ceiling, the safe door was hanging off its hinges, and there were bits of carpet everywhere. The post office staff were treading through inches of safe ballast and a queue of people was standing outside the post office patiently waiting to be attended to. Lying on the floor, near the end of the knotted rope hanging from a ceiling beam, lay a pair of thin rubber gloves, obviously left there by the thief. The chances of finding a finger-print at the scene seemed remote. My colleague picked up the gloves to examine them. Having looked at the outside of the gloves, he carefully turned them inside out completing the operation by blowing the fingers out. At that moment the feeling was similar to that experienced by a pools winner. The safe blower's hands must have been covered in a film of black grease, for on the inside of his rubber glove was a complete set of his finger-prints. So good and clear were the prints that they were identified before lunch time and the thief was arrested later that day, still in possession of the stolen cash and postal orders. By using gloves he had obviously done some thinking, but not enough. I doubt if he will be so slipshod again.

Another successful investigation, and one with which I felt particularly pleased, happened when a house was broken into and a large amount of property stolen. The intruder had spent a considerable time in the house, selecting the most expensive items to steal; obviously he had the eye of a connoisseur. He had entered every room, leaving behind him a trail of havoc and glove prints. It was most frustrating, until unforeseen circumstances came to my aid. When he had reached the kitchen, this less than fastidious criminal, obviously feeling the tension, had felt the need to have an immediate bowel movement and had obliged in the middle of the kitchen floor. My luck was changing, for adhering to the thief's considerable deposit was a makeshift piece of toilet paper. The odds were heavily in my favour that he would have removed his gloves to perform this delicate manoeuvre. Few of us could do it neatly in gloves! I carefully removed the paper and took it back to the Finger-print Bureau, where I subjected it to chemical tests. I was correct in my assessment. There developed on the paper was a perfect right, middle-finger print which, when searched and identified in the files, led to the arrest and conviction of the burglar. Not many of our jobs were resolved in quite such an unsavoury way.

If a thoughtless policeman is the first person to arrive at the scene of a crime and touches articles handled by the intruder, it can be very difficult at a later stage to assess the amount of evidence he has failed to preserve. Sometimes during forensic examination of the scene, finger-prints have been found both smudged and damaged and it has been fair to assume that a careless policeman has destroyed some of the forensic evidence. On other occasions, when a most meticulous examination has been made and none of the culprit's finger-prints found, one is not to know whether or not prints existed or a clumsy officer had removed them during his preliminary examination. When lecturing to young police officers I emphasized this particular point and stressed the care they must take when arriving at the scene of a major incident, quoting the following circumstances.

Early in my finger-print career, along with other experts, I was asked to go to a small terraced house in Manchester and there assist in the investigation into the murder of an old gentleman. It had occurred earlier that day and had all the hallmarks of a burglary which had gone wrong. Someone had climbed up the fall pipe at the rear of the house, opened a bedroom window and then climbed through. Going into the front bedroom, the burglar must have been shocked to find the occupier of the house, the old gentleman, ill in bed and probably watching him. The criminal had obviously panicked, seized an empty lemonade bottle and had struck the old man a violent blow on the head, killing him as he did so.

When I got there the old man was lying dead in bed with the blood-stained bottle lying on the bed alongside him. The rear-bedroom window, which was wide open, was subjected to a thorough examination for finger-prints. On the outside surface of the window were found the merest tips of finger-prints, apparently made by a person climbing through. There were scuff marks on the fall pipe at the rear, but no identifiable finger-prints. Now, it is not possible to search and identify from the files the merest tips of finger-prints. When a person is arrested and his prints are taken, the last joint of the finger, excluding the tip, is rolled on a pad of printers' ink and then rolled on to the finger-print form. These tips of prints found on the window were only useful in that they told us the killer was not wearing gloves when he climbed into the house; they could be used to identify him, but only if he was first arrested and the tips of his fingers then printed.

A lemonade bottle has a good, smooth surface capable of retaining a finger-print. When this murder weapon was examined, our disappointment was acute. Around the neck of the bottle, in a position consistent with its having been held as a weapon, was a set of leather-glove impressions. Our assumption was a simple one. To avoid attracting attention to himself on a summer's day the intruder had approached the house not wearing gloves; but once inside he had immediately put them on.

This theory, however, lost favour. The following day a hitherto unknown set of circumstances came to light. One of the uniformed police officers who had attended the scene of the murder came forward to say that, when he had gone into the bedroom, he had seen the old man apparently gravely injured. He had gone to the bed, which he sat upon whilst he checked whether the old man was actually dead. No soon had he sat down than the lemonade bottle had fallen off the bed and rolled on to the floor. Mistakenly believing that he had to rearrange the room exactly as he had found it, and not wishing to leave his own finger-prints at the scene, the young officer had picked up the bottle whilst wearing his leather gloves and had replaced it on the bed.

Had the murderer put on a pair of gloves after breaking into the house, or did he leave his finger-prints on that bottle? If so, did the uniformed officer's leather gloves obliterate them? The crime was never solved, no person was ever arrested and, barring a genuine confession at some future date, we will never know the answer. Thieving is a thoroughly self-centred business: the man takes it upon himself to have the right to enter your house; to take what you have, and to do with it what he likes; and, if your seeing him puts him at risk, to take your life or to injure you badly, entirely to suit himself. If you are rich, he deems you a more than fair target, though you may have worked long and hard for what you have. If you have little but are old, feeble and thus vulnerable, many a thief reckons you are a prime target because you do not present a threat to him whilst he is engaged in his criminal activities. Either way the thief is self-centred, greedy and mostly quite ruthless. There was perhaps a lot to be said for the system adopted when juries were first used: all its members knew the accused and were thus in a position to say whether or not he had any justification for what he had done; they would know his character as a neighbour and would be able to say whether he was indeed a bad person. The opposite system is now the case, and there are those who feel it is not an improvement.

According to Mark Twain, there are lies, damned lies and statistics. In police circles great value is placed upon statistics as a means of proving whether or not a force or a department is efficient. As each of them produces its own statistics there is a natural tendency for them to prove that they are rather more successful and efficient than they actually are. In this assessment of efficiency the crime detection rate is of paramount importance. This rate is a comparison between the number of crimes reported in an area and the number of crimes detected, and it is expressed in percentage form. You will notice that I refer to the number of crimes reported: that is a very different thing from the number committed. Nobody knows how many committed crimes are not reported, but it is certain there are many, especially where in the case of burglary the attempt to enter has not been successful or nothing has been taken, which does sometimes happen.

The Criminal Investigation Department produces the statistics by which the detection rate is determined and quite often divisional detective offices will vie with each other in an effort to obtain the highest percentage. In this annual game there are certain handicaps to be either enjoyed or overcome, depending on which area you happen to be serving in. A matter of swings and round-abouts; what one department may gain on the swings, the other may gain on the roundabouts.

For instance, the A Division covers Manchester city centre. There are a number of department stores and shops to be protected, but very few people actually living in the area. There the crime detection rate, surprisingly enough, is boosted by the large number of thieves arrested for shop-lifting. I say 'surprisingly' because shop-lifting is the most prevalent of crimes, one which cannot be prevented, and when it is well organized is most difficult to detect. And yet, as if to give weight to Mark Twain's words, shop-lifting possesses, for statistical purposes, vir-tually a 100% detection rate. The reason is that a case of shop-lifting is normally reported to the police only when the thief is caught in the act. However, in the vast majority of cases no one is caught, and no one apart from the stock taker suspects that the theft has occurred; the losses are covered by the store's profit margin and the shortages are not reported. Hence, one person arrested for shop-lifting means that one case of shop-lifting has been reported to the police, a prisoner has been charged, and, because few people are found not guilty, there is a near 100% detection rate. This is a decided advantage for the A Division CID, if something of a mockery for those people who place too much reliance on such figures.

An advantage which the A Division does not enjoy, but which most of the other territorial divisions do, lies with the large amount of juvenile delinquents who live on their patch. When such a person is arrested for commit-ting a crime, part of the art of detection is to wheedle out of the prisoner a great number of TICs. These are 'taken into consideration' offences and the idea is that, when the prisoner is charged with an offence, the detective will interview him and coax out of him admissions to whatever other offences he has committed prior to the one with which he is now charged. These are often of a similar nature, for instance stealing lead and copper piping from derelict houses. When the prisoner appears before the magistrates for sentence, he hopes that, when imposing sentence, they will take into consideration all the offences which he is now admitting and thus his slate will be wiped clean, confession not only being good for the soul but also good for the statistics. This can result sometimes in a juvenile being arrested for committing a felony and perhaps having sixty previous cases taken into consideration.

Even in the Finger-print Bureau we were bitten by the bug of competition, though in truth there was no other department with which we could be compared. We therefore competed against ourselves, comparing the year's results with those obtained the previous year, success being measured not by detections but by identifications, with an expert attempting to identify more finger-prints found at the scenes of crime than he had done during the previous twelve months.

To most finger-print experts the number of identifications made was important, even though some might have denied it. To some extent each would have 'favourite' criminals, a particular thief who, because of his ineptitude, would provide a diligent finger-print man with a harvest of easy identifications. One such person provided me with an abundance of them. I was working as a Sergeant in the Salford area at the time a young boy was having the greatest difficulty in settling in at the borstal to which he had been committed. He was such a frequent absconder from this place that one could only sympathize with the house master in charge of the catering arrangements, as in mid-week it was difficult to predict whether he would come down for breakfast or not. At weekends his movements were far more predictable. Homesick for the bright lights of Salford, this boy would invariably end up there. Obviously, he was not allowed to sleep at his parents' home and in any case if he had done so he would soon have been picked up. He would therefore find accommodation nearby and to do this would break and enter offices and workshops, avail himself of any food or drink he could find and stay there for the weekend. One of his favourite and most comfortable refuges was a small workshop which produced flags for various countries and purposes. After breaking into the premises, he would help himself to tea and biscuits before settling down for the night snugly wrapped in the flags of the nations, united and otherwise.

As the area finger-print officer, I would be asked to visit the scene of this regularly committed crime and would usually find and identify the absconder's finger-prints. With nowhere to go, the lad would be quickly arrested, charged and brought before the magistrates, who would have no alternative but to return him to the borstal from which he would almost immediately depart once more. It reached a stage where, if on a Monday morning a member of the bureau received a request from the Salford CID for me to attend the scene of a burglary at one of the boy's favoured sleeping places, he would write the request in the daily journal and then, without saying a word, retrieve a copy of the boy's finger-prints from the files, which he would hand to me with a wry smile. Whilst not a particularly good capture, the boy was always the source of some dry wit and was 'good for the figures'.

All good things must come to an end, however, and my supply of easy identifications ran out when a young and inexperienced, though optimistic, detective arrested the borstal boy and charged him with breaking into a small workshop. He told the lad that he would be well advised to admit the offence as 'Sergeant Fletcher has found your finger-prints there.' Suddenly the penny dropped and the youngster realized why the police were always one step ahead of him. Shortly after acquiring this knowledge he absconded again from borstal, returned to his beloved Salford, broke into and entered his much-favoured flag shop and settled down for a pleasant week-end near home. As usual, I was asked to attend the scene of the crime shortly after it was discovered on the Monday morning. Upon arrival I saw that the lad had been busy with a paint spray and each surface he had touched had been given a coat of paint. At the point of entry and on each drawer and cupboard he had touched the result was the same. At the door through which he had left the premises I found that not only had he applied a coat of paint to the door knob but had also left a message for me sprayed on the wall by the side of the door. Misspelt but clearly understood, it read, 'Now find my fucking fingerprints, FLECHER!' After completing his farewell message and before departing from the building the boy had left the spray can near the door. I retrieved the can, carefully applied a little powder and for the last time found the finger-prints of my young friend. Borstal can be an education for villains, but perhaps this one had never stayed there long enough to learn about finger-prints before.

A senior detective's heart is guaranteed to miss a beat when he answers the telephone and hears that a murder has occurred on his patch. No matter how experienced he may be he will hope that it is a straightforward killing and relatively easy for him to solve. Whilst all murders cause concern to those who lead the enquiry, some, perhaps because of the circumstances surrounding the case or the apparent lack of clues, appear even at a very early stage as though they are going to be difficult to solve. These are the ones which cause most stress to the senior investigator and are sure to cost him many hours of sleep.

The kind of homicide which causes the least concern and generally no loss of sleep is the 'domestic' one, when in an unpremeditated attack someone kills a relative or friend. In police circles this type of crime is referred to as 'one for one', meaning one murder committed and one murderer arrested.

In the category of those likely to cause most concern is the murder which occurs out of doors, usually late at night with no witnesses present, the alarm being raised only when someone finds the body. In a case in which there has been little or no previous contact between murderer and victim there is usually no quick solution to be found; it is normally a matter of conducting a diligent examination of the crime scene, coupled with extensive routine enquiries, with detectives desperately hoping for a lucky break.

One of the luckiest I ever encountered happened late one Sunday afternoon in July 1976, when I had to visit the scene of a murder in the unkempt and overgrown gardens of a licensed club in Haughton Green, near Manchester. At lunch time that day, whilst exercising his dog in the grounds of the club, a man had found the naked body of a young woman. Efforts had been made to conceal her body, because it was covered with long grass.

Medical examination showed she had been sexually assaulted and then strangled, death being estimated to have occurred late the previous evening or in the early hours of the morning. Even though the killing had occurred out of doors with no witnesses to it, we hoped that once the victim had been identified it would be possible to establish that she had been present in the licensed club the previous evening, and that enquiries made there would lead to identifying the killer. These enquiries were, in the circumstances, found to be unnecessary because an examination of the murder scene revealed something which not even the most optimistic of detectives would dare hope for – the name, address and a photograph of the murderer. An organized search was made by uniformed officers of the long grass in the area surrounding the body. They were looking for objects of evidential value which could have been dropped or torn loose in a struggle, such things as buttons from the murderer's coat or a comb containing head hairs, the sort of thing which could easily be dropped by accident from a jacket pocket.

During the search a young officer found a man's leather wallet. It was dry, clean and had obviously not lain there for any length of time. In the wallet was found a driving licence with all the usual details including date of birth and a Gas Board identification card complete with photograph. It was soon learned that the man was a gas fitter employed by the North West Gas Board and that the card was his authority to enter their customers' homes. He was quickly arrested and, when interviewed, soon confessed to having committed the crime.

On a damp and murky November evening in 1976 two young boys made plans to break and enter a dilapidated,

disused Indian restaurant near the centre of Ashton under
Lyne, a small mill town on the outskirts of Manchester.
The place was due for demolition and the electricity
supply had been cut off some weeks earlier. The young-
sters were ill equipped for the venture, possessing neither
a modern torch nor the means to buy one. Undaunted by
this lack of equipment, they broke into the building and
then improvised a system of lighting similar to that
adopted by Tom Sawyer and Becky Thatcher when
exploring McDougal's cave in Mark Twain's famous
novel. Forming a torch out of rolled-up newspapers, they
lit it and started searching the downstairs rooms. Pressed
closely together and with the flickering torch held out in
front of them, both boys slowly mounted the staircase.
At the top of the stairs they went into a bedroom and
thrust the lighted torch out in front of them. Then, just
as Tom Sawyer and Becky did when they spotted Injun
Joe, these two wayward young Ashton lads got the biggest
shock of their lives. The burning paper torch provided
just sufficient light for them to see that two feet away,
lying on top of a blood-stained bed, there was the body
of a man – but minus a face.

Knowing where to find assistance when required, and
without a thought as to the present trespass, the boys
raced out of the restaurant and dashed to the nearby
police station, where they breathlessly blurted out their
story. Uniformed police officers quickly went to the
disused restaurant and found the boys' story was true.
An immediate investigation began. Shortly after I got
there, officers already present told me the incident was
being treated as a case of murder.

Equipped with a powerful hand torch, I entered the
dilapidated restaurant and made my way upstairs. I went
into the front bedroom and flashed my torch around it.

Against the left-hand wall was a single bed badly stained with blood. Lying on top of the bed, with his feet near the door, was the body of a man dressed in pyjamas, over which had been pulled a pair of grey slacks and a fawn raincoat. All the clothing was heavily blood-stained. The body wore shoes and socks.

Lying at the side of the bed was a large carving knife covered in dried blood. I examined the head; most of the face was missing. Lighting my way by torch, I went into the bathroom. It, too, was heavily blood-stained. I could see bloody footmarks on the bathroom floor. Some person had walked through the blood in bare feet and had left a trail of footprints. Each of them was easily identifiable on the linoleum floor.

I knelt down by the side of the prints to examine the ridge detail with a magnifying glass. As I did so, I could see that the foot impressions appeared to be too large to have been made by a woman. I went back to the bedroom and verified that the deceased was wearing shoes and socks.

As the officer in charge of the crime scene I was now expected to make an assessment for the benefit of the Senior Detective. Experience and an aptitude for the work provides a person with the ability to 'read' a crime scene and I take pride in the fact that my opinion was often sought. Having availed himself of the assessments of the different specialists, the Senior Investigator could accept or reject most or all of these opinions. I now supplied my own view. 'Having regard to all the known circumstances, I think it is fair to assume that the man has been murdered, and the evidence rather points to a homosexual killing.' It is to his credit that he accepted this without comment, but how wrong I was! When the pathologist performed the post-mortem examination, it was found that the 'victim' had died of natural causes. He had been suffering from a stomach ulcer which had perforated, causing him to vomit a large amount of blood and probably suffer considerable pain.

Quickly, I went to the mortuary where I obtained the dead man's footprints and returned to the disused restaurant, where I compared them with the footprints in blood on the bathroom floor. They matched perfectly.

In daylight it became easier to assess what had probably occurred. Some weeks earlier the 'victim', an Indian, had gone to bed dressed in his pyjamas. As he was living alone in this disused restaurant, without any electricity, he had put the carving knife at the side of his bed for protection. A friend of his later confirmed that this was in fact his normal practice. Feeling unwell, he had got out of bed and gone to the bathroom, where he had started to vomit blood on the floor. After walking through the blood in his bare feet, he had returned to the bedroom and had vomited blood again, this time over the bed and the carving knife. Realizing that he needed help and that the telephone had been disconnected, he had started to dress, first pulling on his trousers and then putting on his shoes and socks. He had finally struggled into his raincoat, vomited blood once again and had then collapsed on top of the bed, where he died. His face had been eaten away by rats and maggots. Evidence of identification was later provided for the coroner's enquiry by a finger-print expert.

Evidence is the means by which a thing is proved or disproved according to the law. It will consist of oral evidence, which is normally sworn evidence, real evidence such as weapons, stolen property, etc, or could be of a documentary nature. Additionally, there are different forms of these types of evidence, such as primary evidence, secondary, circumstantial, of opinion and the little-known but very important evidence of presumption.

Primary evidence is that of a person giving direct evidence of something he has seen, heard, touched, tasted or smelled. Secondary evidence is that given when a person produces a copy or a model of the original; it is acceptable only if it is not possible to produce the original. If my memory serves me correctly, circumstantial evidence is defined as 'evidence not of the fact to be proved, but of facts from which that fact can be deduced with a reasonable degree of certainty'. My favourite type of evidence is, for obvious reasons, that of opinion, which is only acceptable when given by a person who is considered by the court to be an expert in his or her particular field: medicine, finger-prints, ballistics, handwriting, art, and so on. The little-known evidence of presumption includes the presumption of fact and both irrebuttable and rebuttable presumptions. The presumption of fact is the inference that a reasonable person will draw when certain facts are presented to him. And I may add here that millions of words have been spoken in court argument as to what is a reasonable person. It usually boils down to what is considered reasonable in the circumstances. One English court decided, if I remember rightly, that a reasonable man was 'the one on the Clapham omnibus' – the ordinary man in the street. The irrebuttable presumption is, in reality, a rule of law. For example, the law presumes that a child under the age of ten years cannot commit crime and that a boy under the age of fourteen cannot commit rape; it also presumes that ignorance of the law will not constitute a defence.

Whether the reader will agree with the first of these presumptions, or will themselves presume that 'the law is an ass', is an entirely different matter. The last of the three presumptions, the rebuttable one, includes both that a sane person intends the natural consequences of his actions, and that a child between the age of ten and fourteen years can form no criminal intent. These presumptions are usually rebutted when evidence is produced to the contrary.

When appearing in court I would quite often give sworn oral evidence in respect of my examination of the scene of the crime, produce real evidence in the form of a finger-print on an object, produce secondary evidence in the form of photographs of finger-prints on unmoveable objects, produce documentary evidence in respect of the prisoner's finger-prints taken on the official form and then give evidence of opinion (expert evidence) as to the identification of the finger-prints.

In order that this next little story be fully appreciated it is necessary to understand the manner in which a witness is examined when he attends an English court of law to give evidence, and the procedures which are followed.

Upon entering the witness box he will first take the oath and then be subjected to examination in chief. This means that he will be examined, usually quite gently, by the side which has produced him, be it prosecution or defence.

This will be followed by the cross-examination, when he is examined, usually not too gently, by the representative of the other side. The cross-examination is followed by the re-examination, when the witness may again be examined by the side which has produced him, usually on matters which have come to light as the result of the cross-examination. In this re-examination new matters may be introduced only with the consent of the court. After the witness has survived the three examinations and has left the box, he cannot be recalled by either defence or prosecution, only by the court.

Shortly after qualifying as a finger-print expert I had

occasion to attend Manchester City Magistrates' Court and give evidence. The case involved a youth who had rushed into a draper's shop, vaulted smartly over the counter and taken a leather jacket before racing out of the shop without being identified. On the counter over which he had vaulted and in that part of the shop to which he had no legitimate access I later found finger-prints which I identified as belonging to a young man with a criminal record. The youth was taken into custody and interviewed in respect of the theft.

Denying the allegation, he said that he had never been in the shop in his life and then made a written statement to that effect. Having regard to the scientific evidence available to him, the interviewing detective promptly cautioned him and charged him with larceny of the coat, finger-printed him in the normal manner and then forwarded those prints to me on the form which the prisoner had duly signed. I compared the prints with those I had discovered in the shop and found that they matched perfectly. As the youth continued to deny the theft, I was required to prepare and produce evidence of finger-print identification. For this purpose I mounted on an exhibit card two enlarged photographs. On the left side of the card I mounted an enlarged photograph of one of the finger impressions recovered from behind the shop counter and on the right side I mounted an enlarged photograph of the corresponding finger-print taken from the accused. Both photographs had been enlarged four times their normal size. On each of the two photographs I indicated sixteen ridge characteristics which were in agreement, the number normally required to prove iden-tification in an English court of law.

On the day of the trial I was standing outside the court room talking to the lady who owned the shop when the youth put in an appearance. He was wearing a leather jacket which the lady strongly suspected was the one he had stolen from her shop. She voiced her opinion to the detective in charge of the case but, as she was not able positively to identify it, no further action could be taken. It was not to be a long trial. There were only three prosecution witnesses to be called: the shopkeeper, the detective and myself. The lady was to give evidence that her shop had been entered and the leather jacket stolen. The detective was to give evidence of the investigation, the arrest and most importantly, as the case was dependent upon finger-print evidence, he would produce the youth's finger-prints on the official form and identify them to the court as the ones he had taken. Finally, I would be required to give evidence of finding the impressions in the shop, receiving the youth's finger-prints on the form signed by him, comparing the two and finding them to have been made by the same person, and then proving the fact by giving evidence of opinion and producing the prepared exhibit card.

At a trial it is important that until such time as he is called to give his evidence the witness remains outside the court room. Being unaware of evidence previously given and the line of enquiry the cross-examination is taking, his evidence will be unaffected by that of previous witnesses.

Shortly before the detective was called into the court I handed him the accused's finger-print form to produce and reminded him of its importance. I then waited patiently outside the court room until I was called to give evidence. When I entered the witness box, I saw the youth's finger-print form lying on the witness box shelf, next to the Bible. I took the oath and then, led by the prosecuting solicitor, gave evidence of the finding of the finger-prints in the shop and the photographing of them. Following this, I explained how I had received the finger-print form signed by the youth and by the detective and produced the form for the benefit of the court. I was then asked by the prosecuting solicitor to give evidence of comparing the finger impressions found in the shop with the corresponding finger-prints on the form, of finding them to have been made by the same person, and finally to produce my exhibit card for the benefit of the magistrates. After completing my evidence in chief, I remained in the witness box, anticipating that I would be cross-examined by the defending solicitor, and was more than a little surprised when he had no questions to ask of me. The prosecuting solicitor finally addressed the bench and concluded the case for the Crown.

Suddenly, the defending solicitor was up on his feet and informed the bench that his client had no case to answer. He patiently explained to the magistrates that whilst the evidence given by the finger-print expert had been well prepared, there had been no evidence produced to the court showing that the finger-prints on the official form were those of his client.

Not only had the detective failed to give evidence of the taking of the defendant's finger-prints but he had also forgotten to produce the form. Worse, the prosecuting solicitor had allowed the oversight to occur without rectifying it.

It was now too late for the prosecution to recall the detective to give the forgotten evidence and the solicitor therefore requested that the magistrates do so. After consultation with their clerk, they, quite rightly in my opinion, refused to do so, and the youth, complete with leather jacket, walked out of the court a free man, smiling broadly at the lady shopkeeper as he did so. It was left to me to explain to her exactly what had happened. It may have been the poor manner in which I offered the explanation that led the good lady loudly to exclaim, 'British justice!' and not blame the two individuals responsible.

I had returned home late one evening after a particularly long day and as I sat relaxing before the television I casually picked up the evening paper to find my attention caught by the front page headline: 'GAIETY GIRL MURDERED'. I started to read the article, curious to find out what problems other detectives were facing at that moment. Only after reading the first two paragraphs did I realize that most of my working day had been spent investigating that particular crime. Earlier I had arrived at a single person's flat in a complex of fairly new buildings in Hulme, Manchester, to assist an investigation there. Most of Hulme's two-up-and-two-down terraced houses had long since vanished, and had been replaced by centrally heated and fully fitted council homes which were certainly far more comfortable to live in. But for many of the older residents, Hulme had lost its character; its pulse was still beating, but its heart had died. I was in charge of a small team of finger-print experts who had come to examine the scene of a murder which had occurred at the flat during the previous evening. On reflection it seemed the newspaper report had been correct, the victim had been a Gaiety Girl and there was evidence to prove it. In the bedroom were newspaper cuttings which showed that sixty years earlier she had danced to enraptured audiences. But the years had taken their toll and for police purposes the Gaiety Girl would be more accurately described as an old lady who lived alone in rather poor circumstances. After the pathologist had examined the body *in situ*, he was of the opinion that she had probably died as the result of manual strangulation.

The team of finger-print experts commenced their examination and I quietly walked through each of the rooms supervising the operation. As I entered the toilet my interest was aroused, for here something was out of place, something which would be unlikely to occur in the flat of a lady living alone: the toilet seat was raised. Had the murderer used the toilet before he left the premises and had he raised the seat to do so? I knelt before the toilet bowl and started to apply finger-print powder to the black plastic lid. I was then aware that I was being watched by a high-ranking police officer, one of the finest detectives I knew, who stood closely behind me watching my every action. I was pleased he had noticed that I was 'on the ball', as one might say, but after a moment to two I got the impression that his interest was a little too close, his scrutiny too intense. At a time when there was plenty else to occupy his mind he appeared to be concentrating far too much on this one small detail. Exactly in the position where I expected it to be I found a left-thumb print. I leaned forward and examined the print with my magnifying glass. He, too, bent forward. 'Have you got something, Tony?' he asked.

'Yes, sir, left-thumb print. Could be useful,' I replied.

A long pause. Then he slowly extended his left arm towards me. 'You'd better check mine. When I got here I was bursting for a pee and I was the last one to use the toilet.'

I checked and identified his left-thumb print on the toilet seat. He placed a forefinger over his lips, 'Not a word to anyone.' But after the murderer had been arrested, he himself let the cat out of the bag.

15

Red Herrings

In the majority of detective novels and plays the story ends with the arrest of the criminal. Quite often the successful sleuth hands over the prisoner to a uniformed police officer, who handcuffs the culprit and then disappears from the set with him, leaving the high-ranking or amateur detective with a rather self-satisfied look on his face.

In fact, the arrest of a murderer will involve only the disbanding of the murder squad (if one has been set up) with perhaps a celebratory drink or two if the prisoner is committed for trial; but this disbandment will mean the beginning of a great deal of work for a small group of officers whose duty it will be to prepare the case for court. It will be their business to tie up all the loose ends and prepare a full and comprehensive report for the Director of Public Prosecutions, affectionately known as 'the Dipper'.

The Office of the Director of Public Prosecutions is in London and is largely staffed with legal experts. Certain kinds of case, murder amongst them, have to be submitted for consideration and the Director, or his representative, has to be convinced that there is more than a 50% chance of conviction.

If he does not think there is a good case, he might suggest how it could be looked at again or recommend that it be merely held and not proceeded with. Believe it or not, one copy of a complete file can stand many feet high upon a desk; it represents a lot of interviewing, a lot of thought and a lot of typing, checking and rechecking, with lists of exhibits and witnesses, in alphabetical and sequential order, so that the legal eagle can refer quickly to whatever he wishes. The whole will be covered by a long report which has annotations indicating which witness statement is referred to. Viewing the whole file, ready for despatch to London can make you wish you had substantial holdings in the paper industry.

Presuming that the DPP has given authority to proceed, and the case is finally presented to the judge and jury by the prosecuting barrister, it is intended that no detail will be left outstanding which could cause controversy. This noble intention is sometimes achieved, sometimes not; many murder enquiries have a red herring, a false confession or clue which has led detectives on a false trail.

Anticipating that the lawyer representing the defence will make capital out of these red herrings, it is often necessary to remove them before the case goes to trial. False confessions must be proved to be untrue and false clues must be proved to have had no bearing on the case. This usually involves much tedious but necessary work.

In the last murder case for which I was to prepare evidence, there occurred a set of circumstances which has puzzled me to this day. It was the brutal murder of a gentle retired schoolmaster in his home near the centre of Oldham. The old man had been battered to death with a hammer which lay, badly blood-stained, on a chair near his body. Under the lifeless and crumpled form lay another hammer which had not been used in the attack.

Both these hammers were the property of the victim and had been taken from a drawer in the kitchen cupboard, which had been left partly open. On a door, just five feet above the victim's body, I found a finger-print which I later identified as that of the killer. On the cupboard drawer from which the murder weapon and the other hammer had been taken I found four finger-prints. These were close to each other on the right-hand side of the drawer and had each been made by the same finger. The marks appeared to have been freshly made and were not those of the dead schoolmaster. As they were on a drawer which contained tools and was probably much used, and as none of the prints had been superimposed with other finger-prints or been damaged in any way, I formed the view that they had recently been left there. The finger-prints on the drawer were not those of the murderer. Had he an accomplice who was never traced? Certainly the two hammers – one badly blood-stained, the other found on the floor under the body – indicated that possibility. Were the finger-prints a red herring, those of a person not connected with the crime? Despite the most intensive of enquiries, the arrest and questioning of the murderer, I still do not know the answer with any degree of certainty.

Robert Collinson was born in Oldham in 1910 and lived there until the time of his death seventy-two years later. The Oldham to which Bob Collinson was so loyal and attached was very much a cotton town. There was also a good deal of engineering by way of textile machinery. Platt Brothers exported their goods all over the world as well as supplying the home trade. Some of their fitters were well-travelled, highly skilled men, going to distant countries, and no doubt teaching many a foreigner to say English words in those peculiarly long drawn out vowels heard in Oldham.

The cotton towns to the north of Manchester are different from each other in situation, accent and trade, now and always have been. Outsiders tended to think of Oldham as scruffy and downtrodden, rows of gloomy terraced houses, dejected millworkers, etc, but this was not so. The houses in Oldham lined some pretty steep streets; great pride went into cleaning the front steps, the arrangement of bright clean curtains, brass door knobs and knockers, black-leaded footscrapers. A man and wife working in the mill might only have to cross the road, perhaps they could even slam the front door when the eight o'clock buzzer started and be at the mill gate, clocking on, before it finished.

Mills were very much community affairs. They not only sent their own candidate for Cotton Queen to the judging, but there were trips to the seaside at Wakes time, when travellers would each pay nine shillings return if the destination was Blackpool, where digs could be had for a pound a week. Blackpool built itself upon the trade of the mill towns. It was a poor and improvident family which could not save up a pound or two for a proper holiday. Doctors used to say that not going away for Wakes week could also prove of benefit, because during that seven days all the chimneys would cease pouring out smoke and for a while the atmosphere would be cleaner; and a bus would take anybody up to Scouthead moors for a few coppers where, on those wind-scoured heights, you really could breathe in something a bit more acceptable to the lungs.

Neighbourhoods, often clustered round their local mill, ran their own informal protection societies. Each stranger would be observed, clocked in and out as it were; and housewives could safely leave their doors unlocked. Children were minded by local women all through the nine-teenth-century growth of the cotton trade, and there is little record of harm being done. Human kindness abounded in many ways, and local women even acted as midwives and nurses when required. Children would do housework for bachelors or the elderly and get a few coppers, called 'odd money', for spending. Money clubs abounded too. Each would have twenty members who would give a shilling each to the organizer. Each member would choose a number between 1 and 20 and then there would be a draw. If your number came up that week you got eighteen shillings, the other two shillings going to the organizer. Funny though it seems to us now, at the time it was worth paying a shilling a week for twenty weeks to possess eighteen shillings to play with one magical Friday. It almost goes without saying that pawnshops were regarded as district moneylenders. Women worked hard, in the mill and out of it; grates had to be blackleaded, front steps had to be cleaned, and in that dirty atmosphere curtains were probably changed once a fortnight. Indeed, it was a life of toil, with two guidelines always to be followed: pay your rent and pay the coalman.

I said that mills started at eight; earlier, they started at seven. The knocker-up with a bunch of wires on the end of his long cane would have rattled away until a pale face appeared at the window. A quick snatch of tea, picking up one's bread and margarine, perhaps a bit of cheese too, very likely wrapped in newspaper, and out of the front door, telling the kids to go to school on time, linking arms with those clattering away down the street in their clogs, shawl wrapped firmly round the head and shoulders against what might be a biting wind. Mill girls often wore a cross-over overall and in the mill had bare arms, because it could be very warm and humid, a necessary climate for the spinning of good cotton. In the mill the noise of the machinery was so loud that girls had to learn to lipread. With the addition of a few gestures it could be quite odd to see a bunch of girls laugh with

obvious enjoyment at something which had not actually
been voiced.

Copster Hill Road is one of the steep thoroughfares in
Oldham, quite a strain on the legs both up and down, and
pronounced 'Copstrill'. The Star Inn too is a landmark for
bus passengers, and the conductors would call out 'Stir-
rinn' in a way which bemused the stranger. Perhaps the
liveliest place was Tommyfield Market on a Saturday
night. The Tommyfield of the 1930s had hundreds of
stalls, lighted by acetylene lamps hissing above one's
head; Granelli's beautiful ice-cream to wrap your tongue
round, hot black puddings with mustard, cold ones
wrapped to take home; bacon ribs, good vegetables and
fruit; stalls of good cotton straight from the mills and of
all kinds of cotton curtainings and ribbons, and a multi-
tude of sellers of cheap pottery and china. There was
almost a carnival atmosphere, because there were also
roundabouts for children and the place was open until
ten o'clock at night. A child could do wonders with
threepence on Tommyfield.

In those days coal was not dear, a shilling a hundred-
weight for first-class stuff, and by burning it the collieries
of Lancashire kept going. What the coal did to the
atmosphere does not bear thinking about, but there is a
good deal of joy in looking at a decent coal fire. The
slogan on council dustcarts at this time was often, 'Burn
More Refuse and Reduce your Rates', which may have
been true if you did it, but that did nothing to help
the atmosphere either. In the trams the Penny Bank
advertised, 'Look after your pennies and the sixpences
will take care of themselves.' The millworkers knew how
to run a Wakes club, how to hoard their money for their
holidays, for Christmas and against bad times. They
needed to do so for the bad times came too often.

Bob Collinson's parents were respectable and reserved, and as a youngster in 1920 he was happy and successful at school. He read avidly and enjoyed the company of a good book. He joined the Boy Scouts, too, remaining an active member until well into his adult life. His natural progression was to teaching and he became well loved, well known and well respected by pupils and parents alike. He was a bachelor with, eventually, no relatives that anybody knew of, but he developed an active interest in church matters and cultivated a wide circle of friends.

Shortly after the Second World War ended, he purchased a small, mid-terrace house at 8 Colwyn Street, Oldham, not far from the town centre, living there alone until the time of his death; he was thus close to the heart of the Oldham he loved. From the time he moved into Colwyn Street he was associated with St Andrew's Church in Middleton Road, which was only a short distance away. Being an active and learned man as well as a bachelor with no wife and family to consider, he became involved in a number of church activities, not least of which was the position of treasurer to the church, something for which he was splendidly suited, because he was literate, numerate and above all honest.

His health was robust and he was always ready to lend a helping hand to elderly neighbours or friends less fortunate than himself. St Andrew's was not a wealthy church and he was not known to have kept church monies or any large amounts of cash of his own at home.

In an effort to raise funds and create a healthy community spirit the church hall was periodically hired to the parishioners for the purpose of holding private functions and over the years many wedding receptions were held there. Being an official of the church and living close by, Bob rarely missed a function because, apart from being very friendly to all, he used his experience as a schoolmaster to keep a watchful eye on the antics of the young.

Bob met his death on the night of Saturday 13 March 1982, and his activities during the earlier part of that evening show not only how active he was but also indicate the type of life he led. That Saturday evening a function was being held in the church hall and Bob had nipped across to see that the lighting and heating were in order, and that the staff had arrived to man the bar.

The eighteenth birthday party of a local girl was being celebrated and at 7.20 the disco was in full swing. Bob was moving about, chatting and sharing a joke with many of the guests. At 7.25 he made his way to the Grange Arts Centre, a short distance away in Rochdale Road. There, the Operatic Society, of which he was a member, was staging its spring production. He was there during the entire performance and was seen to leave at the end, which was 9.45.

He returned to the birthday celebrations at the church hall a few minutes later, and was known to have checked that everything was in order, the bar functioning efficiently and everyone enjoying themselves. Happy about how things were going, he moved over to the buffet for a bite to eat at the invitation of the birthday girl's parents. Supper over, he left the church hall. The only person to see him alive, after his departure, was his killer.

The Oldham which had seen the birth of Bob Collinson was a very different place from the Oldham into which William Lomas was born almost fifty years later. Cotton was no longer king, although the evidence of that reign seemed unchanged. The mill chimneys still proclaimed their names proudly, even though nothing much was going on inside their premises. The atmosphere was certainly much cleaner, mostly of course as the result of the Clean Air Acts but also because of changing industry. A large number of those closely packed, small, terraced homes had gone as people were housed further out, and with them went much of the close community spirit.

William Lomas was born in 1958. On the night of his twenty-fourth birthday he murdered Bob Collinson. Lomas was an unemployed labourer well known to the Oldham police. In complete contrast to Bob, he had made little, if any, contribution to the society in which he lived, spending most of his adult life under the influence of either drink or drugs. He was an enthusiastic user of Citizens' Band radio. Using the pseudonym 'The Exterminator', he held forth with other CB enthusiasts who had both time to waste and were foolish enough to listen to him. Pseudonyms were necessary at one time because CB radio was illegal, but his use of 'The Exterminator' was, you could say, not only pathetic but also strangely prophetic.

If, on the night of his death, the movements and activities of Bob Collinson would be described as those of a normal, decent person, the same could not be said of those of Billy Lomas. His behaviour on the night in question was, to say the least, extraordinary even by his unusual standards. On that fateful Saturday evening Lomas left his sister's home, saying he was going to the Bull's Head public house in Oldham's town centre to meet a girl whose CB radio pseudonym was 'Silver Lady'. When he left home, he was wearing a pair of blue moccasin-type shoes. These belonged to his sister Christine's current boyfriend, Lewis. It had become quite customary for Lomas to use Lewis's clothing, including his shoes.

At about nine o'clock that evening a taxi pulled up

outside the Bull's Head pub. (You may wonder how an unemployed man could afford to travel in a taxi, especially when a good bus service operated.) Lomas got out, paid the driver and went into the premises. He told the licensee, Mr Trimble, that he had arranged to meet his girlfriend there and that her name was Silver Lady. He asked Mr Trimble to put out a call over the tannoy system and announce to Silver Lady that he had arrived, something of a grandiose gesture because it does not take long to look round a pub to see who is there. Whether, in fact, he wanted it to be announced that The Exterminator had arrived to meet Silver Lady is not known. Mr Trimble declined to use the tannoy for such a purpose and suggested Lomas should have a look round and make his own enquiries. He saw Lomas do this, noted that he seemed to be unsuccessful, and then saw him leave.

Silver Lady was later traced by police officers. She turned out to be a fifteen-year-old schoolgirl whose only link with Lomas had been via CB radio. She had never met him and, moreover, had not arranged to meet him at the Bull's Head that night.

When he left the Bull's Head, Lomas made his way to the Roebuck public house in King Street, getting there about 9.30 P.M. He went in and ordered a drink. This was a perfectly normal Saturday night at the Roebuck; it was crowded, noisy but orderly. Customers were drinking peaceably and enjoying each other's company, with the prospect of a lie-in on Sunday morning. Suddenly, and for no reason that anybody could perceive, Lomas became aggressive towards a young man who, in the company of two girls, was standing next to him at the bar. He swore at this young man, pushing his own face close up to him in a most aggressive manner, confronting him unreasonably for a few minutes. When interviewed later by the police, the young man could not offer any explanation for the incident, saying that, whilst Lomas did not appear to be drunk, his eyes seemed to be glazed and staring, and that within minutes of his outburst Lomas left the pub.

Nothing was seen of Lomas for over an hour, but about 10.45 P.M. he went into the Britannia public house in Wash Brook, Chadderton, Oldham, through the back door. Wash Brook is only a short distance away from Bob Collinson's home in Colwyn Street.

It was the barman at the Britannia who saw Lomas enter through the back door and he found Lomas's conduct most unusual. In fact Mr Haslam, the barman, could not remember ever seeing such conduct before: Lomas actually bought drinks for people who were complete strangers to him. Oldham, as you will have gathered, is not a place where you would buy a stranger a drink in order to impress him. Mr Haslam had never seen Lomas before that Saturday night, but knew his name, because around closing time Lomas had made a point of letting him know it. Lomas's exceedingly generous behaviour had made him the subject of a good deal of comment; after all, Oldham is not far from the Yorkshire border and in Yorkshire if 'tha' does owt for nowt tha does it for thesen'. What is more, he informed the recipients of his unusual generosity that he practised the art of Japanese fighting, whatever he meant by that.

He soon had an opportunity to demonstrate his alleged skill when a young man well known to Lomas walked into the crowded pub. Lomas held a grudge against this young man, because it happened that Lomas's CB radio set had been stolen from his home and to his mind this particular young man was the number one suspect. An argument soon began and it went on until after closing time. Lomas declared that he wanted to go outside with the young man and demonstrate his physical prowess. As soon as the bar closed and no more beer could be got, both men left the Britannia and began to fight outside. More sensible people, however, soon put a stop to the silly, drunken affair. Lomas left and made his way home to his sister Christine, arriving shaking and trembling, at about 11.45 P.M.

Naturally enough, Christine asked him why he was in such a state. He confessed that he had broken into Mr Collinson's home with the intention of stealing money and that, whilst doing this, Bob Collinson had disturbed him. He admitted he had killed Bob Collinson, using a hammer he had found in the house. He said he had otherwise been quite alone at the time of the murder.

Living next door to Bob Collinson at 6 Colwyn Street, Oldham, were Mr James Hodge and his wife Elsie. During that Saturday evening they were sitting quietly at home watching *Dallas* on television. At five minutes to ten, shortly before the end of the programme, they heard three very loud bangs which seemed to come from Bob Collinson's front door. These three bangs were loud enough, and unusual enough, for them to think that something was amiss. Being good neighbours, they decided to investigate and find out what, if anything, was wrong. They went to their own front door and looked out into Colwyn Street. There were no lights showing next door, which indicated that Bob Collinson was out; everything appeared to be quiet and normal in the street. Having satisfied their curiosity, they returned to the television set and continued watching their programme.

About fifteen minutes later, they both heard banging sounds which seemed to come not from the front door of

Bob Collinson's home, but from the kitchen. They turned down the sound on the television set and listened, but nothing further was heard, so they both resumed viewing and thought nothing more about the strange banging noises.

Alan Broscombe and Bob Collinson had been close friends for most of their adult lives, and with both of them being retired from business they had developed the habit of visiting each other at home from time to time. Alan Broscombe had arranged to call on Bob on Sunday 14 March and at twenty minutes to two that day he arrived by car. As he drove up he was somewhat surprised to see that the curtains were drawn and that the front door was slightly ajar. When he knocked on the door, there was no response. He pushed open the door and walked into the vestibule, where he saw the Sunday paper lying on the floor. He picked it up and went into the living room, putting the paper on a chair which stood next to the sideboard. On the sideboard, near the chair, was Bob Collinson's flat cap.

As he straightened up from putting the newspaper on the chair he was deeply shocked to see the body of his old pal lying in the doorway which led from the living room into the kitchen. He went towards the body. Even though the curtains were drawn and the room was gloomy, he could see that Bob had sustained massive facial and head injuries. He rushed out of the house, got into his car, drove to the nearest telephone kiosk and rang the police.

Later that day, as most people in Oldham were sitting down to high tea, I was making my way to 8 Colwyn Street in the middle of a cloudburst. The twelve-mile journey from my home was through torrential rain, which worsened as I drove towards the higher ground on the lower slopes of the Pennines. In such circumstances few places appear pleasant, but when I reached Colwyn Street, I was saddened to see the obvious deterioration which had occurred. Many of the small terraced houses which once abounded in the district had been demolished to make way for new major roadways. The open gauntness of the scene reminded me of Manchester following the 1940 German blitz. Colwyn Street and the few streets nearby were like a small oasis in a desert of wasteland. It must have been sad for Bob Collinson and people of his age group to have witnessed such a great change in their life-style, to see the break-up of communities and to know that on new estates it would take years to re-establish the same links, if indeed it would ever be possible.

Inside the front door of Bob Collinson's house there was a small vestibule with an internal stained-glass door leading to what was always called the parlour. This vestibule in itself set a house a little above the kind where the parlour was entered straight from the street, and even now an estate agent will make much of such a feature. A door connected the parlour with the kitchen, and from the kitchen there was a door which opened directly into the enclosed back yard which, before the house had been modernized, contained the outside toilet.

From the kitchen an internal door led directly to the stairs which gave access to two bedrooms, one at the back and one at the front, and to a small bathroom. Being a bachelor and living alone, Bob Collinson's house was comfortable enough but lacked that particularly feminine touch that usually only a houseproud woman can supply.

As I went into the parlour through the vestibule door I found that I was amongst the first of the investigating team to arrive. Immediately I could see the crumpled form of Bob Collinson lying in the doorway separating the parlour from the kitchen. As I stood and took stock of the situation, I was able to see the terrible injuries he had sustained. A uniformed police officer, standing in the vestibule, pointed with one finger to the murder weapon, a large blood-stained hammer which lay on an armchair.

Occupying three walls of the parlour were shelves containing Bob's large collection of books, lovingly acquired and cared for during a life-time of study. Before the main examination of the scene began, I had a quick look around the house. Apart from a drawer in the kitchen cupboard which had been partly opened there appeared to be little that had been disturbed. As I stood in the kitchen I could see a second, smaller hammer lying beneath Bob Collinson's body. He was fully clothed and wearing an overcoat and scarf.

Examination of the Yale lock on the front door showed that it had been forced and damaged. As the curtains in the parlour were still drawn, the light in the kitchen was burning and the gas fire was not alight, I presumed that Bob had arrived home late the previous evening, found his house had been broken into and had then gone into the parlour, put his cap on the sideboard and had then disturbed the intruder in the kitchen, and that this person had then murdered him.

The normal routine began: the body was photographed from many angles and then carefully removed to the mortuary. A detailed examination of the scene commenced. On the outside surface on the bottom left-hand side of the front door, I found the impression of a right shoe print which was pointing downwards, toe towards the floor. About eighteen inches above the heel, in an inverted position, were finger-prints made by a right hand. It looked as thought someone had stood with his back to the front door and kicked backwards with his right foot, forcing the door open. On the floor near where the body had lain was a similar footprint with a mesh pattern sole. I had the door removed from its hinges and conveyed to the Finger-print Bureau at police headquarters.

Next I examined the hammers, a large blood-stained ball-pein one from the chair and a smaller, unmarked ball-pein one from the kitchen floor. Both hammers were very old. The shafts were not polished and I was not able to recover any finger-prints from them. On the kitchen side of the door dividing the kitchen from the parlour I found a finger impression. It was on the opening edge of the door, five feet seven inches from the floor and above the exact spot at which Bob Collinson had apparently been murdered. Of great interest was the tool drawer which stood, partially opened, in the kitchen cupboard. All Bob's tools were kept there and, although he was known to have possessed two hammers, there were none in the drawer. It seemed obvious that someone had taken the hammers out of the drawer prior to the murder and had used one to kill him. On the right-hand side of the drawer I found four finger-prints, each made by the same finger, each one near the other three, and apparently made at the same time.

On that Sunday evening, whilst the initial examination was in progress, the matter was also being discussed and certain theories were being put forward. By this time, back in Christine Lomas's home her brother, William, had completely changed his story. He told her that he had burgled Bob Collinson's home along with an unknown second man, and that this second man had actually done the killing after both of them had been discovered by Bob Collinson in his house.

At the eighteenth birthday party at St Andrew's church hall, where Bob was last seen alive, two uninvited and so far unidentified men had apparently been in the hall at the time that Bob was enjoying the buffet, before going home. Having regard to the two hammers found at the scene, only one of which was blood-stained, it was felt that two men might indeed have been responsible. This assessment was given to both press and television, stressing that, whilst two hammers had been found, only one had been used in the attack. It was hoped that if the killer had been accompanied by someone who had taken no part in the murder, then that person would come forward, name the murderer and clear himself. No one came forward.

On the following morning, Monday, I arrived early at the scene and was told that the finger-prints found on the front door, on whose identification so much of my initial hope depended, had been eliminated as those of the first police officer to arrive at the scene. It was perfectly understandable, but still disappointing.

A little later I looked at Bob's collection of books, and had just returned H. V. Morton's *In Search of England* to its rightful place when my eyes were drawn to a section of the library which appeared to contain a collection of personal diaries. To the left of the parlour window were more than fifty of Bob's personal diaries, dating back to 1924, and also a great number of personal account books dating back several years, in which he had recorded most, if not all, of his household purchases; on one Tuesday morning he had even recorded the price of a lettuce. Small wonder that in church circles he was regarded as such a wonderful choice for treasurer, a job he had no doubt enjoyed. These account books had been balanced each day.

The senior investigating officer was Tom Butcher, the same person who had arrested the murderer James Smith twenty years previously, and it was to him that I handed the diaries and account books.

Later he examined the diaries and in the one which covered 1980 he found a loose piece of paper which bore the name and address Billy Lomas, 46 Park Avenue, Chadderton. Next, Tom Butcher checked Bob Collinson's domestic accounts book for the same year and found the following entries:

Loan W. Lomas (Sept 25)	£5.00
19/10/80 Loan W. Lomas	£5.00
4/11/80 Loan W. Lomas	£5.00

However, before these entries were found in the accounts book, and on the Tuesday evening following the reporting of the case by the media, a young barmaid at the Boat and Horses public house in Chadderton answered the telephone there and spoke to a man with a local accent who identified himself as 'The Exterminator'. The man told the barmaid that he and his mate had murdered an old man in Oldham on Saturday night and that whilst the other man was present it was he, The Exterminator, who had committed the murder.

Billy Lomas was well known to the police at Oldham, but nevertheless the entries found in Bob Collinson's diary and accounts book still came as a surprise. When detectives visited Christine Lomas's home and spoke to Billy, he told them he had known Bob Collinson and had indeed borrowed money from him, but insisted he had always repaid the loans. This was verified after Bob's careful accounts had been further examined.

In the living room of the house a searching detective found a pair of moccasin shoes, the sole pattern of which closely resembled the footprint found on the front door at the murder scene. After comparisons had been made at the Finger-print Bureau, it was found that the fingerprint on the kitchen door, five feet above where the body of old Bob had lain, had been made by William Lomas.

Whilst the moccasin shoes were identified as the property of Christine's boyfriend Lewis, William Lomas admitted that on the previous Saturday evening he had been wearing them.

Lomas was taken into custody and, after further enquiries had been made, he was cautioned and charged with the murder of Robert Collinson, a charge he denied.

An examination of the shoes was made at the Forensic Science Laboratory at Chorley and the right shoe was found to be consistent in size, type and wear with the impression found on the front door at 8 Colwyn Street.

On the morning of Saturday 20 March, less than a week after the murder had been committed, Lomas appeared before the magistrates at Oldham and was remanded in custody at Oldham police station. At lunch time that day he asked to see the officers in charge of the case. When they arrived, Lomas began to cry, admitting to the murder of Collinson. He said that on the previous Saturday evening, whilst alone, he had broken into Bob's house with the intention of stealing cash. Having forced the front door, he found that he had damaged the lock. Wishing to repair the lock and thus make himself more secure whilst burgling the premises, he had taken two hammers from a drawer in the kitchen.

Whilst having these two hammers actually with him and before he had a chance to mend the lock, Bob

Collinson had arrived home and disturbed him. He had attacked the old chap in the darkness.

He then switched on the light and found that his victim was dead. In a panic he rushed out of the house in Colwyn Street and ran to the Britannia public house, where he had become involved in a fight about an allegedly stolen Citizens' Band radio set. After the fight was over, he had returned to his sister's home, where he washed his blood-stained clothes and confessed to his sister that he had committed the murder.

Lomas chose to make a written statement and it was suggested to him that he might wish to have his solicitor present when he did so. His solicitor was duly contacted. When he arrived at Oldham police station, he was made aware of the fact that Lomas was now admitting sole responsibility for the murder of Robert Collinson and wished to make a written statement, in his presence.

William Lomas then made his written statement. He admitted burglary at 8 Colwyn Street during the night of Saturday 13 March. Lomas had been cautioned, of course, as to his responsibility in making this statement and a detective was writing down what he said. Suddenly, Lomas again changed his story and introduced an unknown man named John. He said that earlier on the Saturday night he had met John by chance in a public house in Oldham town centre. He did not know any other particulars regarding John such as his second name or where he lived, and could only say that he had seen him in town centre public houses in Oldham on previous occasions.

On this fateful Saturday he and John had discussed the possibility of breaking into a house together and stealing cash. They had then left the pub and gone to Bob Collinson's home, where they had effected entry by forcing the front door. He said that, whilst committing this crime, they had been disturbed by Collinson's arrival home and during an exchange of words John had murdered Bob by striking him several times with a hammer.

Lomas was later asked if he used the Citizens' Band radio pseudonym The Exterminator and he agreed that he did. It was of importance to identify the finger impression left by someone on the tool drawer in Bob's kitchen cupboard and to this end every effort was made. Elimination prints were taken of all known callers to the house, and compared. The finger-prints of known friends and criminal associates of Lomas were checked against the outstanding print and a search was also made as far as possible in the bureau files. No identification was made and the mark still remains unsolved.

Two days after making the statement involving the unknown man John, at ten o'clock on the following Monday night Lomas again asked to see the senior detectives involved in the case. When this was arranged, he appeared to be calm and composed. He told them that he alone had murdered Bob Collinson and that he had blamed a second man, John, in an effort to get himself out of the actual killing. He declined to have his solicitor present and, after again being cautioned, he chose to make another written statement, which was written down by a detective and signed by Lomas. In this statement he reiterated what he had said in his first statement. Lomas did not retract this statement later.

It is a wry thought that the number of honest people who would have lent money to William Lomas, the out-of-work labourer with a criminal record, could not have been great, and yet, in return, William Lomas had no compunction in robbing Bob of further money.

In many murder enquiries there are red herrings and it

could well be that the four identical finger-prints found on the tool drawer are a good example of such a circumstance. Had they been left in the home of the murdered man by a person completely innocent of the crime, one who was either unaware that the crime had been committed or did know, but for reasons of his own had no wish to come forward?

At the scene of a crime the specialist will present to the senior investigating officer the results of his findings together with his assessment of possibilities and probabilities. All this will cover only a narrow field or a small part of the enquiry. At this particular scene the scientific evidence rather pointed to the involvement of two people, yet the evidence obtained by other members of the murder squad as the result of interviewing witnesses had traced Lomas's movements so well that it was clear he was operating alone. He certainly had not spoken of meeting another man and was alone at the Bull's Head when he spoke to Mr Trimble, the licensee, and asked him to tannoy for Silver Lady. He was certainly alone at 9.30 P.M., less than thirty minutes before Bob Collinson's home was burgled, because at that time he was acting in a most aggressive manner towards a young man in the Roebuck public house. Shortly after the murder was committed, at a quarter to eleven that night, Lomas was alone when he went into the Britannia public house and made his presence known in no uncertain fashion.

So, it was established that Lomas was alone some thirty minutes before the murder was committed and some thirty minutes afterwards. On balance, I feel that the evidence that he was alone when the murder was committed is far stronger than anything which might indicate he had an accomplice. All the circumstances of the case were included in the report eventually submitted to the Director of Public Prosecutions.

On 24 November 1982, Lomas appeared at the Crown Court at Manchester. He pleaded guilty to murdering Robert Collinson and was sentenced to life imprisonment.

Epilogue

In this book I have attempted to show that crime is rarely committed by a master criminal and is never investigated by a super sleuth. In the main, it is committed by very ordinary, often misguided, individuals, with the investigation conducted by a group of ordinary individuals, most of whom have graduated to the CID from the uniformed branch.

If the reader has found this book different from others written by people with police experience, and I hope they have, it is because in each chapter I tried to concentrate on that aspect of the investigation which set it apart from other enquiries. Whether the difference stemmed from the period of time in which the crime occurred, the *modus operandi* of the criminal, the intuition or hopes of the detective, the needs of the court, or, as in the cases of the Yorkshire Ripper and the Black Panther, the widespread alarm caused to sections of the public, one thing is certain – all cases a detective is required to investigate are different.

Without doubt, in my thirty-five years of service the working day of the average detective has changed considerably: much of his time is now spent writing about crime instead of being out on the streets investigating it. Increased case loads dictate that the modern detective can no longer operate as his counterpart did nearly forty years ago. In those days he had time to stroll around his patch, keeping his finger on the pulse, not only in daily touch with criminals and informants but also able to keep a wary eye on the prospective delinquent – a nod here, a look there, a warning finger raised, an arrangement for the would-be offender to attend the 'surgery' (the detective office). Detectives of that kind had their own system. It may not have been well organized, it may have appeared haphazard, most of their work certainly was done on foot, but it was right for the times.

If the workings of the older detective appeared to be haphazard, the same could hardly be said of the uniform branch, whose work was well organized and regimented. With good cause, people look back with affection to the days when there seemed to be a policeman on every street corner on whom they could rely to preserve the law and protect their property. Sadly, times have changed, and in the inner city areas the modern policeman will spend much of his time responding to calls for his assistance; serving the public, but with insufficient time to protect them. For his sake, I hope that times change yet again.

Experience gained in the uniform branch is invaluable, but the most important day in my service was in November 1956, when I entered the Finger-print Bureau. I ceased to be a number and became a name; no longer was I C96, but Tony Fletcher. I was a finger-print man and as I learned how the job had to be done, and qualified as an expert, I became known, along with a few others, not as 'a finger-print man', but as 'the finger-print man'. Thus, I was able to put into the job something of my own character and to develop accordingly. In later years my job satisfaction was enormous; as a specialist police officer not only was my advice and assistance sought at many major crime scenes, but I was also required to give evidence of opinion in many important trials.

If I were allowed to offer one piece of advice to a young policeman, it would be to remain open-minded. Whether, as in the case of Asru the mummy, he needs to be looking into the past or, because of the need for computerization, the future must be comprehended or, as in the case of the ghost Nicholas, the unknown must be respected, he should always try to look at things with a fresh and open mind.

Index